Continuities in Poland's Permanent Transition

Harald Wydra
Assistant Professor
Institut für Politikwissenschaft
Universität Regensburg
Germany

First published in Great Britain 2000 by
MACMILLAN PRESS LTD
Houndmills, Basingstoke, Hampshire RG21 6XS and London
Companies and representatives throughout the world

A catalogue record for this book is available from the British Library.

ISBN 0–333–77472–8

First published in the United States of America 2000 by
ST. MARTIN'S PRESS, LLC,
Scholarly and Reference Division,
175 Fifth Avenue, New York, N.Y. 10010

ISBN 0–312–23135–0

Library of Congress Cataloging-in-Publication Data
Wydra, Harald.
Continuities in Poland's permanent transition / Harald Wydra.
p. cm.
Includes bibliographical references and index.
ISBN 0–312–23135–0 (cloth)
1. Poland—Politics and government—1989– 2. National characteristics, Polish. 3.
Post–communism—Poland. I. Title.

JN6760 .W93   2000
306.2'09438'09049—dc21
                                                            99–053560

This book is printed on paper suitable for recycling and made from fully managed and sustained
forest sources.

10   9   8   7   6   5   4   3   2   1
09 08 07 06 05 04 03 02 01 00

Printed and bound in Great Britain by
Antony Rowe Ltd, Chippenham, Wiltshire

Continuities in Poland's Permanent Transition

For Anne

\

Contents

List of Abbreviations

AWS	Akcja Wyborcza Solidarność (Solidarity Electoral Action)
BBWR	Bezpartyjny Blok Wspierania Reform (Non-Party Bloc for the Support of Reform)
CBOS	Centrum Badania Opinii Społecznej (Centre for Public Opinion Research)
CMEA	Council for Mutual Economic Assistance
EC	European Community
EU	European Union
FPD	Forum Prawicy Demokratycznej (Forum of the Democratic Right)
KLD	Kongres Liberalno-Demokratyczny (Congress of Liberal-Democrats)
KOR	Komitet Obrony Robotników (Committee for the Defence of Workers)
KPN	Konfederacja Polski Niepodległej (Confederation for an Independent Poland)
NATO	North Atlantic Treaty Organization
OECD	Organization for Economic Co-operation and Development
OKON	Obywatelski Komitet Ocalenia Narodowego (Civil Committee for National Salvation)
OKP	Obywatelski Klub Parlamentarny (Civic Parliamentary Club)
OPZZ	Ogólnopolskie Związki Zawodowe (All-Polish Trade Unions)
PC	Porozumienie Centrum (Center Alliance)
PL	Porozumienie Ludowe (Peasant Accord)
PRL	Polska Rzeczpospolita Ludowa (Polish People's Republic)
PRON	Patriotyczny Ruch Ocalenia Narodowego (Patriotic Movement for National Rebirth)
PSL	Polskie Stronnictwo Ludowe (Polish Peasant Party)
PZPR	Partia Zjednoczona Partia Robotnicza (Polish United Workers Party)
RdR	Ruch dla Rzeczypospolitej (Movement for the Republic)
ROAD	Ruch Obywatelski – Akcja Demokratyczna (Civic Movement – Democratic Action)
ROP	Ruch Odbudowy Polski (Movement for Poland's Reconstruction)
SdRP	Socjaldemokracja Rzeczypospolitej Polskiej (Polish Social Democracy)

SLD	Sojusz Lewicy Demokratycznej (Democratic Left Alliance)
UB	Urząd Bezpieczeństwa (Security Service)
UD	Unia Demokratyczna (Democratic Union)
UW	Unia Wolności (Freedom Union)
ZChN	Zjednoczonie Chrześcijańsko-Narodowe (Christian National Alliance)

Preface

This book is concerned with continuities in Poland's transition. To my knowledge, the relevant literature has not yet posed the question of continuities as an analytical problem of its own right. Two central reasons may be adduced for such a state of affairs. First, the events of 1989 were profound political upheavals that have fundamentally changed the map of Europe ever since. A new political and societal order has been shaping up as epitomized in the democratization of politics, privatization of the economy, individual and political freedom, or a fundamentally new orientation of international allegiances. Second, the conceptual apparatus in the social sciences – ruled by systemic variables such as democracy *vs.* autocracy or capitalism *vs.* command economy – prefigured an almost unanimous judgement of the events of 1989. Eastern Europe arguably provides for the richest and most fascinating field of study of political and social change.

Discontinuities have thus been the guiding pillars of research. Under the impact of the demise of communism, researchers have largely eschewed to tackle the problem of continuities. While continuities are generally not denied, they are often attributed to pathological remainders in collective mentalities or dysfunctionalities which, in turn, impede the modernization and democratization of state and society. I am keen to propose an alternative reading of Poland's transition. Making up for an apparent shortcoming in this regard, my intention in this book is to analytically link continuities in post-1989 Poland to the pre-1989 past. Evidence strongly suggests that discontinuities such as democratic and interest-driven politics or civil society have not fully taken roots and are suspended in a lengthy transition. In tackling this problem, I was guided by two intuitions. First, the long-term process of transition suggests that 1989 was not the rupture-point that initiated the transition, as taken for granted in the relevant social science literature. Second, the first reality of political outcomes is dependent on continuities in a second reality which comprises pre-political fundamentals such as passions and identities.

As to the subject matter, this book examines Polish politics and society at the end of the twentieth century under the premise that 1989 has not been the rupture-point for which it is commonly taken. The often-evoked Polish drama has not come to an end, while the achievement of normality is arguable at least. In an alternative reading of Poland's transition, this book conceptualizes several continuities that have kept Polish politics and society in a permanent transition far before 1989. To this purpose, it elaborates a set of continuities in the second reality of political passions. Furthermore, a second concern of this book aims to contribute to theory building in the field of East European politics. It provides an analytical framework that is – if modified and adapted to other countries – essentially applicable to other countries in Eastern Europe. Poland's history is, admittedly, unique as are most national trajectories in history. Yet former Soviet-type societies share a common destiny. The collapse of communism has dismantled political and social institutions and has discredited an ideological project. Internally, the emotional and mental bonds linking each nation with moments of disruption in its own past may be common factors in the former Eastern bloc countries. The focus on the modalities of dissolution of order links up with the theoretical interest on the study of political and social order. Based on an in-depth study of a transitional society, this book proposes an alternative methodological and theoretical framework for the analysis of contingency in politics.

This book emanates from a doctoral dissertation that I wrote at the European University Institute in Florence. The unique environment at the European University Institute has a great share in the elaboration of this book. Throughout my stay there I had the opportunity to meet fascinating people who shared some of their stimulating ideas with me. The inspiring intellectual communion at the European University Institute and the 'transitional' theme of this book are thus interlinked. Manifold suggestions from different angles of the social sciences have enriched the inter-disciplinary approach applied in this book. I have tried to go beyond classical institutional analysis in order to extricate the paradoxes of continuities in discontinuities by taking recourse to conceptual tools from political science, sociology, anthropology, and history. The inter-disciplinary conceptual design links up with the particular blend of cultural backgrounds that underlie this study. Elsewhere than in Florence, it would hardly have been possible that a German should write a book on Poland in English. This intellectual adventure necessarily entails some risks of gaps and shortcomings. Despite several research stays in Poland, first-hand material is necessarily limited and incomplete. As I had to provide myself with translations from the languages used into English, the reader should be aware of shortcomings as to style and content.

Florence, however, was only the second step in my work on Poland. I started working on Poland at the University of Regensburg due to the initiative of Mathias Schmitz and Michael Zängle. Over the years I have had the opportunity to discuss parts of my research with Barbara Heyns, Jerzy Holzer, Tadeusz Kowalik, Kazimierz Kloc, Jacek Kuroń, Michael Müller, Yossi Shavit, Jan Zielonka, Ireneusz Bialecki, Bogdan Mach, Witold Morawski, Edmund Mokrzycki and Tadeusz Syryjczyk. My friends in Poland have helped me by providing practical advice and moral support. I am grateful to Paweł Kuglarz, Joanna Szwajcowska, and Beata Ziorkiewicz. For talks on the topic and for helpful comments I am indebted to Johan De Deken, Etienne Billette de Villemeur, Mario Drago, Simon Dubbins, Vladimir Gradev, Esther Hauk, Julie Lynch, Berta Moreno Torres, Guglielmo Meardi, Ewa Schwierskott, Tessa Storey, Aleksander Surdej, Adolf Trägler and Frederic Vandenberghe. I owe a great deal of my understanding of Eastern Europe to countless spirited conversations with Agnes Horváth. I am particularly indebted to theoretical discussions with Knut Mittendorfer, who left us all too early. Leslie Holmes encouraged me in moments of doubt, and has contributed a great deal to the publication of this book. Richard Sakwa has been unfailing in inspiring amicable advice, while Philippe Schmitter's very critical stance towards the argument of this book has been of great value in sharpening the focus of this study. The editorial quality of this book owes a good deal to Joanne Caddy, who read through and corrected an earlier draft. My copy-editor at Macmillan, Christina Zaba, considerably improved the book's quality of language and style, and her competent engagement in its subject-matter has made it a pleasure to work on the typescript.

Finally, I am particularly grateful to the members of the thesis committee for their help in coming to terms with a complex problem. Zygmunt Bauman and Claus Offe provided sharp and generous criticism, while Colin Crouch has patiently supported several shifts in the direction of my research and always given the right advice at the right time. Above all, this book owes a great deal of its substance to Arpád Szakolczai, who encouraged me throughout four years to continue on an untrodden path of research, and who stimulated many of the ideas to be found in this book. His intellectual guidance and good spirit were coupled with an unfailing friendship. Most importantly, this book would not have been finished without Anne.

Regensburg, May 1999

1

The Continuity of Second Reality

This book deals with continuities in Poland's transition. A book on continuities may be a surprise to the reader familiar with the social science literature on Eastern Europe. Politics and societies in Eastern Europe are nowadays primarily associated with political and social change on a broad scale. The strong impact of change is reflected in different domains of the social science literature. Accordingly, the demise of the communist system has induced research on conceptual alternatives for a new system (Hankiss, 1990; Beyme, 1993; Merkel, 1994; Offe, 1997; Holmes, 1997a). The emergence of individual autonomy and the liberation from a closed system have stimulated works on civil and open society (Keane, 1988; Ash, 1990; Dahrendorf, 1990; Ekiert, 1994; Gellner, 1994). Changes in the regime of Eastern Europe became a major and controversial study of object of transitology and its sub-discipline, consolidology (Linz and Stepan, 1996b; Schmitter and Karl, 1994, 1995; Offe, 1996; 1997; Elster *et al.*, 1998; Holmes, 1997b). In this vein, scholars were recommended to shift their thinking 'from the heady excitement and underdetermination of the transition from autocracy (. . .) to the prosaic routine and overdetermination of consolidated democracy'.[1]

On the whole, starting from the early 1990s, scholars have shifted their attention from examining the foundations of communism to the study of transitions, and have come to emphasize political uncertainty, changing contingencies, structural indeterminacy, and the significance of elite choices (Ekiert, 1996:323–4). The assumption on discontinuity was perhaps most fashionably expressed in the thesis of the end of history (Fukuyama, 1992), a point with which around 1989 'nearly all of Eastern Europe agrees'.[2] In this vein, conceptual givens in the literature on consolidation of democracy

1

work with premises such as the 'finished transition to democracy' (Linz and Stepan, 1996a:15). More generally, and embracing both transition and consolidation, democratization is supposed

> to describe the overall process of regime change to completion, i.e. from the end of the previous authoritarian regime to the stabilization and rooting of new democracies (. . .) This principal objective of consolidation is for the risks and uncertainties typical of transition to be gradually reduced to the point where failure in democratization becomes highly improbable.[3]

On the other hand, the end of communism has not brought about a definitive cut in terms of systemic particularities. Thus, scholars such as François Furet have suggested that 1989 is not aptly grasped by the term 'revolution', because contrary to the French revolution, communism did not leave institutional or ideological principles, nor a historical heritage. 1989 produced no new idea, no new leaders, no real parties, no new society, nor a new economy (Furet, 1995:8–9). Other scholars stressed the importance of the 'old' situation, arguing for a vacuum or the institutional void in the period of transition (Jowitt, 1992). In this vein, post-communism seems to be better understood as the rejection of the communist power system than as a clear-cut adoption of an alternative system (Holmes, 1997a:13). Compared to the rupture-point in 1945, the record of change and continuity seems to be a mixed one at best (Offe, 1997).

Discontinuities and continuities in Poland's transition

The round-table pact and the founding elections of June 1989 are arguably the foremost events that discontinued communist political power (Geremek, 1991, Skórzyński, 1995; Osiatyński, 1996). The round-table pact and the semi-free elections largely dismantled the institutional framework of pre-1989 Poland, thus grounding their uncontested significance as the cradle of Polish post-1989 order. There is a general consensus that 'independent and democratic Poland was born during the Round Table negotiations'.[4] Throughout Eastern Europe the political events of 1989 were equivalent to a systemic disruption which entailed a variety of ideological and institutional discontinuities.

In the wake of these founding events, the first non-communist government in the Eastern bloc opened up the way to the democratization of political and social life. An impressive discontinuities has come to pervade institutional politics Polish post-1989 politics has seen the emergence of a new party system, three parliamentary elections in 1991, 1993, and 1997, as well as the peaceful change of political power in 1993 (from post-Solidarity to post-communist) and in 1997 (from post-communist to the coalition of Solidarity Electoral Action and Freedom Union). After the first years of Solidarity governments, a second wave of reforms as of 1997 has set out to accomplish privatization and the decentralization of administrative units. Furthermore, the regime change in 1989 helped to implement the legitimacy of government, the rule of law, and the freedom of the press. Gradually, the conviction gained ground that traditional Polish dichotomies such as state *vs.* society or communist regime *vs.* Solidarity opposition lost their explanatory power for Poland in the 1990s. As new socio-economic cleavages were supposed to become dominant (Wnuk-Lipiński, 1996; Frybes and Michel, 1996), the consolidation of Polish democracy has become a leading paradigm (Wnuk-Lipiński, 1996; Ziemer, 1998).

A comparably remarkable record of restructuring and transformation has been achieved in the economy. Following timid and politically steered market reforms in the 1970s and 1980s, only the economic shock-therapy of the first Solidarity government in 1989 launched massive economic change (Winiecki, 1992; Sachs, 1994; Slay, 1994; Balcerowicz, 1995). The politics of liberalization, stabilization, an expanding private ownership, and the stopping of arbitrary wage policies were the order of the day. After initial hardship, Poland has become the leading economy in the region, enjoying the highest rates of economic growth, steadily declining inflation rates, and an expansive private sector, which produces up to 60 per cent of its GNP. Such trends are accompanied by substantive changes of property rights and by an increase in foreign investment and consumption. Forecasts for 1999 ranked Poland first in terms of economic strength and rule of law, and runner-up to Hungary and Slovenia, which lead the list of 27 post-communist countries.[5] The reverse side of economic liberalization only confirms the general trend of discontinuities. Economic reforms have largely dismantled the social safety net. Unemployment, poverty, social and economic hardship have hit large parts of the population, and have widened generational and regional disparities.

By the same token, the collapse of communism discontinued the ideological pillars of pre-1989 politics and society. Models of democratic reform and transitions had been harboured inside Polish oppositional thought throughout the 1970s and 1980s. At the end of the 1980s Western-type models of political and economic reform replaced nearly half a century of Marxist-Leninist-type centralism and command politics in the economy. As the Marxist-Leninist model failed, the oppositional strategy of anti-politics became superseded, and liberalism as the guiding principle for economic reform and for civil society made remarkable headway.

> The unmistakable sign of an opening up towards liberalism (which before 1989 was almost non-existent on the East European political scene) was the growing popularity of the two main ideas. The idea of the autonomy of the individuals taken as the starting point of politics (anti-politics in this case), and the idea of civil society as a sphere of activity independent from the state and undertaken spontaneously by individual subjects, who among themselves establish new relationships and agreements and, consequently, create new forms of public life.[6]

Conversely, this ideological shift is accompanied by the disintegration of Catholicism as a dominant 'Polish ideology' (Gowin, 1996).

The scope of discontinuities is perhaps most remarkable in Poland's new foreign policy options that put an end to almost two centuries of international dependence (Prizel and Michta, 1995). After achieving anew full sovereignty in the wake of the concomitant breakdown of the Soviet Union and organizations such as the CMEA and the Warsaw Pact, Polish politics was free to choose its way and orientation in the new post-communist Europe. The magic formula 'return to Europe' embodied the turn towards integration into the West, as was reflected in the increase of political contacts, economic trade and co-operation with EU-countries. Inversely, former communist countries lost in political and economic importance. In the mean time, the association in 1993 with the European Union and the start of negotiations for EU-enlargment in 1998 have marked substantial steps towards the end of Poland's historical limbo position of the last two centuries. Poland's integration into NATO in spring 1999 is the most emblematic step towards the accomplishment of this discontinuity.

This overview suggests that the central characteristics of pre-1989 Poland's political system, legal norms, social and economic conditions, and ideological orientation have to a large extent been discontinued. If measured by what has been normal for the country during the last 200 years, 'it is now commonplace to observe that Poland has become a "normal country"' (Ash 1996). Since 1989 Poland has been free, sovereign, and prosperous; Germany is its best ally in the West, and there is no immediate threat from Russia. There is good reason to reckon that Poland has not been so well placed since the second half of the sixteenth century. Accordingly, 'Poland's transition from normal abnormality to abnormal normality is already a fantastic achievement.'[7]

In the initial effervescence of institutional discontinuities, the issue of continuities kept a low profile. The awareness of continuities in politics resurfaced with the return of post-communist parties to power in 1993. The reappropriation of political control through ex-communist parties was referred to as a second version of the Polish Peoples' Republic, or summed up by 're-communization with a human face'.[8] But cleavage lines throughout the 1990s suggest that Polish politics have been considerably influenced by the heritage of its own past. In 1989, Poland was to draw a thick line under the past and to dispense with large-scale de-communization (Holmes, S., 1994). Yet, political attitudes towards the past keep being stamped by pre-1989 history and tend to reproduce pre-1989 political cleavages which focus anew on the historical antagonism between the post-communist and post-Solidarity camps (Smolar, 1996b; Roszkowski, 1997). Politics of memory and problems of coping with the nation's own past and with accountabilities for communist crimes have been haunting Polish politics and public opinion ever since the early 1990s (Ash, 1998). The quest to assign responsibilities for communist crimes and for the past in general has led to widespread claims for a settlement with the past.[9] As the record of the communist past remains highly contested, Polish history exerts an extraordinary power on collective political mentalities (Grajewski, 1996; Kersten, 1996; Szacki, 1996; Roszkowski, 1997; Ash, 1998; Grabowski, 1998). There are strong indicators that conflict lines of Polish politics will follow those of historical division lines in the future too (Marciniak, 1996; Kwiecień, 1996).

Continuities are perhaps most striking where they are least expected, namely in the economy. On the one hand, the deep intertwining between former political and new economic elites led to the emergence of political capitalism (Staniszkis, 1991b). On the other hand, changes such as the dismantling of state ownership or of the patronage stage were not on the agenda of the round table (Bauman, 1994:21). Furthermore, long-term continuities in Polish economy, such as growth fatigue and pervasive weakness of the state, impede the enforcement of property rights and any effective co-ordination of a market economy. 'Thus, while both these systems, economic and political, have been undergoing change, the mechanism causing growth fatigue in all those years has remained the same' (Poznański, 1996:246). Before the economic recovery of 1994 onwards the Polish economy went through several crises. The deterioration of the national economy during 1990–1 was of a size comparable to that of the 1979–82 crisis. The national product declined sharply in 1990 and again, by less, in 1991, then stabilized in 1992, pushing the real national output below the 1975 level (Poznański, 1996:264). On the other hand, the increase of social poverty and of unemployment led to a 'genuine revolution in the distribution of national income which resembles almost to a text-book illustration of marxist accumulation of richness at one pole and pauperization of the majority of society at the other pole' (Kowalik, 1995:238).

While the official politics of real socialism disintegrated after 1989, the shadow society as its antithesis has survived in various forms. In the mid-1990s people had more confidence in informal ties based on circles of relatives and close friends (or officials who could be bribed) than in the anonymous world of institutions, legal norms, and complicated mechanisms like those of democratic politics (Narojek, 1991; Smolar, 1996c:36; Kolarska-Bobińska, 1994). Furthermore, the revolution of 1989 was accompanied by low psychological involvement and political apathy, and led to a demobilization of the masses and the elites (Mason *et al.*, 1991; Smolar 1996c). Confidence and trust in public institutions has remained low and distrust in political parties and the state high (Sztompka, 1996). Splits both through moral dividing lines and a dividing line of memories are as marked as are ideological divisions on how to achieve political and constitutional consensus (Grabowska, 1997).

Given the evidence above, continuities seem to be highly interlinked with discontinuities. It is arguable at least, whether Poland's transition can be analyzed as primarily ruled by discontinuities. In any case, a considerable set of continuities in political and social life points to the need to examine them in depth. This mixed record of continuities and discontinuities is reflected in assessments of reform politics which are frequently presented in terms of 'the glass half full or the glass half empty' (Gomułka, 1993; Rosati, 1993; Holmes, 1997c). While some approaches try to analyze Poland in the light of the consolidation of democracy (Wnuk-Lipiński, 1995, 1996; Frybes and Michel, 1996; Ziemer, 1998), others have provided pertinent analyses of the afterlife of communism (Kolarska-Bobińska, 1994; Holmes, 1997c; Smolar, 1996a, 1996b, 1996c; Kojder, 1998). On the grounds of evidence at face value one cannot, however, guess whether there is any linkage between change and continuities or whether there is the paradox of continuity in change (Poznański, 1996). 'But there is a sense of "old wine, new bottles" as one looks at the landscape of increasing alienation and disillusionment, voter apathy, and distance between the leaders and the led in post-communist Poland' (Curry and Fajfer, 1996:245).

Transition and contingency

To understand the complex nature of the discontinuities and continuities in Poland's transition, I suggest a reassessment of some given assumptions on transition and contingency in politics. Guided by common methodological reasoning, most studies on change in East European politics and societies are dominated by a dyadic opposition contrasting one systemic variable with another. Scholars tend to draw comparisons between communism and post-communism, between authoritarian order and democracy, or between a closed and an open society. In this vein, early treatises on transitions dealt with 'transitions from' a particular political system, mostly from authoritarian rule. In one of the first conceptual attempts to grasp recent phenomena of change from authoritarian to democratic regimes, 'transition' was defined as the 'interval between one political regime and another' (O'Donnell *et al.*, 1986:6). The concept's nature as a shift or a switch is conspicuous. 'Democratic transition and consolidation involve the movement from a non-democratic to a democratic regime.'[10] Furthermore, transition was understood as being

> delimited, on the one side, by the launching of the process of dissolution of an authoritarian regime and, on the other, by the installation of some form of democracy, the return to some form of authoritarian rule, or the emergence of a revolutionary alternative.[11]

Processual categories were not abandoned, though, as transitions were qualified by the path of transition dependent on the prior-regime type (Linz and Stepan, 1996b:38–65). Yet the problem is the identification of transition paths with political systems such as suggested by the typology of democratic, authoritarian, totalitarian, post-totalitarian and sultanistic regimes. It is not surprising that the suggested transition path, i.e. an inherently processual category, turns out to be one of opposed structures or systems. The concept of transition initiation implies the start of transition and thus fits a dyadic conception.

> Transitions initiated by an uprising of civil society, by the sudden collapse of the nondemocratic regime, by an armed revolution, or by a nonhierarchically led military coup all tend toward situations in which the instruments of rule will be assumed by an interim or provisional government.[12]

This two-step move towards a finished transition is most explicit in the assumption that Eastern Europe is the most recent example of 'waves of democratization'.[13] In the wake of the democratizations in Western Europe after 1945 and Southern Europe and Latin America in the 1970s and 1980s, this third or fourth wave of democratization (Huntington, 1991; Beyme, 1994:85) was defined as a 'group of transitions from nondemocratic to democratic regimes that occurs within a specified period'.[14] Moreover, in any of the four waves of democratization the two-step move – that of the collapse and rebuilding of systems – seems to be as tightly connected as in the case of Eastern Europe.[15]

Standard approaches in the social sciences thus lack a conceptual framework which would allow for a consideration of 'transition from' and 'transition to', and that, in addition, would account for the 'old' and the 'new'. Perhaps the most conspicuous attempt to define the scope of uncertainty between two systems was the claim about a 'genesis-environment' that took hold of Eastern Europe (Jowitt, 1992:262–68). East European societies were seen as left 'without institutions and without a system' (Bunce and Csanádi, 1993). By contrast to Fukuyama's 'end of history' thesis, Jowitt considered his Genesis image to be 'more accurate and helpful in assigning meaning and attempting to influence the type of world we are entering'.[16]

Given the boost in institution-building in post-1989, and its unclear theoretical status, uncertainty seems to be too vague a concept. On the other hand, a framework of analysis must not be determinating. In this vein, it seems more adequate to acknowledge the importance of path dependence, according to which 'it is in the ruins that these societies will find the materials with which to build a new order; therefore, differences in how the pieces fell apart will have consequences for how political and economic institutions can be reconstructed in the current period'.[17] Unsatisfied with transition as a dualist 'from- to' concept, David Stark claimed that East Central Europe was undergoing a plurality of transitions in a dual sense. He argued for the need to 'disaggregate "the transition", perhaps even dispense with it as a concept, and undertake the difficult research work of understanding how changes in the different countries and in the different domains have very different temporalities'.[18] While this approach made a plea for considering the specificities of the starting-point, its main focus was to dispense entirely with the concept of transition. Stark argued that 'in place of transition (with the emphasis on destination) we analyze transformations (with the emphasis on actual processes) in which the introduction of new elements takes place most typically in combination with adaptations, rearrangements, permutations, and reconfigurations of already existing institutional forms'.[19]

Despite its sensitivity towards the dissolution of communist order, the concept of path dependence does not go beyond the common thinking in two steps, those of deconstruction and reconstruction. This two-step move becomes apparent as 'the true strength of the concept of path dependence ... is precisely its analytic power in explaining outcomes where strategic actors are deliberately searching for departures from long-established routines and attempting to restructure the rules of the games'.[20] As a result, path-dependence proffers merely the duality of breach (departure from long-established routines) and outcome.

Responding to the demise of communism, the emerging transition literature emphasized the establishment of new rules, the transition to a new form of political and social organization. Despite the specification of sequences that distinguish between transition and consolidation (Schmitter and Karl 1994; Bos, 1994), the dominant trend in the social science literature conceives of transition as concerned with the shift from one state to the other. While the former was concerned with the destabilization of autocratic orders and possible exit routes from it, the latter addressed the stabilizing factors that would sustain the new order. At any rate, the passage from the old to the new order hinges on two limit-points: the starting condition, and the endpoint to which transition will lead. Thus, the concept of transition itself is heavily rooted in the state 'to', and does not pay enough attention to the state 'from'.

On the whole, the year 1989 appears as a seemingly objective and imposing point of measure of change. Any approaches to continuity and discontinuities pivot on the axis of the year 1989 and its consequences. In Poland and elsewhere in the region, 1989 complies with the requirements of a standard definition in political science that attributes to transition the quality of a starting-point which is characterized by rupture, by a breach of the former order. 'The transition generally starts with a particularly dramatic event (. . .) as a culmination of a series of events. Such an event often results in the public and official commitment of the authoritarian rulers to hold free elections and to revert power to the electorate by a specified deadline.'[21]

This application of a dyadic pattern to Eastern Europe is only partly due to the nature of the conceptual pool in transition literature.[22] Given the long and pervasive division of East and West before 1989, such a dichotomy seems comprehensible, and the desire to replace a failed system with a more successful one seems only natural. Furthermore, to conceive of transitions as a shift from one system to another complies with the tradition in the thinking about social and political change which has been ruled by an essentially dyadic structure: it is interested in the point of departure and in the point of destination of a process. Thus, the tradition of Western thought has usually answered questions of the coherence of societies by emphasizing a state of disorder, the old situation, whose results were detrimental to living and which thus had to be somehow reversed and substituted by a new order (Dahrendorf, 1959:157ff.). In a similar vein, such a dichotomy was inherent in Western sovietology, whose mainstream assumption of systemic dichotomy was reinforced by political and military stalemates. Systemic confrontation contributed to a dyadic pattern of Eastern communism and Western democracies, making a black-and-white scheme the common outlook. The dichotomy in the pool of social science literature is telling in this respect: on the one hand, the theories of the collapse of communist power (Holmes, 1997a:23–62); on the other hand, the burgeoning literature on transition, consolidation or transformation. Rarely, if ever, are these strands of literature interlinked.

As a result of such dyadic thinking, contingency in politics is essentially located in the transitional period which starts off with the breakdown of communism in 1989. If one were to spell out a principle of 'transitology', as Schmitter and Karl named the first branch of research, it could well be 'uncertainty'.[23] For the new branch of 'consolidology' that is concerned with the consolidation of democracy, 'stability' became the catchword (Schmitter and Karl, 1994). Despite this gradual shift from uncertainty of transitions towards the modalities of consolidation, the analysis of variables of contingency in politics is essentially coterminous with 1989. Such a dyadic approach to contingency must associate the end of communism primarily with discontinuities. In order to contain contingency, the systemic change from a centrally planned economy or a monoparty political order to a democratic and capitalist order is analyzed under the heading of rationally designed institution-building. Similarly, approaches that have underscored the high contingency of a new world disorder (Jowitt, 1992) do not escape dyadic thinking either, since they assume the emergence of uncertainty or disorder as a consequence of the end of communist stability.

Standard approaches to contingency in research on Eastern Europe are biased as they work with the assumption that the shape and impact of contingency are decided by its systemic outcome. Claus Offe defined the core problem of the political and economic modernization of former socialist societies as rooted in a lack of noncontingent givens which would be suitable fixed parameters of the politics of reform. 'Precisely because the system is at such a deadlock, everything becomes contingent, and nothing can self-evidently remain as it is.'[24] The absence of a fixed set of trustworthy or at least uncontested social facts and binding institutions forces the reform politicians to some gigantic bootstrapping act. Due to the collapse of communism as system, contingent outcomes must be located in the post-1989 period. While contingency is primarily assumed for the transition phase after the rupture-point, pre-1989 is not treated as a period of high contingency.

This book sets out to elaborate a theoretical framework that problematizes the dyadic structures of transition theory and approaches to contingency in the Eastern European context. It is keen to extend the problem of contingency of political and societal order to pre-1989. The central endeavour of this book is to examine non-contingent givens in the transitory pre-1989 situation and to link them analytically to post-1989. I will elaborate a set of continuities that may elucidate the transitory character of both pre-1989 and post-1989 Polish politics. Such an assumption is sustained by the self-definition of communist regimes as transitional (Kersten, 1991; Sakwa, 1995; Szakolczai, 1996; 1998; Horváth 1997, 1998).

Transitology took its cue from Machiavelli's definition of uncertainty.

The difficulties encountered in attaining power arise partly from the new institutions and laws they are forced to introduce in order to establish their power and make it secure. And it should be realized that taking the initiative in introducing a new form of government is very difficult and dangerous, and unlikely to succeed. The reason is that all those who profit from the old order will be opposed to the innovator, whereas all those who might benefit from the new order are, at best, tepid supporters of him.[25]

Modern transitology has translated this claim into an antagonism of two systems. Such a viewpoint is mainly induced by a focus on the *virtù* of elites whose action is able to transform an old system into a new one. The fundamental experience of dissolution of order, so central to Machiavelli's work, plays a minor role. Experiences such as the long-term decay of political order and corruption, the cyclical nature of constitutions, or the opposed humours in a prolonged crisis as analyzed in parts of the Discourses and the Florentine Histories, therefore, have been neglected by the transition literature.

Looking at the Polish pre-1989 political order, it is at least arguable whether the antagonism of two systems as put forward by transitology complies with Machiavelli's concept. If the state 'from' is assumed to be stable, any analysis of change and continuity must remain linear or evolutionary. A closer look at the instability of pre-1989 Polish politics suggests the cyclical nature of Polish post-war history (Ascherson, 1981; Curry *et al.*, 1996).

The sequence varies little in its broad outline. It begins with the arrival of a shining new government, promising radical economic changes and liberal political reforms. Gradually this ruling group is affected by political decay until it degenerates into the same sort of stifling autocracy which it replaced, a clique out of touch with the needs and wishes of the Polish people Economic discontent finally touches off a working-class revolt. This leads more or less directly to the fall of the political leadership and its replacement by a new team – in its turn flourishing promises of reform and responsiveness to public opinion. A cycle has ended. The next begins as this new leading clique, after a few months in which the newspapers are free and sausage is plentiful, is slowly drawn into the same process of degeneration.[26]

Transitoriness and uncertainty in Poland are here extended into the realm of the pre-1989 order. Systemic coherence and profitability for the incumbents are questioned far before the systemic breakdown in 1989.

Not only was it not a totalitarian system; it was also not even a viable system. Upheavals, even when they were neither mass actions nor successful, were never really brought under control and ended. No communist leader felt strong enough to do away with its opponents. Nor was any leader capable of marshaling enough resources to make the system really work to either control or satisfy the population. Economics, domestic politics, foreign policy, and the processes of social change were so intertwined that Poland could only rock on for thirty years from one half-solved set of problems to the next and back again.[27]

If one sees pre-1989 Polish politics in the light of a breakdown of order, an understanding of the modalities of discontinuities and continuities in Poland can be gained only if the socio-genesis of pre-1989 order is linked to that of post-1989. So far, social science research tends to give insufficient attention to the conditions of how the old order dissolved. Increasingly, studies want to understand 'not so much the breakdown of the old order, but the problematic emergence of the new'.[28] To my knowledge, only a limited number of studies have been dedicated to in-depth analyses of communist societies, acknowledging their fragility and transitoriness (Staniszkis, 1991; 1994a; Engler, 1992; Horváth and Szakolczai 1992; Sakwa, 1995; Szakolczai, 1996; 1998; Horváth, 1997; 1998; Wydra, 1999). Such a focus on the conditions or modalities of dissolving orders was developed in history[29] and historical sociology (Huizinga, 1939; Sewell, 1996; Szakolczai 1996, 1998). Arpád Szakolczai (1996) claimed to shift attention from the second limit-point to the first. He advocated that 'emphasis should be placed on the manner in which a society enters a stage of transition, on the *modality* of the dislocation, the collapse, the *dissolution* of the previous *order* of things'.[30] Thus, the post-1989 condition is not examined by ex-post assumptions of how things should be set together, but rather by the conditions under which the former order dissolved.

If one conceives of pre-1989 as a period of transitoriness and cyclical crises, manifest tendencies of discontinuity inside the communist order must be given more theoretical significance than they have received so far. The dyadic structure of systemic antagonisms hinges on the assumption that 1989 was the rupture-point. Moreover, practical considerations in the agenda of academic research tend to favour analyses of the modalities of the new post-1989 order, discarding the old or reducing them to mere preliminaries. An investigation of continuities needs to re-evaluate the assumed rupture-point of 1989. Thus, the first question to ask of the problem of continuities in transition regards the pivotal moment of 1989. While there is no precise date or period at which to locate the outset of this transitory condition, this book argues that transition is not centred around the focal point of 1989. There is good reason to assume that the demise of communism in Poland, despite being 'by far the most dramatic of the crises that punctuated communist rule there . . . was not the beginning or the end of Poland's transformation process'.[31] Second, and tightly linked to the first point, there must be a shift from the objective-institutional level to the subjective-experiential level.

Summing up, the conception of post-1989 as a highly contingent period as opposed to an essentially stable pre-1989 period is inherent in the methodological apparatus of the bulk of the transition literature. The dyadic approach to transition is reinforced by the dyadic conception of modernization *vs.* totalitarian approaches. Such concepts hardly provide the tools to examine the paradox of continuities in a period of profound discontinuities. I will set out to develop a conceptual tool that permits analysis of continuities through the second reality of expecting discontinuities.

Second reality before and after 1989

If the Soviet system was ideocratic in character[32] – with the single Marxist–Leninist ideology as fundamental to political life and not open to legitimate challenge – East Central European countries were less ideocratic. Several ruptures of social and political order testified to the fragility of countries such as Poland, Hungary, or Czechoslovakia (Simecka, 1984; Arnason, 1993; Holmes, 1997a). It was in East Central Europe and Yugoslavia that the legitimation crisis rendered the communist regimes most fragile, and where individual autonomy, civil society, and anti-politics developed best. 'In Czechoslovakia, during the Prague Spring, or in Poland during the Solidarity period, at least an incipient and imperfect parallel society began to emerge.'[33] This fragility of political and social order crystallized in concepts such as the second society, second polity, or parallel politics (Skilling, 1989 Hankiss, 1990). 'During the period of normalization which followed in the two countries, a system of more or less co-ordinated structures developed which, at least in embryo, represented a "second polity" or independent society at a lower level of development.'[34] Autonomy and spaces of freedom allowed for an independent sphere where people met and established associations within the second society. The emergence of a second society in Poland expressed the increasing conflicts between the communist regime and society and official politics. Similar to the dualism of civil society *vs.* state (Arato, 1981; Keane, 1988), second polities, economies, and cultures were seen as effects of the regime's failure to make society comply with official politics. In this regard, independent organizations, alternative structures, and autonomous activities in some East European societies such as Poland, Hungary, or Yugoslavia showed fledgling attributes of a second polity which, to a certain extent, was detached from the system or partly worked against or outside it.

Second or independent societies were conceived in their institutional dimensions and their systemic results.[35] Less attention was given to the relational aspect with regard to models or images that provided the intellectual and emotional sources on which second realities were built up. Dissidence and opposition grew larger throughout time and engaged the communist regimes in their endeavours to make up for the precariousness of their legitimacy and authority. After initial compliance,[36] the elites and the common people in Eastern European societies, and especially in Poland, became gradually drawn towards imagined, different Western lifestyles. Not only the opposition but also the regime shifted between the first and a second reality. The building of a second Poland under Gierek was about remodelling the national symbolic domain. The regime strove to improve the Polish self-image and cultivate national pride.

'In the 1970s, the propagation of the official ideology in all major domains of public discourse – that is, visual imagery, rhetoric and ceremonial – was constantly amplified.'[37] On the whole, the political, economic, and social reality in pre-1989 Poland was widely associated with cycles of crises (Ascherson, 1981:26; Landau and Roszkowski, 1995:239–254). The frequency of conflict in Polish post-war society was equated with a permanent revolution (Curry and Fajfer, 1996). In pre-1989 Poland, the outcome of politics was contingent, due to the expectations of political discontinuity which remained a steady concern for both the authorities and the opposition.

Given that the authorities in their struggle for legitimacy made extensive use of national and patriotic imagery, I suggest extending the concept of the 'second society' in order to make it useful for an analysis of post-1989 Poland. The long-term dichotomy between foreign repressive systems and society have made the recourse to alternative modes of organization a guiding theme in Poland's history since the late eighteenth century. 'A real authentic, non-illusory Poland only existed where a group of citizens met and took their own decisions. The most spectacular "self-organizations" were of course the national conspiracies themselves ... Their mere existence as genuine Polish centres of debate and decision was revolutionary ... Where such a band of people gathered together, a small space appeared which in this nationalist perspective could reasonably be named "Poland".'[38] Not by chance, the overall aim of the Polish Solidarity opposition was the subjectivization of society. The second reality almost became the primary reality for a short moment, when in late 1980 'Solidarity was simply Poland'.[39] Second reality referred not only to the questioning of authorities in society but also to private life, where norms were rejected (Wedel, 1988). The experience and the perception of realities was so different that one could even think of writing two different histories of the PRL (Szacki, 1996:68–74). A political history would account for the development of the Polish political system, while a history of its society would tell how people lived under the pressure of the regime but were mainly busy with their small affairs. Such a distinction would not follow a black-and-white dichotomy, but should be understood as a 'second life' (Szacki, 1996:74).

To maintain the appeal of a second reality is impossible without the conviction that there is a mode of being more worthwhile to be lived in than the actual reality one lives in.[40] Similarly, in Hungary, a 'double' or 'split consciousness' was a common phenomenon in the 1950s and early 1960s (Hankiss, 1990:97). The subjugation of the subject into a self-imposed different reality was still gripping Polish society in the late 1970s. In the concrete life-world of the people, national and patriotic romanticism linked with religious belief were crucial aspects in the pursuit of a second political and social reality. The essence of communist systems was not massive physical constraint, but rather, an opening-up towards the West, given in small doses. A second economy can hardly exist without inflow of economic goods from outside and a fascination for the richness of Western market economies. The image of democracy[41] was essentially double-edged, as it originally referred to the systemic enemy, but increasingly shifted towards universal humanitarian values, individual and political liberty, and a fully-fledged opposition movement such as Solidarity in Poland. As a consequence, the prolonged collapse of communism left these countries caught up in a situation of the irreality of the real (Engler, 1992:80–2). Such a situation bears resemblance to processes of substitution.[42] Following upon this, 'the power of the authorities relied upon the desire of the governed to leave the social community temporarily, and upon the principle to do nothing that could counteract the fulfillment of this desire'.[43]

On these grounds, I suggest detaching the concept of second reality from a functional meaning in the service of the antagonism of state *vs.* society. In a situation of the menacing dissolution of order, second realities should be regarded as subjective-emotional expressions of the desire to leave an unwanted or unsatisfactory situation. In this regard, the mixed record of continuities and discontinuities in Poland's transition makes a strong case for the assumption that, in many accounts, post-1989 Poland remains pervaded by the irreality of the real. At face value, the achievement of political and individual liberty coupled with democratic legitimacy ended the second reality of a split consciousness. In this vein, the guiding postulates of dissident movements, such as the claim for living in dignity, living in truth, or anti-politics set out to create spaces which were free of a double reality. One can, however, also argue that the period of transition is the lapse of time necessary to fill the gap between reality and mentalities (Frybes and Michel, 1996b:74–5). This regards not only Poland's return to Europe and the adoption of Western models of institutions and norms, but is also about detachment from the reality of habits and mentalities that had developed throughout a period of unstable and contested normative, ethical, and institutional order. In this regard, the pluralization and liberalization of public and political life in post-1989 Poland does not necessarily coincide with a subjective perception of such a process. It is, as it were, a question of whether the glass is half full or half empty.

The economic and social gains from political liberty, moreover, have been restricted to certain segments of Polish society only. It was reckoned that the third republic was a one-third society, pointing to those who profited from the new order and who actively participated in shaping it. Another third, mainly retired people and those living in the countryside or structurally weak regions, bear the burden, and the last third is still undecided which attitude to take.[44] Under the impact of rising 'citizens' movements' in Eastern Europe at the beginning of the 1990s, Claus Offe warned that 'the initial "atomized" state of the post-totalitarian society would not be somehow overcome, but rather reproduced and reinforced'.[45] Juxtaposing this assessment to the picture given by Aleksander Smolar for the mid-nineties, the parallels are striking. 'One gets the paradoxical impression that society today is no less – indeed, perhaps even more – atomized than it was in the final, years of communism.'[46] Similarly, the theme of the invisibility of the authorities and the weakness of the state in East Central Europe has been pervasive since the end of communism.

> By now, millions of people have lost, or fear that they may lose, their traditional roles and positions in the sphere of production and distribution. They have lost their way in the labyrinths of social and industrial relationships, which are in the midst of a chaotic transformation. People do not know any more, or yet, what are the rules of the games, what are their duties and rights, what they have to do for what, what is the cost and reward of what. There is no authority to tell, there are no values to refer to.[47]

It might be objected that a separation of two realities in post-1989 Poland cannot go beyond the standard distinction between state and society. Such a viewpoint, however, ignores the fact that second or double realities can maintain their appeal despite institutional ruptures. I would maintain that the second reality exerts considerable power.[48] Persistent images of national salvation, the myth of enchanted politics or the antagonism between (post-)communists and anti-communists indicate the continuity of myths and beliefs despite a revolutionary break in institutional politics.[49] In moments of crisis, elites may be subjectively convinced that they are guided by reason, while objective reality may distort this subjective perception (Pareto, 1968:93ff.). As Jerzy Szacki argued, 'our society to a considerable degree consists of people whose biographies are not stamped by any profound disruptions. Neither was the founding of the PRL for them the end of the world nor was its breakdown the beginning of the world'.[50] Indeed, for many Poles the year 1989 did not signify an experience of change. After the return from more than 40 years of exile, the former Radio Free Europe director Jan Nowak-Jeziorański asked a member of staff in a Polish hospital when, to her mind, Poland really obtained its liberty. She replied that it was probably under Gierek (in the 1970s), because from that moment one could freely travel abroad. As Nowak-Jeziorański commented: 'In that moment I understood that for her and me the year 1989 (. . .) was lived on a different level, and that in current Poland a part of society thinks like me, and a part like her.'[51]

The impact of second reality in post-1989 politics is reflected in the radical but widely unsuccessful desire for large-scale changes. In both pre- and post-1989 Poland second realities or meta-realities (Ekes, 1994; Michel and Frybes, 1996b; Kowalski, 1997) are difficult to escape. In order to identify the continuities in Poland's transition I propose to reframe some fundamental theoretical and methodological assumptions that have guided social science research on Eastern Europe. In methodological terms, this means reconsidering the dichotomy that confronts pre-1989 with post-1989 and which also pervades the discussion of second reality.

The theoretical dichotomy of systemic oppositions, such as autocracy *vs.* democracy, or state socialism *vs.* the market, lines up with the established dichotomies in methodological approaches. One such methodological dualism contrasts the tradition of area studies (such as Sovietology) with that of democratization studies. Consequently, post-1989 Eastern Europe is often squeezed into a two-tier scheme of interpretative accounts. On the one hand, political developments in Eastern Europe should be analyzed as primarily dependent on linear heritages from the past. On the other hand, the emphasis is put on the autonomy of political actors in a situation of uncertainty. In offering a dual choice in the research agenda, Philippe Schmitter asked which represented the better strategy, and he favoured the second one.

Should the scholars of post-communist transitions rely primarily on the unique cultural, structural or behavioral features inherited from the "marxist-leninist-stalinist" past in their effort to understand what the outcomes of these momentous transformations will be? Or, should they focus on a more generic set of issues and utilize primarily non-area-specific concepts that presume a less historically constrained range of choices and hence a greater autonomy for actors?[52]

By the same token, current scientific discourse on Eastern Europe has revived an old cleavage. Change and progress in democratization and marketization are mainly associated with modernization theories, while pathologies and continuities are mainly summarized under the totalitarian paradigm.[53] This dualism does not seem appropriate in identifying the inherent linkage between discontinuities and continuities. Rather frequently, institutional changes do not correspond to the expectations of important collective groups. While the social sciences have predominantly focused on the discontinuities at the objective institutional reality, the subjective reality of individuals and collective groups arguably appears to be at odds with the rapid changes in the institutional framework of politics, economy, and society (Sakwa, 1995). The two levels can be made explicit by comparing post-1989 with post-1945 Eastern Europe and Russia. In this regard, sociological and political analysis in the early 1950s coined the concept 'totalitarianism'. The classical analyses focused on the institutional and ideological principles of Soviet-type systems. While modernization and convergence approaches came to dominate the social sciences in the 1970s, 'totalitarianism' had shifted in meaning throughout the late 1960s and 1970s. While violent repression and coercion decreased (Paczkowski, 1997), the reality of the totalitarian lie in common life prevailed among Eastern European intellectuals (Rupnik, 1988).

Given the changes of concepts and contexts, this book surmises that a study of continuities must step back from dyadic thinking. This corresponds to the lack of a clear-cut separation of the first and second societies. Elemér Hankiss has pointed out that most of the second sphere was characterized by the absence of first society rather than by the positive working of the opposite principles. 'This twilight existence of alternative world-views in the second social consciousness had little in common with the open articulation of well-developed, autonomous world-views.'[54] On these grounds, the second or alternative society in Eastern Europe remains essentially an indeterminate sphere of a hypothetical nature.

The 'second society' failed to develop into an autonomous sphere of social existence, into an alternative society governed by organizational principles different from those of the first society. It was a no man's land, where the governing principles and the rules of play of the first society did not work, but the principles and rules of a different type of social existence had hardly emerged. They had not clustered into a more or less consistent new configuration.[55]

As the above examples show, dyadic methodologies can hardly pay heed to the mixed and often confusing record of discontinuities and continuities in Poland's transition. In an attempt to theorize the East European transition, Arpád Szakolczai (1998) has argued that much of modern thought, from the heights of philosophy down to the mundane details of politics, is dominated by the number 'two'. While philosophy as well as current economics and politics uses dyadic opposition between two sides as the central tool for analysis, he has advocated a shift to a three-tier scheme of explanation.

In this vein, historical and sociological research on Eastern Europe has offered some models of triadic approaches. In his ground-breaking essay on the three historical regions of Europe, Jenö Szücs (1988) argued that East Central Europe is a unique formation in between the Western and the Eastern model. Through the crisis at the beginning of the sixteenth century, the career of Western absolutism led to the subordination of society to the state. On the other side, the East nationalized society. In between the two poles of a Western and an Eastern model, a third region emerged.[56] Another three-tier scheme of explanation equated the rise of democracy in Eastern Europe to a civilizing process by applying Norbert Elias's figurational approach (Wydra, 1999). Elias repeatedly stressed the importance of networks of interdependence and reciprocity for the understanding of processes in society. Methodologically, relations between collective groups in societies or between societies cannot be analyzed without taking into account the disposition of collective groups and their mutual relationships (Elias, 1978; 1991). Furthermore, in his study on the national conflicts in Yugoslavia, Rogers Brubaker (1996:55–76) convincingly showed the triadic nexus in the war between Serbia and Croatia. What is commonly presented as a dyadic conflict actually hinged on a triadic relational nexus of reciprocal perceptions and images between national minorities, nationalizing states, and external national homelands.[57]

Triadic frameworks that focus on structures must be complemented by a three-tier scheme to conceive of the process of change. In her work on processual analysis the legal anthropologist Sally Falk Moore distinguished between 'processes of regularization' and 'processes of situational adjustment'. While the first process is ruled by a 'philosophy' of determination,[58] the second one concerns indeterminacy. Processes of 'situational adjustment'

> are those by means of which people arrange their immediate situations (and/or express their feelings and conceptions) by exploiting the indeterminacies in the situation, or by generating such indeterminacies, or by reinterpreting or redefining the rules or relationships. These strategies continuously reinject elements of indeterminacy into social negotiations, making active use of them and making absolute ordering the more impossible. These processes introduce or maintain the element of plasticity in social arrangements.[59]

Two realities of continuity

While explanations of triadic kind have been provided for historical dynamics, there is good reason to assume that Poland's pre-1989 instability was ruled by processes of situational adjustment. Moreover, in Poland and in other countries in the region, the appeal of myths and utopias is fundamental to an understanding of contingency in politics. As I will argue throughout this book, the processes of normalization in pre- and post-1989 Poland can be read as situational adjustments hinging on a vision of social and political utopia. In this vein, second realities materialized as political realities.[60]

In order to extricate continuities of second realities one must distinguish between different levels of analysis. Taking up a conceptual device introduced by David Easton, one can distinguish three hierarchical levels which make any political system operative (Offe, 1997:32f.). At the most fundamental level, a 'decision' is taken as to who 'we' are, that is, on identity, citizenship and territorial, as well as on social and cultural, boundaries of the state. At the second level, rules, procedures and rights must be established which together make up the constitution or the institutional framework of the 'regime'. The highest level, within the parameters of the two previous premises, includes processes and decisions – in terms of both political power and economic resources. This three-tiered model clearly suggests links of upward determination: the 'normal politics' that is going on at the third level is embedded in identities and constitution.

As identities break down and passions rise, the significance of human nature in politics increases. Throughout pre-1989 but, in particular, in an environment of the collapse of habitual beliefs, hopelessness, and the irreality of the real, Polish politics were characterized by low predictability and a lack of far-sightedness. This permanent uncertainty of stable reference-points for political and economic order had a serious impact on the convictions of elites (Horváth, 1998). Drawing on the importance of second realities, the methodological framework in this book will stress not the hard variables that dominate transitology, but the soft variables such as those relating to culture, mentality, and collective consciousness and subconsciousness.[61]

I thus propose to study Poland's transition based on the continuity of second realities which draws on political passions (Furet, 1995; Tocqueville, 1988; Horváth, 1997;1998). Tocqueville emphasized two principal passions that prevailed in the French revolution: first, the hatred of inequality and the desire to destroy old-fashioned institutions in order to build a society according to humanity's yearning for equality; second, the desire to live not only as equals but also in liberty (Tocqueville, 1988:296). The theme of equality in Poland's transition has commonly been under-estimated, as the end of communism highlighted the importance of liberty. Yet both political passions shared an inherently utopian character. The egalitarian goal as the driving force of communist modernization was farcical and illusionary (Arnason, 1993; Furet, 1995). Similarly, liberty has temporarily lost its bearings in post-1989 Poland (Gross, 1994; Szacki, 1995). While the theme of equality in terms of social justice has indeed lost its bearings,[62] equality has played a crucial role in the forging of communities for a social contract for national salvation. The peaceful consensus at the round table, and the enthusiastic return to Europe, have thus continued the most pervasive theme in Polish politics and society since the nineteenth century.[63]

To explore the qualities of the revolutionary passions of equality and liberty, the pillars of contingency in Poland's transition are treated in an anthropological spirit. The dissolution of political order must be treated as the dissolution of the body politic. As Reinhart Koselleck showed in his groundbreaking study *Critique and Crisis* (1988), the Enlightenment as the century of critique and moral progress came to ignore crisis as the central concept. Yet Rousseau grasped its diagnostic content by postulating crisis as a dissolution of order leading to anarchy (Koselleck, 1988:134–140). While Rousseau innovates by fully applying the medical implications of the *corps politique*, this medical understanding of the state as body politic is already inherent in Machiavelli. Machiavelli's use of humours was embedded in a long tradition of the use of medical analogies in classical and medieval political philosophy (Parel, 1992:102ff.). Not by chance, arguably the most controversial policies in the Polish post-1989 transition, such as the economic shock-therapy and the politics of lustration, were taken from medical language or referred to ritual purification.

After 1989, all over Eastern Europe the importance of national identities, ethnic traditions, and universal economic models has been on the rise. It was argued that 'these attempts at inventing traditions, exemplary models, and dogmas are hardly promising, as the element of arbitrariness is evident with which the political movements and elites choose these allegedly "prepolitical" fundamental truths and proclaim them as their program.'[64] Dyadic perspectives that are interested in change or transition from one system to another must assume that newly arising reference-points are not uncontested social facts, but that in the system everything becomes contingent, and nothing can self-evidently remain as it is (Offe, 1992:882).

This book conceptualizes continuities in Poland's transition by drawing on non-contingent givens which essentially belong to the second reality. The second reality of pre-political passions will be elaborated in six different types of continuities. To assume that post-1989 Eastern Europe dispenses with non-contingent givens means to under-estimate relational figurations, such as the historical interdependencies between East and West. Similarly, it would downplay the conflict between communist regimes and opposition movements on behalf of images of normality. To grasp these non-contingencies in a methodological framework one needs to step back from approaches such as political economy, democratic theory and systems theory. I surmise that these non-contingencies are not institutionally stable principles, but have an essentially utopian quality. The resurgence of irrational reference-points in the guise of 'prepolitical fundamental truths' in the process of establishing political order disturbs social scientists. Passions and emotions are at odds with contractual or consensual reordering of things. To unravel this paradox, this book has opted for a new methodological framework that focuses on the pre-political quality of the fundamental reference-points in post-1989 Poland and Eastern Europe.

Given the dyadic impasse of standard approaches, my methodological approach is based on a three-tier scheme. In order to examine the starting-point of transition, I will make use of the works of Arnold van Gennep (1960) and Victor Turner (1969; 1974; 1985; 1987; 1992). Van Gennep developed a scheme of rites of passage, while Turner conceptualized the in-between stage as a liminal phase, a threshold situation. As I will argue throughout the book, Polish politics were stamped throughout pre- and post-1989 by various threshold situations. In most cases, these situations were moments of nationwide communities, as will be exemplified by the Solidarity community in 1980 and the round-table community in 1989. In order to grasp the continuity of cleavage-patterns, I will rely on René Girard's theory of mimetic conflict (Girard, 1965; 1977; 1987; 1988; 1989; 1990; 1994). Based on broad studies on the epistemology of Western literature, myths, and the biblical texts, his work is concerned with the basis of cultural, social, and political order. The central argument holds that in moments of disruptions in cultural and social order, the reciprocity of desires creates conflicts. Such a relational approach to conflict in politics assumes that antagonists in a situation of crisis pursue utopian projects which can essentially be regarded as mirror images. A third conceptual tool aims to examine the role of Solidarity elites for the modernization of politics and the economy as a way to leave behind the state of backwardness. By applying Bruno Latour's concept of action at distance, I will examine the modalities of the imitation of models in Poland's transition. I will argue that Polish political elites resembled disoriented explorers of utopian islands.

To study the modalities of continuities in Poland's transition by connecting the hypotheses of Turner and Girard seems to be contradictory. Rites of passage may come closest to integration theories of society, while an approach to imitation based on reciprocal appropriative mimesis suggests a coercive and violence-based vision of conflict in society. Turner's conception highlights the creation of a spiritual unity in an existential community and thus conceives of it as a consensus-based reordering of social, cultural, or political order. Girard's approach to imitation breaks with the long tradition of mimesis as representative (Girard, 1987). While imitation is a fundamental mechanism of learning in human life, it becomes most acute in situations of crisis, when it becomes appropriative. In a mimetic perspective, desires are by definition endless, but the availability of desired objects is limited by definition as well. The pursuit of utopian projects is assumed to be reciprocal, while the shortage of desired objects makes it impossible to satisfy all desires and thus may lead to potentially violent conflicts. As their application to the Polish case will show, both these theories are not only compatible, but gain full power only in their conjunction. William Sewell's in-depth analysis of the attack on the Bastille as a historical event brought together the emotional and rational-normative foundations of the French revolution.[65] Linking the idea of a social contract to large-scale crowd violence, it shows convincingly how a liminal period may produce and sustain conflicting states such as emotional unity and common feelings in moments of *communitas*, and may trigger the mimetic ravages of crowd violence (Sewell, 1996:864–871).

As I will argue throughout the book, dependence on second realities has entailed the repetitively changing allegiances of political elites. The autonomy of political actors, assumed as crucial in most approaches to political order in transition, is thus contested by a relational triadic framework. The passions of equality and liberty are examined in terms of short-term communities and pervasive utopias that guided pre- and post-1989 Poland. The core principles in the continuity of second reality are pre-political passions that are constitutive for the anti-structure of *communitas*, the mimetic conflict of historical antagonisms, and the backwardness of elites. Hence, the approach taken in this book does not offer an analysis of Poland's transition towards a clear-cut political system, but elaborates analytical categories in order to show how Poland's post-1989 politics has been pervaded by non-contingent continuities. A comparison with Easton's scheme suggests that the continuities are fundamentally located at the first level of normal politics, while they strongly influence the second and the third level. Continuities in Poland's permanent transition are not visible at face value and can only be extracted by looking at the second reality of images, myths and mentalities.

The first reality has produced a variety of discontinuities, while continuities persist in the second reality. In the first part of this book, I am going to examine pre-1989 politics with an expectation of political discontinuities in the second reality. I will argue that permanent instability hinged upon the passions of equality and liberty as crises and conflicts were driven by social and national communities as well as by widespread tendencies for political utopias. In the second part of this book, second realities are conceptualized as guided by the ideological and institutional impact of images that are temporarily weakened but recurrently become essential reference-points for Polish politics and society. This continuity of non-contingent second realities provides the crucial link between Poland's permanent transition before and after 1989.

Part I

In the first part of this book, I examine political change in post-1989 Poland by linking it analytically to the continuities of second realities in Poland's past. My primary objective is to probe into socio-genetic causes for the lengthy transition to Western models of political and societal organization. Analyzing long-term political instability and conflict in pre-1989 Poland, I will argue that the permanence of transition can be conceived as recurrent experiences of threshold situations, in which collective actors and political elites have found themselves in both pre- and post-1989 Poland. Examining these continuities, some pre-political non-contingent givens in Poland's transition are developed.

In Chapter 2, I examine the round-table pact in view of the dissolution of communism in Poland. I argue that 1989 was not the rupture-point for which it has been taken in most of the social science literature. As shown in this chapter, political events in 1989 constituted a further crisis in a series of recurrent crises. The round-table pact in 1989 was a moment of communion across ideological and historical enmities. This community differed from pre-1989 communities such as the Solidarity community in 1980 only in kind, not in principle. As in pre-1989 Poland, the round-table community as a moment of anti-structure came to shape political order on the basis of emotions. Being another threshold situation which did not bring about a normalization of political order, it did not constitute a rupture-point in the continuity of transition.

Chapter 3 deals with political conflict in Poland's transition from the point of view of identity-politics. I will examine the causes for the replication of historical antagonisms between the post-communist and post-Solidarity camps as they re-emerged throughout the 1990s.

I will argue that in pre-1989 Poland both antagonists pursued social and political utopias. In a society with a low degree of class-differentiation, antagonists aimed to totalize their own utopian project of a second Poland in direct negation to the mirror image of their political opponent. As pre-1989 Poland experienced contested norms and legitimacy, both antagonists were in liminal conditions. In this vein, a reciprocal imitation of utopias – which aim to develop totalizing visions of political legitimacy and social power – came to constitute the passion of liberty in Poland's transition. Chapter 4 examines causes for the continuity of backwardness in post-1989 Poland. I will argue that problems of political and economic modernization are rooted in the lack of fully-fledged political elites. The continuing backwardness of the political elites in Poland's transition is a consequence of their imitation of blurred images of democracy and capitalism and their recurrent reference to images of the past.

The continuity of second realities that link up pre-1989 with post-1989 underlies the recurrence of three fundamental processes in Poland's transition. First, communities such as those in 1980 or in 1989, as short-term situations of anti-structure, have had a deep impact in Poland's transition as they left their stamp on the political order. Second, competition with each other on the basis of commonly pursued utopian images has been characteristic for the continuity of historical antagonisms between (post-) Solidarity and the (post-) communists. Finally, the continuity of backwardness can be seen as caused by the lack of fully-fledged elites that imitate blurred models from the West and reorient identity-politics towards the own past.

2
The Continuity of Transition

Two assumptions about the significance of the year 1989 for Poland's political future have guided scholars. The first holds that Poland's transition from state socialism was initiated in 1989 by consensual elites, and thus amounted to a revolution from above (Staniszkis, 1991a; Osiatyński, 1996; Higley *et al.* 1998). The second assumption suggests that neither the state power nor Solidarity were weak (Ekiert, 1996; Poznański, 1992). 'In 1989, the regime of Jaruzelski was not particularly weak, and there were no signs of rapid demoralization of army or policy. There was also no evidence of unusual lack of order, with people feeling afraid for their lives or property ... power was taken over by the opposition through negotiations or rather handed over to them by the Communist party.'[1] Ekiert's argument holds that demobilization policies pursued by the communist regime failed because of Solidarity's particular strength, which was not fundamentally affected by martial law and the underground period (Ekiert, 1996:286–9).

As happens frequently in the social sciences, disruptive events of great importance suddenly promote concepts such as transition,[2] which appear to be so self-evident that scholars hardly bother to define them precisely. Moreover, under the premises of such concepts, other strands of the literature dealing with interrelated problems are considered less. As regards the round-table pact, the rich tradition of historical, political, and sociological analysis of the Solidarity movement gave way to actor-oriented interpretations in the new field of transitology.[3] The assumed rupture point of 1989 absorbed most of the attention in academic literature, to the extent that scholars hardly ask under which conditions the dominant actors of the round table actually arrived at this unprecedented situation.

For elite-oriented approaches in transitology, the initiation of transition is coterminous with the convergence between the communist regime and a coherent Solidarity elite. The round-table pact is considered to be an intentional proposal for a social contract, a 'bargaining between the government and society' (Elster, 1996:3). In a path-dependent spirit, this refers to the attitude of strategic actors that deliberately attempt to restructure the rules of the games. Accordingly, the widely accepted slogan of a negotiated pact or a revolution from above[4] was supposedly rooted in a 'consensus of termination among elites' (Przeworski, 1993:136) towards an anti-crisis agreement between the communist government and the Solidarity opposition in the late 1980s. In this respect the failed referendum on the economic reform in November 1987 had a signalling function, since 'in autumn 1987, the day after the referendum, Solidarity took the decision to propose an anti-crisis agreement'.[5] In these circumstances, the Polish case enters the category of transplacement, where 'democratization is produced by the combined actions of government and opposition'.[6]

A further variant of the convergence-pattern tries to extend the 'Rokkan hypothesis'. It argues that transitions to democracy are characterized by a 'convergence of pressures from below and from above'.[7] With hindsight, Adam Michnik, one of the most influential Solidarity advisers and a central figure in the round-table process, characterized it as 'a great political achievement, as the application of the Spanish evolutionary way to the Polish reality of abandoning dictatorship'.[8] This emphasis on convergence in the round table of 1989 complies with an actor-driven vision that defends the centrality of pacts as a means of transition from authoritarian to democratic order (O'Donnell *et al.*, 1986).

In contrast to the convergence pattern, analyses of pre-1989 Polish politics and society largely concur in stressing the separation between Polish society (*społeczeństwo*) and the communist regime (*władza*) as the most notable systemic characteristic of pre-1989 Poland. After initial compliance between elites and people with the communist regime in the 1950s, oppositional tendencies in the 1960s and early 1970s were limited to particular groups such as workers, the Catholic Church, or intellectuals (Raina, 1978; Kuroń, 1978; Karpiński, 1982; Michnik, 1985). The state–society dichotomy gained full force only in the second half of the 1970s. This separation, however, only came about and was sustained by a great convergence (Ash, 1991:19ff.) of opposition groups that developed during the 1970s, and it reached its peak with the emergence of the Solidarity movement in 1980. The dichotomy in Polish society was aggravated by the proclamation of martial law in 1981.

In the following I will examine the systemic dichotomy with a view to characteristics of convergence and separation. This chapter postulates that dyadic conceptions of situations of contingency in politics are not appropriate to account for the mixed record of continuities and discontinuities in the Polish transition. Drawing on this apparent lack, the present chapter develops an alternative concept of transition by focusing on the modalities of the breakdown of Polish communism. Analyzing the points of departure of the political antagonists, according to which systemic dichotomy was resolved by convergence at the round table, I will show that the antagonistic groups in Polish politics before the collapse of communism went through different processes of convergence and separation. On these grounds I will set out to elaborate two arguments. First, I shall take issue with the dominant vision that regards changes of social and political order fundamentally as a two-step move. As arguments on the permanence of crises in post-war Poland have shown (Ascherson, 1981; Curry and Fajfer, 1996; Poznański, 1996), there is strong evidence that 1989 did not constitute a fundamental rupture-point in this cycle. Second, I shall argue that Poland has been in a permanent transition for a long time, long before 1989. The history of communism in Eastern Europe, epitomized by the Polish case, amounts to a series of attempts to arrive at a desired endpoint while never achieving it.

To a considerable extent the mass experience of Solidarity in 1980 and 1981 reversed the atomization of society. Given its breadth and intensity, the emergence of the Solidarity movement was due to a successful mobilization of societal forces. At the same time, the constitution of a fully fledged mass movement made a peak in a lengthy process of society's separation from official rules and norms imposed and defended by the communist regime. 'Creating Solidarity, society rejected the system. . . . Before August [1980], society, if it rejected the system, did so only in the verbal-emotional sphere, not in practice.'[9] Hence, it managed to achieve the subjectivization of society. 'Since August 1980 the real form of Poland is slowly emerging.'[10] While society started to 'feel at home', communist power became rapidly marginalized. 'The complete isolation of the authorities is no outstanding phenomenon in the history of the Polish Peoples' Republic. But such a clear and demonstrative isolation is a novelty.'[11] The separation from the objective-institutional, 'first' reality became generalized in a genuine mobilization from below. Contrary to earlier crises, where only single-status groups such as workers or intellectuals deviated from the established norms, the emergence of Solidarity was distinguished by the fact that it was sustained by an ideological and organizational *rapprochement* between intellectuals, workers, and the Catholic Church.

> The non-communist Polish left now abandoned the outdated stereotype of the bigoted, nationalist, 'reactionary', anti-Semitic Church (which lived on as a terrible phantom in the mind of the western Left); . . . Catholic and non-Catholic intellectuals found more and more common ground in the defence of common values, common sense and basic rights against the late Gierek regime; and . . . the church of Wyszyński and Wojtyła cast its protective mantle around an increasingly outspoken opposition.[12]

Such a large-scale convergence intimated the institutionalization of a second reality which was reflected in the rationale of Solidarity. 'The spirit of 1980 was not: "How can the system of power be reformed?", but: "How can one defend oneself from the system?"'[13] As a consequence, this convergence of Polish society against and outside the communist state entailed a breach of the established communist order in post-war Poland in the subjective realm. 'It was a moment when individuals, brought up in the totalitarian situation (characterized by a gap between common-sense morality and rules imposed in the name of "objective reason"), were able to overcome their own moral indifference to society and to themselves.'[14] This separation also applied to objective breaches of communist norms through the denial of rules and the legal framework.[15] 'Even within the theoretical confines of state socialism, inevitably a societal autonomy and diversity of individual interests seem to have developed. This progress toward a pluralistic political life gained momentum with the founding of Solidarity.'[16]

In the aftermath of the proclamation of martial law in December 1981, the focus shifted anew to the antagonism between state and society, crystallized in the 'civil war'. Few studies have traced back the structural change of both antagonists, Solidarity and the communist regime, during this period. Ekiert (1996) argued that, contrary to the normalization strategies in Hungary (1956) and Czechoslovakia (1968), the communist regime failed to achieve the demobilization of the Solidarity opposition and its popular support.[17] Given that in the aftermath of the Polish 'revolution' of 1980–1 both antagonists were subject to deep changes in organizational structure, political legitimacy, and popular mobilization, there is good reason to argue that the survival of the Solidarity spirit can be attributed to the processes of separation. In the following, I will outline the most remarkable separation processes experienced by political activists during the 1980s.

The 16 months of Solidarity's existence reflected not only a deep legitimacy crisis of the communist regime. Already as of April 1981 Solidarity itself had succumbed to an identity crisis which became manifest in tensions over future political strategies, demobilization and diminished strike activity (Staniszkis, 1994b:123ff.). As differentiation processes inside Solidarity led to the foundation of independent clubs (Holzer, 1984:168 and 325f.; Cecuda, 1989:31), its identity became more and more contested.[18] With the proclamation of martial law in December 1981 Solidarity's fall into the underground aggravated the processes of separation from formerly defining attributes. As its leading figures were arrested, the trade union was delegalized and stripped of its mass activity in enterprises. Similarly, it was deprived of the powerful weapon of the strike, and had to renounce the realization of a self-governing republic in state enterprises.[19] During the 'long march' formerly successful strategies such as strikes or large-scale trade union activities at enterprise level became widely obsolete, since 'the Solidarity cells were so deeply underground that many workers did not even know they existed'.[20] While the basis of the trade union and the self-management structures in enterprises waned away quickly, on the scale of society, 'in 1987 we Solidarity people already were only a waning margin'.[21] Moreover, declining public approval for Solidarity, and the waning identification with it, testified to Solidarity's increasing loss of legitimacy.[22] In 1985 55.7 per cent of Poles polled approved of the introduction of martial law. (Marody, 1988, 280–5.) In February 1989, Solidarity was still virtually banned from public discourse by a censorship that only allowed reference to 'talks with Lech Wałesa and a group of persons'.[23] As mentioned earlier, Solidarity's rejection of a reformist path in 1980 and 1981 was recognized as a strategy of negation. The willingness to negotiate with the communist regime in 1988–9 meant the end of the negation, and at least partly, the end of the Solidarity of 1980 (Skórzyński, 1995:42).

Conversely, the economic and political reforms undertaken by the Jaruzelski regime in order to stabilize the political situation only produced an 'unstable equilibrium' (Poznański, 1996:139) and failed to achieve a normalization of the country (Ekiert, 1996). From 1980 onwards the Communist Party became increasingly drained of its members.[24] While this tendency petered out in the mid-1980s, the party continued to lose its proletarian character and its share of young members went into sharp decline.[25] Generally speaking, in the wake of 1981 the regime lost its former attributes, a process that crystallized in the 'withdrawal of the state' (Kamiński, B., 1991). The state had to withdraw on various fronts, including those of the economy, its political monopoly, and national 'rituals'.[26] One remarkable withdrawal from rituals concerned the increasing number of people refusing to vote. In three elections[27] during the 1980s, between 25 and 40 per cent of eligible voters did not participate (Kamiński, B., 1991:178; Ekiert, 1996:284).

These simultaneous processes of separation in terms of organizational structure and ideological orientation were complemented by the declining legitimacy of both the communist regime and the underground Solidarity. Most importantly, throughout the 1980s society showed low psychological involvement and a generalized detachment from civic affairs, linked with a retreat into private affairs and growing work emigration to the West (Mason *et al.*, 1991:215). At the same time Solidarity's monopoly of opposition to the regime was slowly giving way to a developing 'quasi-pluralism' in the late 1980s (Smolar and Kende, 1989:12ff.; Kamiński, B., 1991:186ff.). As of 1989, a general trend appeared that can be termed a 'separation of power from responsibility'. In this regard, Jadwiga Staniszkis has pointed to a separation of politics ('reason of state') from any ethical argument formulated from the perspective of the individual. Furthermore, 'one could sense the severance of earlier bonds (obligations) in the power apparatus', as well as 'a sharper separation than before between the sphere of power and that of social life'.[28]

The collapse of the formerly defining attributes of political antagonists was accompanied by society's rising zeal for separation from superseded political and economic structures. A comparison between 1980 and 1989 is telling in this respect. Adam Michnik has described the crisis of the late 1980s as the 'deepest of the crises', a 'general crisis of communism. . . . whose changes and shocks will entail a rupture (a non-continuation) of the communist system'.[29] The Communist Party's crushing defeat in the June elections of

1989 is commonly equated with the end of communism in Poland, as it paved the way for Solidarity's takeover of governmental responsibility (Ash, 1990:369–70). As Michnik has pointed out, the deputies to the *Sejm* took the results of the June 1989 elections as a mandate to conduct structural reform in Poland. However, 'the majority of society was not at all conscious that it had voted for such a reform in June 1989'.[30] In 1980 the emergence of Solidarity had been as a 'mass-movement which became the acknowledged representative of society against the regime'.[31] The elections of June 1989, on the other hand, were a referendum against the established party without clearly attributing representation or legitimacy to the other side either. The refusal of the old power structures was not a clear legitimization of a particular new force.

> And while the Poles threw the communists out in June 1989, they did not empower legislators. They did not give a mandate to make laws to anybody. It should have been understood that the June elections were but a rehearsal for a 'velvet' revolution and nobody elected at the time should have considered himself or herself an empowered representative of the people.[32]

The election results showed to what extent the loss of differences between 'we' and 'them' were welded together, and how Solidarity acquired the attributes of a mirror-image of the communist regime. 'The strong relationship between support for civic committee candidates and rejection of the national list clearly indicates that anti-regime feelings are virtually inseparable from pro-*Solidarność* attitudes in Poland.'[33] By the same token, a similar intermediate status in terms of political legitimacy applied to the semi-free elections in June 1989. Finally, governmental responsibility in the first Solidarity government had to be shared with the communists, as the far-reaching competences of the president and extra-constitutional institutions curtailed democratic legitimacy (Staniszkis, 1991a:213).

Separation and the 'in-between': liminality

Commonly, 1989 is regarded as the starting-point of transition made up by a convergence of elites that ended a dichotomy of political antagonisms. However, the above analysis suggests that the round-table pact should rather be seen through the perspective of the separation processes that preceded convergence at the round table. To my knowledge, Zygmunt Bauman was the first to draw attention to this obvious tendency of sep-aration processes. In his view, the East European revolutions have been marked by 'separation between the interests that brought the fall of the old regime and those which the new one serves or promotes. They are, so to speak, two-step revolutions, with a void separating the two stages.'[34] In the following, I will examine more thoroughly the meaning of 'void' and 'separation'. Bauman took his cue from the French anthropologist Arnold van Gennep, who introduced the notion of rites of passage, and from Victor Turner, who elaborated upon them (Van Gennep, 1960; Turner, 1969; 1987). Following Van Gennep, any transition in social and cultural life is marked by three phases: separation, margin (*limen*),[35] and aggregation. In its wake, Gennep spelt out the importance of those margins which acquire a certain autonomy. As an analytical framework, van Gennep introduced three steps that make up the rites of passage: the pre-liminal, liminal, and post-liminal rites (Van Gennep, 1960:14). More interesting than each isolated part is their sequence. The first phase marks the detachment of the individual or group from its former attributes or identities, usually uncoupling it from an 'earlier fixed point in the social structure, from a set of cultural conditions (a "state"), or from both'.[36] The third phase (reaggregation or reincorporation) regains a relatively stable state anew and, by virtue of this, has rights and obligations *vis-à-vis* others of a clearly defined and structural type. The central phase in the rites of passage is that of liminality. As Turner defined it: 'Liminal entities are neither here nor there; they are betwixt and between the positions assigned and arrayed by law, custom, convention, and ceremonial.'[37]

In Turner's ideal type, the liminal state embraces the in-between stage between two stable orders. As Turner has argued,

> rites of passage are found in all societies, but tend to reach their maximal expression in small-scale, relatively stable and cyclical societies, where change is bound up with biological and meteorological rhythms and recurrences rather than with technological innovations. Such rites indicate and constitute transitions between states. By 'state' I mean here 'a relatively fixed or stable condition' and would include in its meaning such social constancies as legal status, profession, office or calling, rank or degree.[38]

The picture of confusion and reversal of roles and competences during the systemic changes in 1989 highlight their conditions of uncertainty and ambivalence.

> Underdetermination and ambiguity of the liminal condition cannot be said to serve any specific purpose, and even less a purpose deliberately set and pursued by the elite currently in charge. It is, rather, a combined outcome of the dissolutions of past meanings and the nebulousness of promised new ones. Liminality is inherently ambivalent. It is a condition without any clear time-span, obvious exit or authoritative guides.[39]

This state of non-ending or missing reaggregation calls for a reconsideration of Turner's ideal-type, which needs to be adapted to societies.

> Turner's vocabulary is strewn with references to purpose and function. This is well justified when liminality serves the reassertion of a relatively stable structure – its continuous reproduction over time. It is not permissible, however, in our extension to the passage of societies rather than their individual members. The decisive difference is that the end-structure to which liminality would eventually lead is 'given in advance', if at all, solely in the form of a vague utopia which more likely than not would bear little resemblance to the actual state of affairs established at the other end of the liminality ordeal.[40]

Bauman confined the liminal condition to post-1989 Poland, and thus logically continued to see 1989 as a rupture-point. There is, however, good reason to assume that in terms of the continuity of second reality, the processes of separation in pre-1989 and post-1989 Poland are interwoven. The cyclical political crises in post-war Poland, the emergence of a fully fledged systemic opposition, and the institutionalization of a second reality show that dissolutions of past meaning and the nebulousness of promised meanings were determining characteristics of Polish politics well before 1989. When Solidarity appeared in 1980, it did not fall in the interstices of the existing social structure, but in the infinitely broadened, multiplied and publicized interstices which had already been existing for decades. It was not by chance that 'the opposition of the 1970s did not represent the deviation, but the norm of societal thought'.[41]

The processes of separation that disaggregated the political antagonists from their formerly defining attributes suggest that a state of liminality not only applies to the 'official' transition as of 1989, but can arguably be extended over the whole 44 years of communist rule in Poland and even before.

Poland in permanent liminality

Taking his cue from Bauman, Arpád Szakolczai has argued that Eastern Europe has been in a period of permanent transition since the very beginning of the Bolshevik Revolution in 1917 (Szakolczai, 1996;1998). Throughout post-Second-World-War history, communist state and ideologies had a strong taste of being between a societally contested reality and the utopia of a better future (Malia, 1994:29ff.). The liminal condition of communist regimes squared with their self-description as transitional regimes who regarded themselves as 'socialist', being on the way towards communism, but not fully there. Furthermore, the socialist regimes took power in Eastern Europe in the wake of a world war, that is, during a major period of transition and the collapse of order (Gross, 1989, Kersten, 1991). During the Second World War the Polish underground state was deprived of any chance to re-establish independence and came under the rule of a big ideological empire for whom it had been an enemy nation for centuries (Paczkowski, 1998:117–42). Because of this, the dissolution of the Polish state created an authority vacuum and a normative void.[42] Most of Polish society experienced a loss of values and a loss of confidence for having failed twice, first in not maintaining the Polish Second Republic in 1939 and again in 1944 in not liberating Poland from foreign occupation (Kersten, 1991:169). As a consequence,

> psychologically, Polish society found itself in a situation defined by both defeat and victory. The result of this combination was a certain ambiguity of attitudes, confusion, a lack of consequence, disparity between views and behaviour, hesitation, and an inclination to adapt. Fear was an additional factor, caused by repression aimed at the organizations of the Underground State.[43]

This psychological state of disruption was aggravated by Poland's territorial displacement from east to west, and by its blood tolls, one of the highest, as a result of the Second World War. The population of the present territory of Poland declined by 7 million, or 12 per cent, between 1939 and 1950.[44] As in Europe as a whole, 'the Pole of 1945 (and of the next two years) was a wanderer'.[45] The disastrous social consequences of violence, forced migration, and increasing hatred of enemies entailed a 'widespread psychological regression, i.e. a collapse of adult norms and standards of speech, behaviour and attitude, and a reversion to less mature patterns'.[46]

When Stanisław Gomułka defined the Polish version of the People's Democracy in March 1945 he could not have been more explicit on the liminal character of the project. 'The People's Democracy' was to be merely a transitional stage for the Polish state. If 'the consistently democratic people's forces (the PPR[47] and their allies in the PPS[48] and the SL[49]) that have designated socialism as the final goal', were to win over or isolate 'the liberal-agrarian and liberal-bourgeois forces' and defeat 'the reactionary-fascist forces', then 'the road of evolutionary social change and an evolutionary transition to a Socialist system will be entirely possible'. Others asserted that 'socialism (. . .) is not an issue for today'. It lay on the horizon, 'but we must concentrate on today's problems, and speak in a way that will be understood today'.[50]

The modalities of the establishment of communist power in Poland stamped the course of Polish politics for decades to come. In Turner's definition of the interstructural character of the liminal, the relationship between instructors and neophytes in non-liminal periods (that is, in situations of order) is characterized by complete authority and complete submission. 'Nevertheless, it must be understood that the authority of the elders over the neophytes is not based on legal sanctions; it is in a sense the personification of the self-evident authority of tradition. The authority of the elders is absolute, because it represents the absolute, the axiomatic values of society in which are expressed the "common good" and the "common interest".'[51]

Although formally valid and implemented in power relations, the distinctions between communist authorities and oppositional neophytes were constantly questioned in communist pre-1989 Poland. Despite an initial compliance of society with the communist regime, its cyclical crises (1956, 1970, 1976, 1980/81) demonstrate fundamental discontent on the part of the layer of society that ideologically and politically was supposed to be the power base of the authorities: the workers. Moreover, resistance against the authorities appeared to be institutionalized, as is shown by the considerable number of independent circles (*środowiska*) of oppositional thought and private or semi-public spaces of freedom and dissidence (Wedel, 1988; Kuroń and Żakowski, 1995:155–205). In this respect, the inner-party opposition by the revisionists (such as the open letter by Jacek Kuroń and Karol Modzelewski in 1965), the myriad of Catholic and intellectual circles, and the Committee for the Defence of Workers (KOR) founded in 1976, shared the same objective: their subordination was contested by the subordinated themselves. Polish post-war history was a history of its society's resistance, of which Solidarity's emergence was the culminating point as a unbloody insurrection of the oppressed (Kowalski, 1990a).

Other aspects of a protracted liminal threshold situation in Polish politics can be readily recognized by the symbols of opposition and the beliefs that attach to them. Such are 'the powers of the weak', or, in other words, the permanently or transiently sacred attributes of low status or position (Turner, 1969:109). The weak or the powerless in a communist system are those who are either excluded from the unitary mechanism of power, or who voluntarily renounce participation in it.[52] In Poland, the second factor especially played an important role, making the power of the weak a national trait, as argued by Adam Michnik.

> We are much less vulnerable to sovietization. Why? Our singularity is made up by different factors: historical tradition, the Catholic Church and the courageous but very realistic politics of the episcopate (. . .) The whole of society keeps on exerting pressure. This pressure is sometimes manifest in violent explosions (Poznan´ 1956, March 1968, December 1970, Radom 1976), but its usual characteristic is a silent, daily and obstinate resistance. (. . .) We in Poland can breathe a cleaner air than elsewhere, an air of spirituality which is renewed every day, invisible but essential for culture and national consciousness. All this has not been provoked by the mere perusal of publications by the opposition. It is the result of a whole multiplicity of actions.[53]

Liminal conditions tend to eliminate distinctions and graduations between legitimate or absolute power and inferiors (Turner, 1987:99). The communist authorities in pre-1989 Poland could hardly ever be certain about the acceptance of their authority. Moreover, the oppositional forces (whether workers, intellectuals, KOR, or Solidarity) aimed at a reshuffling of the attributed power positions.

In the end, the communist governments' opponents learned more about getting and using power effectively than their rulers did. Actors who did not win one battle returned to fight again, with their tactics adjusted to avoid failure. Rulers who were supposed to have total power ultimately retreated from their challenges and recognized the hopelessness of their situation.[54]

In Turner's view, a breach of norm-governed relations – which means the commencement of crisis – is 'signalled by a public transgression of a salient rule normally binding on members of the group being studied. This may be an overt flouting of a law or custom to make inevitable a testing political process, or it may result from an outburst of previously suppressed feelings'.[55] Such activities appeared more frequently in the Poland of the 1970s, as proved by rising strike action, mass protests, and the formation of a counter-public, a public political opposition. It also led to the forced withdrawal of two party chiefs, Gomułka in 1970 and Gierek in 1980.

The only moment in which this drawn-out liminality – consisting of contested political authority and questioning of the legitimacy of the communists – seemed to be suspended may apply to Gierek's project of a 'second Poland'.[56] At the outset of the 1970s his economic policy based on credits from the West caused an 'economic miracle', rising investments and booming consumption. In this context, Jacek Kuroń's account is particularly illuminating: 'Almost the entire society accepted the power (*władza*) and the dominating order. It was the only period in my life-time, when I was afraid of society. I felt being marginalized, I felt that Gierek had bought the Poles.'[57] This temporary reversal of roles only reinforced the liminal Polish condition when a massive political opposition emerged as a result of this fake reform. As Kubik has shown in his detailed analysis of public discourse in the Gierek era, the fight for authority and political legitimacy was led not only through economic liberalization, but also through the appropriation of national and patriotic symbols, ceremonies, and rituals (Kubik, 1994a:31–74). Large segments of the populace rejected Gierek's master fiction and undermined the regime's monopoly on social communication, thus furnishing the people with the conceptual and symbolic tools with which to define social reality afresh (Kubik, 1994a:73). Long before 1989, the instability caused by these separation processes generated a 'peculiar aura of being in a sort of limbo situation – between two systems (when socialism's arrangements no longer exist but a new system is not yet created)'.[58]

To a significant degree, the Polish economy too was affected by transitoriness and the failed attempt to arrive at a desired situation. 'The practice of "real socialism" . . . meant not only a reversal of the time sequence in relation to the expected course of events . . . but a basic shift in the perceived line of dependence: socialism was to be not the outcome but the major vehicle of overtaking other nations.'[59] As Poznański has demonstrated, the process of transition to capitalism was under way at least from 1970 (Poznański, 1996). 'With many elements of the past continuing unchanged or only partially changed, the overall (social) system assumed yet another transitory – mixed – form.'[60] There is good reason to assume that economic reforms in post-war Poland amounted to a 'cycle of crises' (Landau and Roszkowski, 1995:239–54). Privatization only started from 1987 onwards and promoted political capitalism (Staniszkis, 1991b) as the guiding principle of the transition towards a new state of economic structure. Political capitalism as a *nomenklatura*-driven privatization can, however, also be conceived as a process through which the centrally planned economy lost its defining attributes. Such a view is supported by the fact that the particular forms of political capitalism did not have a transformative interest; that is, they did not aim at dismantling the state's control of the economy (Staniszkis, 1991b).

Furthermore, empirical analyses of post-1989 Poland confirmed that there was a state of separation from the 'old' economic order without having reached a 'new' order, and that the situation was consequently that of being stuck in a vacuum.

> The decisions made by the authorities in the second half of the 1980s dismantled the planned economy, without installing any market-oriented features. The economy was no longer controlled by the plan and decisions made by the central authorities, nor was it guided by market regulating and co-ordinating mech anisms. The resulting vacuum was tentatively filled by various adaptive mechanisms and rules dictated by scarcity.[61]

In this vein, 'regardless of political changes, the average citizen has the impression of still living in the same world, the world of permanent crisis which has become a kind of curse on Poland'.[62]

To sum up, the Polish situation pre-1989 squares with Szakolczai's view, according to which 'one can safely argue that for at least six or seven decades the East European region has been in a permanent state of transition, having left a regular state of affairs and never arriving to a point of safe repose that in the "West" in a certain sense happened, e.g. with the New Deal, the Marshall Plan, or the establishment of the EC'.[63] While it is not possible to specify a precise starting-point for liminality in Poland, there are strong indicators for a condition of permanent liminality even before the war. The occupation of Polish territory throughout more than 150 years by foreign powers had prompted a series of insurrections and the establishment of underground states. The failed insurrections in 1830 and 1863 had entailed not only severe losses of life, but had also weakened Polish elites and Polish identity through repressive measures such as anti-Polish education policies and policies of Germanization in the Prussian and Russification in the Tsarist provinces (Wandycz, 1974:193).

During the occupation of their country, Poles used to feel neither here nor there, or to use Turner's term, betwixt and between. 'Long years of foreign domination had left their mark on the outlook and mentality of the Polish citizens of Russia, Austria, and Germany. Overawed by the might of the three empires, the average Pole could not readily see how he could affect his own and his nation's fate.'[64] It is not by accident that Alfred Jarry in 1896 gave his play *Ubu Roi* a Polish setting. He declared: 'The action takes place in Poland, that is to say, Nowhere.'[65] Following the partitions and the short interlude of the Second Republic in the 1920s and 1930s, under German occupation the Polish lands were literally given the label *Zwischenland*, the status of an area in-between, presumably between the *Reich* and some other 'over-there' yet further removed.[66] Prolonged statelessness and resistance against occupational authorities thus generated a deep distrust among Poles towards the state.

The continuing inter-structural character of the liminal conditions in Poland points to striking parallels between nineteenth-century and post-1945 Poland. A long record of uprisings and resistance accompanied a strong longing to attain national independence and become a modernized nation by means of political and cultural Westernization. In this vein, Hugo Kołłataj, the main architect of the May Constitution of 1791, interpreted modernization in terms of a nation-building process: as a transition from the nation of the gentry to the 'new nation'.[67] Thus, the continuity of romantic nationalism in the Solidarity movement was not surprising (Kubik, 1994a; Walicki, 1997). The anti-politics of the 1980s, with their pursuit of living in dignity and truth, share characteristics of liminality with Polish romanticism, which was generated under the impact of failed insurrections, the refusal of the norm, and forced emigration. In a similar vein, the nineteenth-century version of anti-politics abstained from practical politics and was based instead on spiritual and ideological leadership. 'The notion of revolution was . . . presented in lofty moral terms, and emigration was conceived as a pilgrimage, a purifying process in the search for freedom and justice.'[68]

Another aspect of liminality concerned the appeal to solidarity and unity between opposite social groups and ideological orientations. In this vein, the permanent revolution in Polish romanticism pointed to the unification of inimical social groups such as the nobility and the peasantry (Wandycz, 1974:118–19). Such an attempt to achieve community across borders does not substantially differ from the rapid and extreme swings between right and left and back again which constituted the normal condition of communism (Borkenau, 1971:414). Again in 1980, Solidarity produced a set of apolitical symbols and discourses that mirrored such an intermediate state of terminological and ideological concreteness. 'They were apolitical in the sense that they stood for neither "left" nor "right", neither centralization nor decentralization; neither authoritarian leadership nor participatory democracy.'[69] On the whole, a clear-cut identification of political currents in communist systems was difficult, if not impossible. This was mirrored in Solidarity's aspiration to be a catch-all movement outside the traditional categories of Polish politics. 'I claim that Solidarity is neither leftist nor rightist, neither oriented towards Social democracy nor towards Christian democracy. Solidarity is a new movement that cannot be understood or made understandable by means of the political categories of the Second Republic (1918–1939).'[70]

What distinguishes permanent liminality from systemic approaches such as, for instance, those presented by Juan Linz and Alfred Stepan? In their categorization, Poland – as the most advanced country in the Eastern bloc in terms of institutional pluralism during the 1970s and early 1980s – figures as being between the ideal-types of post-totalitarian and authoritarian regimes. Post-totalitarianism conforms to a relative de-ideologization and the weakening of the belief in utopia as a foundation of legitimacy (Linz and Stepan, 1996b:49). By contrast, permanent liminality points to recurrent rupture-points and a prolonged confusion of norms and coercive relationships. Furthermore, the evolutionary and dyadic conception of totalitarianism as a system as opposed to liberal democracy disregards the socio-genetic pillars of Polish communism, which could only be established in a situation of shattered identities and normative confusion. The period before 1956 is commonly referred to as the totalitarian period, after which totalitarianism rapidly transformed itself into authoritarian communism uniquely within civil society (Linz and Stepan, 1996b:258). Such a vision assumes a consolidated system, whereas in fact this had become progressively weakened after 1956 and, by means of growing political space for the opposition and for individual liberties, had come to constitute what might be called a more liberal authoritarian system. One can object to such an evolutionary view, as did Krystyna Kersten, by arguing that 'totalitarian communism in Poland never gained a fully-fledged shape'.[71] Although the confusion after 1945 and the subsequent Stalinist policies had not developed into a self-sustained system, they undoubtedly stamped the spirits and behaviour of the Poles. Despite the complexity of the relationship between communist power and Polish society, it is safe to say that the weakening of totalitarian structures in Poland after 1956 enhanced political freedom. None the less, the first post-war decade had left its stamp on spirits and behavior (Kersten, 1996:24–5). This meant that politics in moments of high contingency such as in 1945 and 1989 were liminal, with political mentalities suspended between a disaggregated and confused former state of things (war and the breakdown of communism) and vague utopias of a future state in which new structures (communism and democracy) would be consolidated.

The principles of communism drew on maintaining the state of confusion and of disaggregation as the only way of staying in power. The weakness of the communist regimes was rooted in their pathological need to rule by maintaining hatred, imaginary enemies, and a perpetual process of destroying patterns of civility and independent centres of power (Gross, 1989:208f.; Horváth, 1998). 'The Communist/socialist ambiguity of official discourse was achieved by constantly switching emphasis (through time and space) between such pairs of principles as centralism and democracy, hierarchy and egalitarianism, internationalism and patriotism and nationalism.'[72] The extreme fragility of countries such as Poland and other Eastern European countries (Gross, 1989:209f.; Arnason, 1993; Holmes, 1997) could thus only be redressed through a widespread belief in utopia. While utopia is commonly outcome-oriented, and associated with a complete social structure and political system, it was in fact the anchoring point in a situation of confusion and high disapproval in society. The drawn-out transition, and, as a consequence, an extended transitional stage, was characteristic of state socialism, since 'the objective of catching up has not been achieved, both because socialism has failed to run as fast as expected, and because capitalism has refused to stand still'.[73] The communists were thus pursuing a phantom that permanently escaped them. 'Ever and again Russia and the communist parties abroad imagined that in this or that country revolution was approaching, victory was near . . . then instead of success, there was always failure.'[74]

Recurrent experiences of *communitas*

As the above analysis has suggested, the inquiry into continuities in Poland's transition has good reason to reconsider the standard claim that the consensus of the elite at the round table was intentional. If one considers the modalities of the dissolution of political order before 1989, it is possible to see the round table as a further link in a series of events that are stamped by liminal conditions of confusion between authorities and opposition. 'We are not dealing with structural contradictions when we discuss liminality, but with the essentially unstructured (at once destructured and prestructured), and often the people themselves see this in terms of bringing neophytes into close connection with. . . . the unbounded, and infinite, the limitless.'[75] In this respect, the round table 'embodied a form of "bargaining between government and society" that bore no resemblance to the usual relationships between the two entities'.[76] As the mirror-image relationship between the communists and the anti-communist opposition crystallized, intimations of anti-structure became manifest in a confusion and lack of strategies. Such liminal moments of authority vacuum and normative void appear regardless of historical time-frames. The authorities of the foreign partitioning powers in Poland were in state of confusion just before the 1863 upheaval. 'The authorities were horrified, disorientated. One day they withdrew and tried persuasion, the next they gave the order to shoot.'[77] During the preparatory talks for the round table, 'two different faces of power were represented in one week by General Kiszczak, who on Monday threatened martial law, only to offer a dialogue at the round table on Friday'.[78] It seems that the convergence of communist and Solidarity elites before and during the round table bears key attributes of a process of situational adjustment.

These situational adjustments occurred in moments of particular weakness of antagonists which comply with Turner's concept of *communitas*. For Turner, 'beyond the structural lies not just the Hobbesian "war of all against all", as such contrasting figures as Konrad Lorenz and René Girard have argued, but something else – which I have called *communitas*.'[79] In this regard, liminal conditions such as disruptions of political order, authority vacuum, or high contestation of power legitimacy tend to support experiences of *communitas*. The dissolution of the Polish state in 1939 created an authority vacuum which needed to be filled. In turn, the main thrust of the underground state was to work against social atomization and normlessness (Gross, 1979:287). The underground polity as a community was a moment of anti-structure, thus levelling differences. 'The most sweeping result of the occupation was the democratization of Polish society: differences of class, status, and power among Poles disappeared under the weight of German terror. This period also saw the mobilization of large masses of people into politics and the rapid growth of patriotic consciousness and national identification.'[80] By the same token, the Polish crises in 1956, 1970, and 1980 were characterized by communities of different scope and intensity. In 1956 Gomułka was widely acclaimed by society as the redeemer of the country. In the wake of the workers' revolt in Gdańsk, Gierek's speech of 20 December 1970 appealed to the national community, intimating a social contract in the emblematic workers' readiness to co-operate: 'We will help'.[81] The first visit by Pope John Paul II to his native country in June 1979 sparked nine days of public happening when millions of Poles assembled in peaceful manifestations and defined a 'national community' outside the communist state (Kubik, 1994a:145). 'That intense unity of thought and feeling which had previously been confined to small circles of friends – the intimate solidarity of private life in Eastern Europe – was now multiplied by millions.'[82] Inspired by these events, the heyday of Solidarity in 1980 can be seen as signifying an existential community in Polish society.[83] Most succinctly, Jacek Kuroń summarized the overwhelming success of the general strike of 3 October 1980: 'Solidarity was simply Poland.'[84] During the August of Gdańsk 1980 society, as it were, came into existence. Events from the Gdańsk Accords onwards altered the consciousness of Poles, making individual Poles come alive.[85]

A look over the southern border confirms the significance of communities for the Czech case. Václav Hável put it as follows:

I know from thousands of personal experiences how the mere circumstance of having signed Charter 77 immediately created a deeper and more open relationship and evoked sudden and powerful feelings of genuine community among people who were all but strangers before. This kind of thing happens only rarely, if at all, even among people who have worked together for long periods in some apathetic official structure. It is as though the mere awareness and acceptance of a common task and a shared experience were enough to transform people and the climate of their lives, as though it gave their public work a more human dimension that is seldom found elsewhere. . . . these small communities, bound together by thousands of shared tribulations, give rise to some of those special humanly meaningful political relationships and ties . . .[86]

Although on a different scale, both in Czechoslovakia and in Poland the power of the powerless institutionalized the second reality through spontaneous or existential *communitas*.

The round table *communitas*

Given their mirror-image relationship, the withering away of communist power during the 1980s allowed underground Solidarity to rise from the ashes. The drive for assuring and reaffirming existence was thus a mutual one. While the subjectivization of society through mass mobilization and public manifestations of *communitas* in 1980 had no equivalent in 1989, there is ample evidence for detecting elements of institutional and individual *communitas* at the round table. The usually conflicting relationship between neophytes (Solidarity) and authorities (communists) suddenly developed into warm, even harmonious contacts up to a point where allegiances could no longer be distinguished. While a *rapprochement* between the antagonists had already begun in the mid-1980s, the elimination of distinctions and graduations reached a peak during the autumn of 1988 and the winter of 1988–9. During the talks between the regime and Solidarity at the Magdalenka Palace, it became clear that one side could not do without the other, that two fates had been welded into one. As the government co-chairman of the political reform table put it: 'If we do not come to an agreement, then all we who negotiate at the round table will be the losers. . . . It does not concern only us, on this side of the table, for you will be wiped out by more radical forces, too.'[87] At the round table, formerly fundamental divergences and distinctions between 'we' and 'they' were drastically reduced. According to Osiatyński, the decisive change occurred through the increasing gap between the party and government side. Inside the party apparatus, there was a growing split between top party and government negotiators on the one hand, and the rest of their delegation and the *nomenklatura* on the other. 'This gap grew throughout the entire process. By the end of the round-table talks, top party negotiators perceived the apparatchiks as "them" and included themselves along with their partners from the other side of the table in an "us" category.'[88]

Since Solidarity was the only large-scale opposition in Eastern Europe, it seems reasonable to see the reform or pacted rupture (*reforma* or *ruptura pactada*) as one based on a well-developed civil society (Linz and Stepan, 1996:51). Yet the crumbling of formerly defining attributes and an ideological confusion generated weakness as a common characteristic of the political antagonists. Although Solidarity was the only large-scale oppositional structure in Eastern Europe, its essential feature seems to be not its independence from, but rather its deep intertwining with, the communist regime. While Jaruzelski's regime was grappling with waning political legitimacy and an open economic crisis, throughout the liminal underground period Solidarity's very existence was at stake.

> The first [problem] concerned the further existence of Solidarity. Was it worthwhile to continue the existence of something that was growing weaker from day to day, that by its weakness was being transformed into a caricature of itself . . . And on the other hand: was it worthwhile to look for new forms of legal existence for the structures of Solidarity?[89]

As a consequence, many proposals in the course of negotiation were spontaneous, momentary and lacking of even a short-term strategy. Solidarity was a legendary monument, but it was politically immature and lacked identity (Skórzyński, 1995:111).

The uncertain and volatile strategies at the round table and beyond have their roots in the reciprocal weakness of both regime and opposition that unfolded during the 1980s.

> The absence of resistance justified mild repressions. This created an illusion of restoring governability, which in turn deprived

the authorities of a sense of urgency in looking for long-term solutions to the Polish malaise. The sequence of self-limiting revolution followed by a combination of self-limiting repression also produced self-limiting reforms. This sequence assured political stability, but at the expense of a persistent stalemate between the government and the opposition. The crux of the matter is that the opposition was not able to directly challenge the government, while the latter was unable fully to suppress it.[90]

On these grounds, it seems safe to argue that the convergence of political antagonists at the round table was not primarily induced by any intentional consensus or strategies. In this respect the attributes of the participants at the round table comply with the key characteristics of *communitas*. Following Turner, 'the subject of the passage ritual is, in the liminal period, structurally, if not physically, invisible'.[91] Not surprisingly, the Polish 'revolution from above' was a 'discrete' or 'invisible' one (Staniszkis, 1991a:211). Solidarity and the communist regime occupied low rungs, the first in terms of factual power, the second in terms of legitimacy. In early 1989 Solidarity was an illegal group of people gathered around Lech Wałésa, while its organizational mass potential together with its most powerful weapon, the general strike, had faded away during the underground. Within society as a whole Solidarity's round-table delegation was a faction, if a dominant one, from which different oppositional splinter-groups, political parties, and individuals had separated. The detachment of considerable parts of these formerly supporting groups reinforced its lack of structure. The Solidarity dissident unions refused to recognize the Solidarity delegation at the round table as representing society; and this view was shared by the Confederation for an Independent Poland (KPN). As the president of the first opposition party – founded in 1979 – Leszek Moczulski declared: 'The round table is not competent enough to decide on the elections because the delegation of society's side is fundamentally only a Solidarity delegation. There is no political opposition.'[92] Despite its undeniable anchoring in society, the position of Solidarity very much resembled that of a neophyte, both as regards political expertise and popular support (Michnik *et al.*, 1995:527). A series of clandestine meetings in the Magdalenka palace gathered a handful of delegated negotiators from both the Solidarity opposition and the communist party. In these meetings, the official (that is, structural) differentiating labels, such as 'party discipline', were reduced to a minimum.

Such a picture is in line with Turner's viewpoint when he claimed that 'liminality implies that the high could not be high unless the low existed, and he who is high must experience what it is like to be low'.[93] Long-term opponents like Jerzy Urban and Adam Michnik approached each other. Former hard-liners like General Kiszczak noticed the patriotism of Solidarity activists, acknowledging that in direct contact they did not remind him of scoundrels. Similarly, Jacek Kuroń agreed that at the negotiating table his counterparts not only were not Stalinists, but were not even ideological communists.[94] Facing the unique experiment of the round table, both sides were initiates who, in Turner's terms, were 'stripped of their ascribed structural being' and 'were wholly in becoming'.[95] Furthermore, the degree of merger, or mixing, between the two camps was most intricate at this point of time. Taking his cue from Martin Buber's definition of community, Turner pointed out:

> Community is the being no longer side by side (and, one might add, above and below) but with one another of a multitude of persons. And this multitude, though it moves towards one goal, yet experiences everywhere a turning to, a dynamic facing of, the others, a flowing from I to Thou. Community is where *communitas* happens.[96]

As a result, the formerly opposed blocs broke up from within, while their central, reconciliatory parts fused together in 'mutual forgiveness of each vice'.[97] Former antagonists such as leading party figures and eminent opposition figures suddenly found words of comprehension for each others' actions, of appreciation, and even of esteem. Among such moves were mutual recognition of each other, such as General Jaruzelski's approval for all the projects of Adam Michnik.[98] The round table staged a short-term community which suspended distinctions between ascribed social roles and ideological origins. 'The longer the debates in the palace were going on . . . the more frequently Solidarity leaders popped up on TV screens, in the company of their partners in the talks, the more the differences between both sides were wiped out.'[99]

Such an intertwining and mutual dependence blurred the distinctions between the regime and the opposition. The existential importance of the communist party concerned its survival as the leading force in the Polish state, while Solidarity struggled for its revival as a legalized trade union. Linking up the concepts of 'revolution from above' with the 'round-table' syndrome, Jadwiga Staniszkis has compared the round table to a kind of political 'happening' (Staniszkis, 1994a). This existential or spontaneous event is 'approximately what the hippies today would call "a happening", and William Blake might have called "the winged moment as it flew", or, later, "mutual forgiveness of each vice"' (Turner, 1969:132). Due to its characteristics as an anti-structural community, the round table has clear affinities with what William Sewell characterized as an event that reverses the usual process where ritual induces emotional excitement. As he showed for the taking of the Bastille, 'the emotional excitement and sense of communion induce those present to express and concretize their feelings in ritual'.[100] In this vein, the round table pact was a convergence of elites. Yet it was nurtured by a desire for identity, and crystallized in a community of emotions.

The continuity of permanent liminality

This chapter has argued that the round-table pact was not the beginning of Poland's transition. As the analysis of Poland's cycle of crises has shown, the continuity of liminality can be regarded as one non-contingent given in the second reality. While the economic and social processes at work in Eastern Europe are assumed to have no defined endpoint, 'they certainly do have a clearly defined starting point which serves – given the lack of a better instrument – as a point of measure and evaluation of what is happening'.[101] In the case of Poland and Hungary, the beginning of the transition process was attributed 'to negotiated openings' and to the establishment of 'preliminary pacts' (Ekiert, 1995:287). The foregoing analysis has suggested taking the round-table experience as an event in a series of liminal experiences of short-term *communitas*. In this perspective, 1989 does not constitute a rupture-point. What is more, the objectives of the preparatory projects for the round table of the second half of 1988 and in early 1989 were transitory, that is, liminal in substance. They looked for 'formula of a "common government" (*współrządzenie*) for a transitory period between a monoparty system and a parliamentary democracy. Nobody planned violent or singular changes.'[102]

According to one standard definition of transition, 'it is characteristic of transition that during it the rules of the political game are not defined. Not only are they in constant flux, but they are usually arduously contested'.[103] Such a scenario applies to Poland not only starting from 1989, but for the whole period of Polish communism. The relationship between authorities and neophytes was usually ruled by contested norms and authority vacuums. For the Spanish case, Juan Linz has argued that 'transition is only possible through a complex process that involves both reform and rupture'.[104] In pre-1989 Poland, the rupture of norm-governed relations was permanent. 'The Polish revolution, after all, did not start in 1989 or even in the denouement of martial law; it began more than three decades earlier.'[105]

Conceiving of Poland's transition as permanent liminality refers to a state which is characterized by instability, uncertainty, and prolonged attempts to overcome such a state by reaggregation.

> After half a century of application first of Hitler- and then Stalin-inspired meat grinders Polish society is indeed beaten up into an unfamiliar, featureless shape. Social bonds, group identities, have been shattered and they have to be identified, newly dis-covered, or nurtured back to reconstruct orderly political intercourse.[106]

The party regime and the Solidarity opposition arrived in 1989 as already disfigured and stripped of their formerly defining identities and attributes. The communist system had failed to achieve compliance and was constantly challenged by society's opposition. This permanent jeopardizing of norm-governed relations rendered uncertainty permanent, which thus gave it a certain normality. On these grounds, the Polish case casts doubt on the assumption according to which East European transitions should be considered 'analagous to events and processes happening elsewhere . . ., they should be treated as part of the same "wave of democratization" that began in 1974 in Portugal.'[107]

The standard concept of transition assumes some modification of rules and norms at the outset of transition. 'The typical sign that the transition has begun comes when these authoritarian incumbents, for whatever reason, begin to modify their own rules in the direction of providing more secure guarantees for the rights of individuals and groups.'[108] In the Polish case, there is ample evidence that the official authorities modified their stance in 1956 (liberalization *versus* the Church and the workers), in the wake of 1970 (Gierek's Western-credits-financed project of the 'second Poland'), and in 1980 (the acceptance of a free trade union, the acceptance of the Law on State Enterprise).[109] This transitoriness in the normative framework of Polish communism appears also in the intermittent mode of revisions of the Polish constitution, when 'amendments happened in the rhythm of subsequent thaws that were interrupted by periods of "tightening the regime"'.[110]

Given this evidence, no clear initiating phase of transition, be it in 1989 or earlier on, can be detected. As I will argue throughout this book, the prevalent characteristic of the continuity of transition is the recurrent convergence of political and societal forces in small and large-scale communities, as epitomized in the concepts of negotiated transition or consensual elites. As political elites and large segments of society are in liminal conditions, identity-creating processes tend to unfold in anti-structural communities.

3
The Continuity of Historical Antagonism

Political conflict in pre-1989 Poland is commonly attributed to the antagonism between state and society (Ascherson, 1981; Arato, 1981; Ekiert, 1996).

> In Poland the self-limiting revolution resulted in a sharp divison between the state and society and a well-defined political polarization. Almost from the beginning of the crisis the party-state elites confronted a mobilized society organized in complex territorial and professional networks. Faced with such massive pressure, the ruling elites were forced to surrender their control over vast areas of political and social life. This newly opened political space was immediately taken over by independent organizations.[1]

While many demands voiced by the political opposition concerned the material conditions of life, working conditions, or social justice, the core of the division in society was the alienation of the Polish nation.

> The central charge laid against the Party in 1980 was not that it had offended against human rights, not that it had ruined the economy, not that it had betrayed its trusteeship for the proletariat and not even that it had bound the state too closely to Soviet politics (. . .) It was that the Party had divided the nation and set Pole against Pole.[2]

As a result of the pluralization of politics in the wake of 1989, a de-ideologization of this historical conflict could be expected. After 1989 the differentiation and pluralization of public and political life became associated with the destruction of central myths such as the myth of political unity, the myth of the national and moral unity of Polish society, and the myth of Solidarity. The rational and realistic acceptance of Western models seemed to leave no space for new utopias (Frybes and Michel, 1996:18–19). Despite the unprecedented extent of systemic collapse in Poland, and the experimental character of both the round table and the economic shock-therapy, 'the catchphrase of the transition from communism was that "there was nothing new to invent"'.[3] Moreover, the pluralization of conflict-patterns seems to be the ordinary course of a transitional society. Social and political processes in transition are considered to be asymmetric and irreversible due to the high degree of indeterminacy of social and political actions and the inordinate degrees of freedom that guide collective and even individual action (O'Donnell *et al.*, 1986:18–19). While the anti-politics of civil society were based on a moral discourse of truth, the open society of post-1989 allowed for pluralism in autonomous social life (Ekiert, 1993; Gellner, 1994). The development of interest politics rather than ethical anti-politics was supposed to replace identity-based or ideological cleavages of conflict. Accordingly, the round-table community inspired the reconciliatory stance of the first Solidarity government, whose premise was to draw a thick line under the past. Historical antagonisms seemed to wither away entirely as Poles opted for a change in politics by bringing former post-communist parties back to power in autumn 1993. The we–they dichotomy, so crucial in the 1970s and 1980s, ceased to be the key for understanding the situation in the 1990s (Wnuk-Lipiński, 1996:147; Frybes and Michel, 1996). Strengthening socio-economic cleavages and political interests, the victory of post-communist parties was interpreted as a second thick line, drawn by society, 'that invalidates a significant part of the divisions that ruled the political scenario in previous elections'.[4]

Examining political conflict in Slovakia, Bulgaria, the Czech Republic, and Hungary, Claus Offe argued that identity-based and ideological conflicts constituted the most significant obstacles to consolidation in Eastern Europe (Elster *et al.*, 1998:247–70). His analysis concluded with a distinction between 'easy' cases, such as the Czech Republic and Hungary, and 'difficult' cases, such as Slovakia and Bulgaria. In the 'easy' cases, conflicts in politics and society shifted towards patterns of class conflict with a greater potential of reconcilability, which is expressed in a more advanced system of interest-representation. Offe evaluated the commonalities and differences between these two groups according to five criteria.[5] If this picture was transposed to Poland, it seems likely that in at least four of these five points of inter-group differences, Poland would be included in the 'easy' cases. The points are: Poland's advanced economic situation in the region, the low minority population on its territory, its relatively high fragility under communism, and its establishment of a politics of competition. While the stability of Polish democracy during the inter-war period is indeed arguable, the economy in inter-war Poland experienced considerable growth.[6]

Although the systemic criteria identified by Offe seem to make the case for a transformation from identity-based to interest-based conflict patterns, Poland has been far from debunking historical antagonisms in its politics. Despite the pluralization of its politics, the socio-economic turn in its society, and the autonomization of its individual life, political conflict in Poland has arguably remained rooted in pre-1989 values and discourses. Various analysts have argued that the conflict lines of Polish politics will follow those of historical divisions, implying both a moral dividing line and a dividing line of memories (Marciniak, 1996:122; Smolar, 1996b:171).

> After the 1995 election of Kwaśniewski ... the number of Poles perceiving a restoration of society's division – now a split between ex-communists and the post-Solidarity opposition – has increased. In the seventh year of the transition to democracy and a market economy, Poles' political identifications are still decided more by attitudes towards the country's recent history than by views on economic and social issues.[7]

The tight margin in the presidential elections of 1995 between the new president, Kwaśniewski, and the former president, Lech Wałęsa, was reminiscent of familiar division lines:

> As in the first ballot, electoral attitudes were not clearly decided either by any hard separate sociological variables, or by attitudes towards socio-economic reforms in the last five years. What matters, rather, are historical traditions and societal ties, including religious ones, as well as what had been experienced during the Polish Peoples' Republic.[8]

Electoral polarization continued in the referendum on the Polish constitution in May 1997 and in the parliamentary elections of September 1997. While the preferences of voter groups in 1997 were divided in a more complex manner, the perception of a historical antagonism between post-communists and post-Solidarity was overwhelming (Ziemkiewicz, 1997). There are clear tendencies to indicate a division in current Polish society on attitudes towards religious values and the communist past. Most importantly, this split is reflected in politics. Pro-church atttitudes and anti-communist attitudes are to a large extent shared by supporters of the right-centre political spectrum, while anti-religious feelings and reconciliatory attitudes towards the communist past are shared by the left-wing spectrum. This division applies both to the population and to political elites (Grabowska, 1997). 'As a result, the recently revived polarization of the Polish political arena involves values rather than interests.'[9]

Socio-economic variables and interest-politics have not succeeded in establishing new cleavage patterns in political conflict. Given such a scenario, some authors attribute conflicts in post-1989 Poland to the dysfunctionality of the pre-1989 values and language, in an environment of a politicized society within a consolidated democracy (Linz and Stepan, 1996b:272). Relying on a dyadic systemic distinction between a non-democratic and a democratic system, such explanations seem rather inadequate to account for the continuation of historical antagonisms in Poland. What needs to be explained is how the replicas of attitudes and expectations can be transposed from pre-1989 to post-1989 Poland.

Such a way of posing the problem must elaborate the conceptual patterns of conflict in pre-1989 Polish society, which in turn casts doubt on another dyadic view about antagonisms which draws on class conflict. Due to a low degree of systemic differentiation in Soviet-type societies, and a persistent fragility of the political system, collective conflict in Poland has not been mediated by class or party politics (Kamiński, B., 1991; Elster *et al.*, 1998:247f.). The Solidarity revolution was carried out by a 'cultural-political class' constituted above and beyond socio-economic and occupational division (Kubik, 1994a:230f.). Rather than carrying a dichotomy in class terms, Solidarity's mentality in 1980 could be expressed in terms of one-dimensionality. Despite the very complicated constellation of forces and political pressures which existed, 'the image of the political situation shared by Solidarity members was simplified by taking into account only two forces: "us" and "them"' (Staniszkis,

1984:144). To a considerable extent, post-1989 has seen a revival of this one-dimensionality, as political choices are determined by accepted values, self-identification on the 'left–right' scale and, first and foremost, by people's earlier political biographies. In all the Polish elections between 1989 and 1995, despite many fluctuations and shifts, there existed two basic, consistent groups of voters forming two opposing 'strands': the postcommunist and the Solidarity strands (Ziólkowski, 1998:36). The replication of undifferentiated attitudes between political antagonists in post-1989 Poland can only be extricated by having recourse to the socio-genetic and relational aspects of conflict in pre-1989 Poland. Subsequently, I will show that the conflict between the communist regime and society in pre-1989 and the replica of this antagonism in post-1989 are driven by very similar forces.

The continuity of utopian images

As argued in Chapter 1, the state of permanent liminality is characterized by the instability of norms, contested legitimacy, and recurrent events of anti-structure which reinforce the appeal to utopias. These disruptions are maintained by a vague utopia by which collective groups aim to reaggregate the anti-structure of an intermediate state. From such a perspective, post-1945, communist Poland failed to develop stable political structures. The regime could neither achieve its proclaimed transition to communism, nor could society's opposition – except in the first months of Solidarity's existence – measure up to its claim for its own subjectivization. Such a reading is not in line with the widespread conviction that the exit routes into democratic transition were prepared by a decline of utopian beliefs in Poland (Kennedy, 1995; Mokrzycki, 1995; Linz and Stepan, 1996b). The decline of utopia is reflected, instead, in the long-term decline of totalitarian approaches and their replacement by modernization and convergence approaches (Rupnik, 1988; Lipset and Bence, 1994; Hassner, 1995). From the early 1950s onwards, Western observers emphasized the totalitarian character of Soviet-type regimes. Their analyses focused on the violent character of Soviet-type regimes and on the techniques of totalitarian government that pervaded society (Arendt, 1951; Friedrich and Brzeziński, 1956). Seen in this way, Soviet communism was a dehumanizing[10] empire of evil, one or several steps backward in the development of human progress. Historically, Eastern Europe was charged with the totalitarian heritage of a regime whose power was based on suspicion, indoctrination, ruthless spying, purges, and aggression against its own population. In the wake of Khrushchevian reformism, however, totalitarianism became associated with a different meaning from the Eastern European viewpoint.[11] From a Western point of view, on the other hand, the rationalization of Soviet-type government, decreasing violence and rising dissidence, sustained the persuasion that both systems would converge. Not by chance, fledgling civil society and the growing autonomy of independent groups in politics distinguished Poland as an authoritarian system (Linz and Stepan, 1996b). On these grounds, Poland was considered to be particularly well equipped for the modernization of politics and the economy. Several studies of the Solidarity trade union as a social movement or a movement for modernization reflected this conviction (Touraine, 1983; Tatur, 1989; Ost, 1990).

Essentially, modernization approaches assumed that economic and technological rationalization would lead to intensified co-operation and opening up of the East. East and West would gradually converge, as politics and the economy would adopt the systemic attributes of Western-type democracies. According to this reasoning, practical considerations prompted constant redefinitions of even the most basic tenets of Marxism–Leninism. The later phase of communism was thus portrayed as a withdrawal of utopia and the emergence of criteria of efficiency and realistic adaptation (Kennedy, 1995; Mokrzycki, 1995). 'For it was within and through this process that the utopian and abstract idea of egalitarian collectivism was painstakingly moulded and remoulded over 70 years so as to match an ever more evasive reality. In the end, reality gave the verdict that the utopia had failed.'[12] In this view, utopia declined both in its importance as a design of reality and as the carrier of enchantment with the communist project. A further indication of the rationalization of the communist system and the waning of utopia was the decrease of open political violence in Poland from 1956 onwards, when a system of selective repression was installed. In the 1970s the Security Service (UB) focused more on the control of technological and economic production (Paczkowski, 1997:420–2).

Philosophically, utopia is commonly seen as the mystified consciousness of a real historical tendency (Kołakowski, 1967:128). Even though utopias penetrate the consciousness of mass movements and can influence practical reasoning, they cannot be realized. The utopian consciousness – despite its powerful grip on political and social forces – must remain an inadequate and pathological conscious-ness that constitutes a distorting attempt to impose an extra-historical aim on historical reality (Kołakowski, 1967:128). In this regard, any utopia constitutes an ideal 'nowhere' which, if tried out, would develop into a total or closed society (Dahrendorf, 1990: 58–9). As a consequence, a coherent systemic variable such as democracy or democratic politics must necessarily be at variance with any kind of utopia. In this regard, for Linz and Stepan, Poland in particular exemplifies the dwindling of utopia.

> The relative de-ideologization of post-totalitarian regimes and the weakening of the belief in utopia as a foundation of legitimacy mean that, as in many authoritarian regimes, there is a growing effort in a post-totalitarian polity to legitimate the regime on the basis of performance criteria. The gap between the original utopian elements of the ideology and the increasing legitima-tion efforts on the basis of efficacy, particularly when the latter fails, is one of the sources of weakness in post-totalitarian re-gime . . . The weakening of utopian ideology as a charac-teristic of post-totalitarianism thus opens up a new dynamic of regime vulnerabilities – or, from the perspective of democratic transi-tion, new opportunities – that can be exploited by the democratic opposition.[13]

This chapter will present a different vision of democratic politics. Subsequently, I will examine how utopian aspirations ruled Polish politics and society before 1989. For liminal conditions, that is, when authorities are weak and the opposition is bare of any con-crete political power, evolutionary or progress-oriented understandings of utopia remain in a dyadic impasse. Yet I conceive the signifi-cance of utopia neither as a mere consciousness which looks for alternatives to which the current decadent situation should be re-duced, nor as an eschatological ideal society which will accomplish evolutionary progress. I will put forward the thesis that utopias are reciprocal, as they are based on experiences of communities. I will argue that in a prolonged state of anti-structure, political action of both antagonists (state *vs.* society) was recurrently driven by de-sires for identity and by the search for utopias. Conflict in pre-1989 Poland thus can be read as originating in the mutual desire for the construction of a utopian second Poland.

In the wake of the Poznań riots and the Polish October 1956, the new first secretary of the PZPR, Stanisław Gomułka, was acclaimed by the masses as selected by Providence, as the redeemer of the country (Kuroń and Żakowski, 1995:94). In the wake of the events in 1956 some concrete policy changes were accomplished. Policies of normalization and realistic adaptation in 1956 abolished collectivization, achieved reconciliation with the Church, and installed works councils (Korboński, 1996:52). The 'October' settlement loosened the Soviet grip on Poland, which ceased to be a penetrated system and opened up a 'national road to socialism' (Ascherson, 1981:75–6). Yet in Gomułka's discourse the utopian appeal of a second reality was inherent. His abstract phraseology mirrored a nonsense discourse which encountered awed admiration. Central concepts such as creative criticism, democratic centralism, or socialist realism were deprived of specific meaning (Raina, 1978: 60–2). In this vein, Gomułka's discourse bears a clear resemblance to Rákosi's double-edge evocations of a utopian second reality (Horváth, 1998). Structurally, Gierek's 'second Poland' and Jaruzelski's bid for market socialism leaned on the same principle: they pursued a utopia nurtured by Western images of success and prosperity. Gierek's credit-financed economic boom in the early 1970s created an unprecedented offer of Western goods and spaces of freedom for travel. The building of a 'second Poland' on credits from the West created a model of a consumer society.[14] Normalization and economic reform pursued by the Jaruzelski regime focused on the myth of the economic reform and on the inclusion of the opposition. As Polish communism went through different crises, a ritualized recourse to an ideal 'nowhere' became essential to the survival of the system. While the basic tenets of the communist regime, such as democratic centralism and a centrally planned economy, remained intact, methods of coercion and social control became more rational. 'As time went on, in communist Poland there was less utopia and more Yalta.'[15]

Yet I would maintain that the repressive and utopian aspects of this are interlinked. Such an assumption is sustained by the fact that disillusionment with policies of realistic adaptation became all the stronger. The enchantment with Gomułka's reforms was short-lived. 'In Gomułka's Poland there was no place for terror, but neither was there a space for independence of attitudes. In this sense, Stalinism endured.'[16] After the bloody suppression of the workers' revolt in Gdańsk in December 1970 and Gierek's emphatic appeal to the workers for help, the content of the requested help was not specified. Gierek had set out to make Poland politically more free, culturally more tolerable and economically more prosperous. In substance, however, little of significance was achieved during the years 1971 to 1977. In terms of the basic rights of individuals, censorship or political trials, little change with regard to the Gomułka period occurred (Raina, 1978:204-9). Gierek's import-led growth and economic convergence with Western Europe only revealed the utopian and irreal attempt to create a second Poland from above. When the boom petered out, hard currency debts and growth fatigue re-emerged in the late 1970s. The impressive rise in national income, industrial production, and westward orientation was followed by a subordination of the Polish economy to the eastern CMEA (Poznański, 1996:95-6). 'In practice, Gierek's strategy plunged Poland into a deepening economic crisis marked by a burgeoning foreign debt, gross distortions in the domestic economy, lasting inefficiency and competitive disadvantage, dependence on grain imports, and a progressive loss of control by the center over economic processes.'[17] In a similar vein, Jaruzelski's attempt to normalize Poland by a Kadarism *à la Polonaise* failed (Ash, 1990:261). 'Such a potential of deviation was missing at the end of the 1980s.'[18] The extreme weakness of the communist regime after 1981 derived from the lack of any credible strategies for political and economic reform. The senselessness of economic reform suggested the end of any possibility to 'normalize'.

> After all the bitter and vain experience of this society, the reform cannot prove unsuccessful, partial, insufficiently elaborated. . . . This will be too much for society to bear. History knows the measure of the useless shedding of blood. There is also a measure of the useless shedding of sense. We cannot take it any more. . . . We are giving up. Yes, this is the last Reform. Alas.[19]

Thus, the lack of exit routes only strengthened beliefs and desires for utopias. In a mirror-image fashion, the pursuit of the second reality was not confined to the communists. Disillusioned by the failures of the communist projects, Poles in turn came to cherish cravings for a second reality.

> In Poland of the late 1970s the communist ceremonial was minimally effective because it neither reflected everyday knowledge (or its fragments) nor concealed the actual features of everyday reality; its ability to produce a credible utopia had run out. It

was common knowledge that the economy was collapsing, the standard of living was declining, and the food lines were growing longer. The ubiquitous propaganda of success lacked credibility. . . . Poles lived in a cognitive limbo, in a state of ever growing existential inchoateness, hoping for new ideas, ready for new promises.[20]

As Sergiusz Kowalski showed in his seminal critique of Solidarity's reasoning (Kowalski, 1990), the trade union in 1980 developed two visions, divided by Kowalski into 'realistic adaptation' and 'eschatological relativism'. In the first variant, Solidarity was seen as the finishing act of resistance in the name of dignity. According to Kowalski, such an attitude was pushed aside gradually (Kowalski, 1990a:76–8). In the second vision, Solidarity was conceived as an instrument to attain full liberty. 'The mentality of eschatological relativism was linked to an assumption of a "future" orientation, an attitude towards quasi-aims, which could be some values, to be realized, eventually, only in the future; such a vision was characterized by its proneness to look at today through the prism of tomorrow.'[21] The actions in the frame of eschatological relativism

> did not refer to the current state, but were entirely related to an anticipated state of full freedom – the connection of the spiritual revival of the individuals, which will become what they really are, with the collective revival, identical with the recovery of independence and, consequently, with the reconstruction of society.[22]

Similarly, oppositional activity was to be in line with moral principles of ethical and non-violent behaviour. Hence, in the nationwide community of 1980, equality and liberty were not merely a political formula, but had a strong moral appeal in order to destroy unrighteousness. 'If a social movement wants to realize a social utopia it needs to free itself from the use of force and constraint.'[23]

Solidarity's adherence to the political heritage of the national tradition intimated further aspects of political utopias. First, it adopted the tradition of the democracy of the gentry – the only form of democracy to have taken strong root in Poland – dominated by a strong penchant for direct democracy and hostile to the principle of representation. It is notable that the collectivist ethos of gentry democracy was endowed by an ideal of unanimity and a corresponding image of a unitary and single national will that referred to a myth rather than to reality (Walicki, 1988:10–13). Second, Solidarity represented the legacy of national romanticism. Thus it was suggested 'that the Polish workers, united in "Solidarity", have become a "national class" not only in the sense of representing all national interests, but also in the sense of inheriting the traditional values and faults of the Polish national character'.[24] This Polish national character, backed up by Messianism and a loyalty to the national idea, essentially replaced responsibility for current national affairs by a 'concern for maintaining the memory of an idealized past and by dreams of an ideal future. In other words, "Polishness" was transformed into a lofty idea and the national existence was accordingly conceived of as keeping this idea alive by the power of the spirit'.[25] The state of permanent liminality made it necessary to 'make national existence completely independent of political circumstances by firmly grounding Poland's foundation in the realm of the spiritual. The Romantic generation did this by defining the nation as a community of tradition and spirit, but above all of a universal historical mission.'[26]

As conflict in Polish politics was aggravated in the 1970s, antagonistic groups in society succumbed to social and political utopias in this simultaneous pursuit of second realities. The reciprocity between the power holders in search of legitimacy and the opposition in search of emancipation showed clear signs of a double-bind. 'In 1956 the masses had turned a face of hope towards the party. In 1970, they had turned towards the party in anger and reproach.

In the summer of 1980, the Poles simply turned their backs.'[27] Although the will to rule was lost, the distance between the rulers and the ruled provoked police violence against demonstrators in 1956, 1968, 1970, 1976, and 1981 (Curry and Fajfer, 1996:252). This distance, however, was mainly one of ascribed role. In a condition of permanent liminality, relations between authorities and society were confused, norms and rules often questioned. As a result, political utopias were not limited to the communist regime but were reciprocal. As regards expectations, both antagonists were linked by an underlying community that can be detected in their mutual dependence on each other, of which Adam Michnik's personal account is an early but remarkable testimony:

In 1965 I was arrested next to Kuroń and Modzelewski, an extremely public affair. Kuroń is a well-known former leader of the

Scout movement. Modzelewski was a very well-known historian. I was not even 19 years old and suddenly I had made a career, everybody spoke about me, I was becoming known. . . . I am well-known, I have made a career thanks to the fact that the communists arrested me. In a word, I owe everything to the communists. If there were no communists in Poland, I don't know what I would do.[28]

The communist regime could only temporarily redress crises by violence[29] and evoke compliance by promises of a better future. Stamped by the disruptions of both 1917 and 1945, the violent communist state formation could only maintain itself by constantly evoking utopian aims (Malia, 1994; Horváth, 1998). Simplifying the relationship of violence and utopia, one could argue that each outburst of disorder not only prompted violence but also boosted utopia in its aftermath. Polish permanent liminality lingered between ritualized violence and utopia.[30] The importance of utopia shows how communism differs from other forms of dictatorship. 'It is utopia that allows for large-scale coercion. It is this that distinguishes the Soviet Union from a General Stroessner in Paraguay or from Idi Amin Dada, for instance. Without utopia, these dictators of the classical type could not do what Lenin and Stalin had done, nor could they have lasted some 75 years. A routinized KGB replaced the Gulag.'[31]

It seems safe to assume that the understanding of utopia must not be confined to a modernizing ideology which supports policies of realisitic adaptation. As the above analysis has shown, the lingering on between realistic adaptation and political and social utopias intimates a mentality in Polish politics which recurrently orients policy-options towards imaginary orientation-points. In contingent liminal situations, these reference-points were mutually shared by antagonists. It was the Polish writer Witold Gombrowicz[32] who argued that, in the fight with communism, a recourse to the national religious tradition was nothing else than substituting one utopia with another. He identified a danger in the stereotyped anti-communist attitudes of the Catholic Poland. His advice to revolt against Poland must be read as an admonition not to combat the communist lie by falling prey to another second reality. Gombrowicz's concern was 'to pull the Pole out of any secondary reality', that is, to bring him in touch with the real world, to free him from the idealized vision and values of the great Poles of the past. His plea to liberate

Poles from their Polishness took its departure-point from the specific Polish condition:

> What does it mean, exactly, to be Polish? Poland, that is our life
> in society, as it had been shaped throughout the centuries. But
> were these not centuries of a permanent and desperate struggle,
> of a fight against too-powerful enemies, centuries of frantic and
> cramped existence, centuries of backwardness? Is not this Poland
> a completely imperfect thing, weak, and consumed with all the
> poisons of weakness, disfigured and disgraced? Is not the Pole
> charged with the heritage of this Poland, that is, with the con-
> vulsive past of this people and with a constant, gradual dying?[33]

The desire to create a second reality was shared by the communist regime and society. Utopia was characterized by a symmetry not in the envisaged outcome but in the common underlying mentality of both antagonists. In search of legitimacy, the communist regime admired the broad support which the opposition enjoyed in society and, as a consequence, courted Polish society by imitating the opposition's methods and goals. A good example in this regard is the regime's envy towards society's capacity for mobilization and national self-organization. Such was the case with the 'canalization of ideals', the use of national and societal values for communist power's purpose (Kowalski, 1990a:57–8). Gierek's public discourse was also a mixture of appeal to and use of patriotic and nationalist items (Kubik, 1994a:33ff.). As a consequence, the communists came to court society by appeals to national reconciliation.[34] This strategy was temporarily successful. The national upswing in 1956 – when Gomułka for a moment had the entire nation behind him – was perhaps the peak of the party's acceptance by society. Under the spell of Gierek's economic miracle, 'almost the whole of society accepted the regime *(władza)* and the dominant order'.[35] On the other hand, Solidarity imitated some central organizational features of the communist parties. In this vein, the similarity and reciprocity between the mentalities and methods of Solidarity and the Soviet communist party in the revolutionary phase was striking (Staniszkis, 1984:36–7, n.47). Rather than confining the meaning of utopia to an eschatological certainty as pursued by either the communist party or the Solidarity opposition, it seems more appropriate to see the politics of both antagonists as guided by utopian images. These images were at the crossroads of the 'nowhere' of the permanent liminal condition, coupled with a reciprocal attempt to create spaces of second reality in politics.

The antagonism state *vs.* society as mimetic conflict

The tradition of Western thought has regarded conflict and conflict resolution in society in an essentially dyadic way. On the one hand, a consensus of all with all *(volonté générale)* is established so as to balance conflicting interests among the members of the community. On the other hand, stab-ility is gained through the imposition of power or force by one party and the compulsory subordination of the other party. Such is the concern of Hobbes' Leviathan as well as of the Marxist-Leninist version of the proletarian revolution and the victory against capitalism (Dahrendorf, 1959:157).

The end of communism is generally seen as a victory of the rationalization of politics and the abdication of utopian aspirations. As I showed in the first part of this chapter, Poland's permanent revolution was characterized by the reciprocity of political passions in a state of permanent liminality. Utopias in pre-1989 Poland must not be understood in terms of systemic entities or clear-cut sets of ideological premises. Rather, the reciprocal pursuit of utopias by both political antagonists came down to a predominant mentality in Polish politics. The appeal of utopian images in pre-1989 Poland was of a relational character, as it concerned expectations and desires of both antagonists. Gierek's second Poland and Solidarity's revolution were distinguished in so far as the former project aimed to strengthen the legitimacy of the communist regime, whereas the latter project built up a counter-system based on a self-determining society. Yet they were almost identical in terms of envisaging utopia, since their original driving force stemmed from the pursuit of a second reality of national and political community. It is these mental and emotional interdependences with their vision of second realities that needs to be explained.

Subsequently, I will argue that political conflict in pre- and post-1989 Poland can be read as a triadic conflict based on the political passion of desire. Standard approaches to political conflicts have often had recourse to Machiavelli's definition of the origins of conflict in society as based on opposed humours.[36] The modern tradition has come to read this opposition in terms of class conflict. Yet the divisions in society have their basis in desires and humours which belong to the realm of natural passions (Parel, 1992:110–11). As

Tocqueville argued, the instability of social order promotes the natural instability of desire.[37] In this connection, the breakdown of communism had been accompanied by a progressive loss of faith in the ideological and institutional reality of communism (Horváth and Szakolczai, 1992; Engler, 1992; Maier, 1997).

Girard's theory of conflict assumes the reciprocity of desires in a situation of breakdown of order (Girard, 1965; 1977; 1987; 1988; 1989; 1990; 1994). In his early works he showed how in literary masterpieces desire is the central category of action (Girard, 1965), and argued that imitation is the basis of conflicts. More precisely, it is desire that is at the source of imitation. The anthropological premise holds that imitation and mimesis are not representative but essentially appropriative (Girard, 1987). Human and social life is ruled by three-tier or triadic dependencies in mutual acquisitive mimesis (between two or more imitators and commonly desired objects). For liminal situations such as the permanent Polish systemic crisis, mimetic theory assumes the symmetry of utopian desires of political antagonists.

Imitation was recognized as perhaps the most important means of knowledge transfer in East European transitions (Dembiński, 1991; Morawski, 1994; Offe, 1996a:213ff.; Smolar, 1996c; Ziółkowski, 1998). Yet no comparative analytical framework has so far been provided. Soviet communism was a competitive arrangement that emerged as a rival version of its democratic counterpart in the West and aimed to catch up with or to overcome it.[38] In addition, imitation (of the West) persisted as a defining pattern of communism, as 'imitation is one of the classic features of the System, and is particularly evident in the economic field'.[39] While standard concepts in the social sciences regard imitation as a linear or dyadic relationship, mimetic conflict relies upon a triadic scheme. The objects of imitation, such as knowledge, position, or the love of a person, are desired because they are believed to be desired by another. The relational aspect is given in the convergence of two antagonists on the same desired object. This is what Girard calls desire 'according to the Other', or triangular desire (Girard, 1965:4). 'What desire "imitates", what it borrows from a model, is desire itself, prior to gestures, attitudes, manners and everything to which mimesis is usually reduced when it is understood only as representation.'[40] This proneness to reciprocal imitation is based on an inter-individual psychology (Girard, 1987) through which antagonists in liminal situations compete for a way out of crisis. Appropriative mimesis and thus reciprocity is aggravated when differences are brought down. This was already shown by Tocqueville, for whom a situation of crisis was due to the breakdown of farsightedness and the narrowing down of prospects to give way to short-term desires.[41] Mimetic desire is a condition that is most acute in situations of crisis, breakdowns of order, and loss of belongings.

> When a society breaks down, time sequences shorten. Not only is there an acceleration of the tempo of positive exchanges that continue only when absolutely indispensable, as in barter, for example; but also, hostile or 'negative' exchanges tend to increase. The reciprocity of negative rather than positive exchanges becomes foreshortened as it becomes more visible, as witnessed in the reciprocity of insults, blows, revenge, and neurotic symptoms.[42]

Against this background, mimetic conflict must be distinguished from standard concepts of imitation. Thus, conflictual imitation is not an imitation of abstract concepts such as modernity or postmodernity (Ziółkowski, 1998). In this regard, it was held that 'the imitation of some Western patterns is either unfeasible, or not necessarily desirable'.[43] Similarly, it was asked whether it is 'realistic to attempt to imitate the Swedish model under such radically different circumstances'.[44] Finally, the assumption of a dilemma between 'imitation or a proper third way' (Michnik, 1995:384) misses the point. In all cases, a dyadic vision of imitation prevails and assumes imitation to be at one's discretion.

By contrast, mimetic conflict implies the identification of antagonists in mirror-images. Such mirror-images could frequently be detected in pre-1989 Poland, as reflected in the nationwide confrontation in 1980 and 1981, or in the simultaneous weakness of communist power and opposition in the wake of 1981 (Gross, 1989; Curry and Fajfer, 1996). Solidarity was commonly acknowledged as a movement of negation, be it in its programmatic dimension or in its 'philosophical stance'. Sergiusz Kowalski's analysis painstakingly elaborated the mirror image to these traits of the communist system. In 1980 the total character of the 'system' was perceived as a total attack on society. In Kowalski's reading, the communist system was perceived as follows: first, the system was a phenomenon of totality, one which was entirely binding. As a Solidarity publication of 1980 put it: 'The system binds from top to the bottom – its 100 heads stick on the common body of the hydra.' Second, it is the bearer of anti-values, the sum or the source of everything that is evil. Third, it hides its real nature, pursuing a 'game of appearances'. Fourth, the system is of a hostile essence, a base and evil monster. And fifth, it is situated outside society and outside the human being.[45] In short, Solidarity fought against the mechanisms that permitted the communist authorities to keep society powerless. The isolation of societal subjects, the division of society as such were seen as the foundation of real socialism. Solidarity's desire was to kill the hydra with 100 heads that stuck in the tissue of society and sucked its blood. What was desired was not to overthrow the system, but to clean society from its noxious intertwining with the communist system. For Solidarity the consequence of this total attack by the system was a total answer:

After August [1980] a counter-system shaped up against the [communist] system. It was similarly uniform and binding from top to bottom, i.e. where parts such as lower floors mirror the whole, as if they were identical with them. The system addressed society; if it attacked particular individuals or groups, that was because they represented the whole, or to weaken the whole. The total character of the system appeared in its total attack on society as a collective existence. The answer thus had the same total character.[46]

In conventional terms, one could equate the objects of mimetic desire with power or institutional control. The features of a mimetic conflict between communists and opposition become discernible here.

Everything that one of the partners to violence experiences, thinks about, or carries into action at a given moment, will sooner or later become observable in the other partner. In the last analysis, there is nothing that can be said of any one partner that must not be said about all partners without exception. There is no longer any way of differentiating the partners from one another. This is what I call the relationship of *doubles*.[47]

Such a situation of doubles in the Polish crisis was intimated by one commentator at the end of the 1970s.

The idea of a partnership between *społeczeństwo* and *władza* is a theoretical novelty. Partnership (. . .) is a funny notion, which is ignored by democracy and by dictatorship. Such an idea presupposes a divided sovereignty: a subjective autonomy of society and a subjective autonomy of communist power. In Poland, neither society nor the power are sovereign (. . .) In the days of a complete downfall of the government's authority, towards which everything seems to point to, the alternative of societal organization will be only societal disorganization, ochlocracy, lynch-justice, and blood.[48]

This reciprocity of doubles produced both patterns: the Solidarity community in 1980, which was followed by the confrontation under martial law, and the round-table community which soon afterwards developed into the replica of pre-1989 antagonisms.

In a Girardian reading, both political antagonists pursued utopian images. Solidarity's project of a subjectivization of society bears resemblance with the pursuit of a mimetic image. By the same token, the communists' aim of achieving the transition to communism can be read as a mimetic image. In pre-1989 Poland political conflict was ridden by a reciprocal search for identities and belongings. In post-1989, political identities and belongings were shattered as a result of the dissolution of the former order. The collapse of communism was thus a consequence of this desire for utopias, 'precisely because its utopian project of catching up with the West had not been achieved'.[49] With the institutional discontinuity of communism, however, utopian images did not peter out. As Szacki argued, Eastern Europe was ruled by the conviction 'that the Western process of civilization is always beneficial and, at least potentially, of a universal character'.[50] In this vein, liberalism as the main supposed ideology leading from communism to Western democracy has been fundamentally utopian in the Polish context (Szacki 1995:210). On these grounds, Michnik's definition of the post-1989 period as the return of the past in the shape of a 'hotchpotch of utopias' seems to be adequate. Among these one can mention the utopia of nationalism, of a Catholic state, a European utopia as well as an egalitarian one (Michnik 1995:338). Not by chance, authors that were convinced of the waning of utopia in pre-1989 Poland had to acknowledge its persistent influence in post-1989. 'Unfortunately, Poland's pioneering and heroic path to democratic transition via ethical civil society inevitably created discourses and practices that, until they can be transformed, will generate systemic problems for the creation of democratic political society. (. . .) Anti-politics is dangerous for democratic politics.'[51]

Thus, the transitory period after the breakdown of communism bears resemblance to what Miłosz argued for post-1945 Poland and Eastern Europe: a period of breakdown of order and confusion (Miłosz, 1953:20). Those who compensate the state of disorder by swallowing pills of happiness become schizophrenics. 'The events of today bear out his vision, even in this respect. One can survive the "crisis" and function perfectly, writing or painting as one must, but the old moral and aesthetic standards continue to exist on some deep inner plane. Out of this arises a split within the individual that makes for many difficulties in his daily life.'[52] In post-1989, the sudden shock of freedom

> opened a Pandora's box of horrendous conflicts that had remained unsolved for centuries . . . It brought the colorful bazaar of the market economy and destroyed the jobs of tens of millions. The people of Eastern Europe were not prepared for the realities of freedom. They have lost the protection of their old paradigm . . . they have lost the moral grandeur and the beatific simplicity of their lives. They have lost their identity, self-esteem, and dignity. They have become the poor and irrelevant relatives of the rich living in the West.[53]

Thus the pursuit of utopias in the Polish case must not be regarded as an ideology or the deliberate pursuit of a model. The replacement of ideology with mentality to describe Solidarity's emotion-loaded and action-oriented 'anti-political' political culture comes much closer to the point (Staniszkis, 1984:135). Moreover, the importance of images in Polish politics in areas such as nationalism, patriotism, and the economy, conforms with such a view (Kolarska-Bobińska, 1990; Bauman, 1992a; Kubik, 1994a; Brubaker, 1996; Walicki, 1997). It applies too to concrete political, social, or economic issues, as was shown both for the communist regime and for the Solidarity opposition (Staniszkis, 1984; Kowalski, 1990a; Ost, 1990; Kubik, 1994a).

Mimetic conflict can perhaps be defined best as a set of historically rooted images that guide the ideas and actions of collective groups in their fight for power and social control in a state of permanent liminality. Many features of Solidarity's second realities, such as the subjectivization of society, a life of dignity, or national resurrection, were as utopian as the party's desire to achieve political legitimacy by constant appeal to traditional or national values or import-led growth. Post-communists and post-Solidarity alliances diverge in their vision on issues such as abortion, national independence, religious education, and so on. However, they share a common desire to leave a liminal situation by recourse to the second reality of transition to democracy. In both cases, it is the distance between political elites and social reality that creates and maintains patterns of mimetic conflict. One of Solidarity's central traits was the tendency 'to use detachment as a way of coping with social reality. This trait was based on a cultural matrix rooted in over one hundred years of partition, when the society existed without its own state and nearly all social programs were built on a myth of the possibility of organizing a substitutional society' (Staniszkis, 1984:36–7).

Thus, Solidarity did not want to reform the state, but created a self-governing republic in order to be self-sufficient and independent of the state. Several currents and movements of opposition have pursued the common goal of accomplishing the self-determination, the subjectivization of the Polish nation.[54] As Richard Kearney argued for the antagonists IRA and Northern Ireland, their crucial desire is to be their rival, to possess the self-sufficiency of the other (Kearney, 1979:40). In the case of Northern Ireland, the two antagonists (Republicans and Loyalists) appear to maintain a mysterious intimacy, sometimes having confidence in the complicity which is completely absent from their relationships with their respective allies (Great Britain for the Loyalists, Ireland for the Republicans).[55] In Poland the representatives of society, first the dissidents, then KOR, and finally Solidarity, were in a double-bind with the communist regime.

Mimetic images are not a *homo clausus* phenomenon or merely a psychological state of mind. In a situation of crisis and shortage, the desire for discontinuities is reciprocally shared among those concerned. Such a reciprocity applied before 1989 as well. The systemic antagonisms between East and West gave rise to two paradigms. In the East, it created the 'paradigm of the prisoner' (Hankiss, 1994:116–18).

> People living in the East had hopes for a new and authentic life, an earthly paradise beyond the Wall. For them Western freedom and prosperity was not only a goal to emulate but also invincible proof that life was worth living, that it was not devoid of value and meaning, that oppression, humiliating compromises, and an existence without dignity were only a transitory episode in their lives.[56]

The reality of the Iron Curtain in turn was an indispensable source of meaning for Western identity in its missionary zeal towards the East, developing the 'paradigm of the Missionary' (Hankiss, 1994b:118). To a high degree the existence of the Eastern bloc stimulated and maintained technological, cultural, and social superiority and political stability in the West (Offe, 1997:196).

Similarly, the roots of political conflicts in post-1989 Poland can be explained as an intensification of the reciprocity between antagonists. However, it is important to specify this relationship of doubles. All too easily it could be taken for a state of mind that pursues an evolutionary or progress-oriented, utopian consciousness.[57] In pre-1989 Poland, the antagonists pursued similar objectives which can perhaps be summarized as attempts to constitute idealized images of the Polish nation. To a considerable extent communists and anti-communists were doubles who developed an intimacy as they were progressively drawn into totalizing conflict patterns.

By conceptualizing utopias as mimetic images, pre-1989 and post-1989 patterns of conflict can be analytically connected. Persistent references to self-images have been dominant in post-1989 politics. Identity-formation in Polish politics depends on the creation of self-images that manifest an identity without identity (Roszkowski, 1997:19). In pre-1989 Poland images referred to the evil communists and the West as the provider of welfare, or models for democratic and capitalist order. 'There is little doubt that the life of the affluent West, "as seen on TV", holds a tremendous and unqualified attraction for "the people" (. . .) Most likely, it is the very plenitude and putative accessibility of material goods that arouses desire.'[58] After 1989 identity politics dominated the political scene. Each of the opponents was attracted by a vision of a second reality to be pursued and established for the sake of the redress of unsatisfactory status-quo situations. In this regard, Gierek's second Poland aimed to compensate the shortage of legitimacy by the acquisition of commodities and goods, while Solidarity's revolution aimed to compensate the shortage of self-determination, participation and dignity by imitating the totality of the communist regime. The basic pattern of conflict was not inherent in any established group, class, or system, but appeared to be based on political passions, rooted in memory and collective experiences. In all this, the models remained 'deceiving images' (Dupuy, 1982:132). New political and social identities often rely upon such deceiving images. The malleability of new political identities and a profound sense of disorientation has thrown both political antagonists back to recapture the past.[59] While the post-communist camp shows a tendency to blur their image of the past, the post-Solidarity camp aims to link up with the claim to represent the Polish nation.

It might be objected that it is problematic to speak about a relationship between the opposition and the communist regime as being bound up by mimetic images. Mimetic images are expectations, hopes, shared by several protagonists, and thus point to an equality of desires in a situation of near-sightedness and instability. One could adduce in this regard that the images pursued by either party were radically different. The opposition aimed to build a second society outside the communist system. Conversely, the communists had increasingly to grapple with waning political legitimacy and their contested status as the representatives of the Polish nation. Hence the communist regime pursued ideological unity, political coercion, and social repression, while the opposition fought for liberty of expression, pluralization of political and social life, and democratic rights. Yet mimetic conflict is primarily engendered in the situation of dissolution of order itself, and only secondarily concerns outcomes. In all this, mimetic images do not refer to an ideal state of affairs; they are historically rooted, but their pursuit is conditioned by a double that is real and present. In the anti-structure of permanent liminality, the antagonists in Polish society experienced serious shortages. In a shortage economy, the authorities lacked legitimacy and therefore society's trust. Society lacked economic wealth, political and social rights, and national self-determination. Furthermore, deficits of political legitimacy, economic efficiency and legal authority enhance confusion and arouse desires. A situation of shortage, a loss of belonging, the breakdown of identities reinforce the appropriative dimension of desire. The reformers of the Soviet model in the 1980s turned to the notion of civil society because it conveyed 'precisely that which they most lacked and most desired'.[60] By the same token, 'Many of us in the West took it [civil society] for granted (and some still do), as a kind of normal human condition, while those in the East learnt to love it more ardently by being so thoroughly deprived of it, and by seeing the utter falsity of the faith which declared it to be redundant and fraudulent.'[61] Even if the object is out of reach, desire is there. A sentence by the French philosopher Simone Weil may serve as an illustration: 'Hunger: you imagine food but the hunger itself is real.'[62] Outbursts of public discontent in pre-1989 Poland were manifest in the propensity for crisis induced by the 'meat reason of state' *(mięsa racja stanu)* (Kuroń and Żakowski 1995:131). Following price increases for sausages and ham in 1970, 1976, and 1980, communist norms and rules regarding the mass mobilization of resources were breached several times.

Long-term political projects such as the transition to communism or society's subjectivization were heavily influenced by mental and emotional disruptions. Short-lived moments of imaginary communities boosted initiatives for national reconciliation or for solidarity among different oppositional groups. In this regard, oppositional thought in the 1970s postulated that the desired democratic socialism should not only – and perhaps even not mainly – be a legal and institutional structure, but should be above all a real community of freed individuals, created anew each day.[63] The strategy of new evolutionism which relied upon the unification of the workers, the Catholic Church, and the leftist intelligentsia set out to create a community of oppositional forces in order to offset the lack of social justice and a democratic culture. By the same token, Gierek's project of a second Poland injected commodities and goods, and allowed for personal freedom to travel. Similarly, the Solidarity community in 1980 was charged with images of national patriotism. In this way civil society was not an abstract notion, but became concrete in a semi-free press, the freedom to associate and hold public meetings, and alternative modes of political and social organization, epitomized by Solidarity.

The importance of mimetic conflict is reflected in the frequency of scapegoating in pre- and post-1989 Poland.[64] In the crisis of 1976 'violence was used by both sides. The balance of forces, however, favored the police and the authorities'.[65] Even in 1968, a stability was achieved by a campaign against the 'enemies of People's Poland', 'Zionists', who were threatened with getting their 'bones broken'.[66] After Gomułka's demand that each citizen of the PRL should have but one home country, Poland's Jews were denounced and a great number of them were expelled from the country.[67] The scapegoat effect also applied to the leadership of the communist regime. 'In retrospect, however, it is clear that the primary culprit was the Gierek leadership itself.'[68] In 1980 the communist party lost more than one million members and experienced a serious delegitimization. In turn, Solidarity was victimized by martial law in December 1981. Repression by the communist regime, however, had no lasting effect on the opposition. Poland's lingering between violence and utopia before 1989 can be expressed as a mimetic conflict between the communist state and societal opposition. The anti-system, created by Solidarity as the regime's double, was finished by the regime's violent crackdown on the Solidarity opposition in December 1981. When the doubles met again, eight years later, their potential for creating second realities was exhausted. The general weakness of both antagonists led to the round-table community which, in turn, became a yardstick for the new emergence of mimetic images. However, while the double-bind between the communist regime and Solidarity came to an end in 1989, new double-binds emerged. In spite of the absence of violence in the demise of communism, the war at the top of the hierarchy in post-1989 Solidarity showed the key characteristics of a witch-hunt for scape-goats. In a similar vein, the politics of memory and the politics of lustration are ridden with reciprocal accusation based on images without any great possibility of clearly attributing accountabilities. The desire for identification with images was clearest in the case of Solidarity.

At the outset of the round table, each side had a primordial aim. While Solidarity envisaged a guarantee for its own re-legalization, the PZPR hoped for Solidarity's collaboration in the elections in order to legitimate and stabilize its own position. While at first sight the latter demand might seem to be an attempt for inclusion, it is in fact much more. Both demands and the final outcomes of the round-table agreements needed either to help reassure (for the communists) or revive the existence itself of each side. The crucial point is that post-1989 Solidarity identified with the Solidarity of 1980. Adam Michnik poignantly formulated the role of the original Solidarity for its successor at the end of the 1980s: 'The world was different. So was Europe. Poland was different and Solidarity wanted to be the same.'[69] Solidarity's mimetic image was its main source of identification. One of the experts on Solidarity, the historian Jerzy Holzer, wrote on the occasion of the tenth anniversary of Solidarity's existence: 'Many Poles have difficulties in accepting the real or imaginary differences between the people of Solidarity, and also their evident human weaknesses: rampant ambition, personal envy, fascination with possessing power. Identification with Solidarity has led to a loss of distancing towards it.'[70] This rejection of differ-ence came along with a high differentiation, epitomized in the disintegration of the Solidarity movement.

> Gradually, step by step, we lost our trumps. Poland squandered its chance. Consecutive 'wars at the top' smashed Solidarity into

pieces and destroyed Lech Wałęsa's charisma. Successive 'accelerations' and catchwords such as de-communization ruined the philosophy of the round table, which did not consist in dividing the power but in choosing a way of compromise solutions in the name of the common good.[71]

The continuity of mimetic conflict

This chapter has argued that the replica of historical antagonisms in Poland's transition can be explained by the non-contingent given of the second reality of mimetic images. Political contingencies in post-1945 and post-1989 Polish politics are strongly related to each other through the binding power of utopian political projects. The mythical quality of images such as those of the West or Solidarity was directly relevant to institutional choices or political decision-making. The pursuit of a new political order is charged with the painful process of searching and redefining new identities and belongings. For political elites, the way out of communism was not primarily a leap into the liberty of an open society but became a falling back on deceiving self-images and mirror-images of presumed antagonists. Moreover, such a thrust could be sensed in the scepticism on the option of a third way such as a social market economy, which simply would have impeded Poland in its drive to catch up with the West (Balcerowicz, 1995:3).

This chapter introduced the notion of permanent mimetic conflict as a non-contingent second reality in Poland's transition. The conflict between Polish society and communist state power can be read as based on the desire for mimetic images. As Offe argued, two diametrically opposed forms of pathological reactions are typical of post-communist countries, namely the rejection and simultaneous strategic exploitation of difference. The former implies the 'clinging to "communal", informal and "primordial" forms of social organization, perception, thought and action'.[72] In a mimetic reading, the rejection of differences comes close to the utopian quality of reference-points for political organization or long-term policy-options. Conversely, the exploitation of difference can be sensed 'in ethno-nationalist civil wars at the macro-level, for party, factional and inter-organizational struggles at the meso-level and for forms of predatory, aggressive and parasitic type of mercenary or 'smash-and-grab' capitalism at the micro-level'.[73]

In a mimetic reading, these pathological reactions appear as inherent to the communist period. Moreover, mimetic conflict implies tendencies to unity and of undifferentiation. As the Polish example shows, the scattered opposition of workers, leftist intellectuals, and the Catholic Church accomplished unity in the late 1970s. The great convergence of the opposition in the late 1970s laid the basis for the institutionalization of a second reality. In turn, Solidarity was ruled by a fervent desire to avoid party-like division and to maintain unity at any price (Kowalski, 1990a:133–5). A similar desire was overriding in 1989 and 1990. As will be elaborated in depth in Chapter 5, the disintegration of Solidarity after 1989 simultaneously highlights a process of high differentiation (expressed in the new dynamics of institutional pluralism) and high undifferentiation (expressed in the utopian-like unity of its own image). As long as the mirror image of the Communist Party was a serious competitor, its attacks and culpability did not fully threaten Solidarity's existence. Once the mirror image had disappeared, Solidarity entered into a double-bind with its own image.

Standard approaches see the antagonism between the communist regime and society in the lines of dyadic opposition such as class conflict. This chapter has developed a framework that permits us to analyse political conflict both in pre- and post-1989 Poland as a result of the reciprocal attraction of mimetic images. A mimetic reading postulates that both antagonists are disoriented, deprived of long-term visions and prey to past images. Throughout the 1990s, political cleavages between post-communists and post-Solidarity have intensified. In a permanently liminal condition, conflicts are not based on clear-cut interests or strategies, but develop around the competition for reciprocal images. In the conflict with the communist regime, the Solidarity opposition aimed to imitate the state's totality by creating a counter-system. The round-table community did not discontinue the imaginary reference-points for Polish elites. The images of the West and of Solidarity remained the yardsticks of the expectation of discontinuity before and after 1989. The liminal character of institutional change since 1989, and the widespread conviction of having missed the break with the past, entailed the construction of a third image, which has stamped post-1989 Poland with the burden of a politics of memory.

4
The Continuity of Backwardness

Backwardness and distance

The East's position is commonly defined as backwardness, a concept that points to the lack of specific features characteristic of a modernized state or economy of a Western type (Gerschenkron, 1962; Janos, 1982; Chirot, 1989b; Schöpflin, 1993; Stokes, 1997). Throughout the centuries, Eastern Europe had been deprived of modern categories of political, social, and economic organization that were perceived as successfully implemented in Western Europe. In this vein, the

> political traditions with which Eastern Europe entered the contemporary period can be generally characterized as backward. This backwardness manifested itself in the significantly different relationship between state and society to what had evolved in Western Europe, in attitudes towards modernity and the definitions of modernity, as well as the demands that modernization makes on any society.[1]

Endowed with a distinctively discriminatory leaning – especially for Easterners – backwardness is associated with belated political, economic, and social development. Moreover, the recent renaissance of this concept stresses the importance of historical fault-lines for understanding the current conflicts in Eastern Europe. This might be one reason for the fact that if backwardness is evoked as useful for analysis, it remains explicitly descriptive (Stokes, 1997).

The comparison between the backward East and the modern West comes down to a juxtaposition of two entities or systems, one being stronger, richer, and more innovative, while the other is weaker, poorer, or dependent. As a consequence, modernization approaches have been keen to develop arguments for bridging this distance. They assumed that political change would come about as the central political and economic functions in Soviet-type societies would become more and more similar to Western-type societies (Lindblom, 1977). Others categorically denied this distance between East and West by arguing that totalitarian functionalism was eminently modern. It had only a totally negative social structure which negated personal freedom (Feher, 1995:61). In this vein, 'it is unfounded and misleading to describe Soviet societies, after nearly seventy years of existence, as the embodiment of "backwardness" as against the West, alias modernity'.[2] Feher argued that regardless of its per capita production or the absence of democracy and capitalism, Soviet-type societies competed with the West on the very grounds of modernity which he identified as industrial logic, a universalizing telos and an apparently unstoppable and dynamic growth (Feher, 1995:61). However, several utopias (that of functionalism, of industrialization, of a complete subjection of the work-force to the commanding centre) show that Soviet functionalism is not 'backwardness' but an eminently modern and totally negative social structure.

For the Polish case, this seemingly paradoxical assessment allows us to identify two different realities of distance. On the one hand, before 1989 its objective institutional distance from the West was rather high as regards economic efficiency, political legitimation, and the eminent role of the elites in society (Szacki, 1995; Kersten, 1996). On the other hand, Poland was hardly distanced from the West at all in terms of its collective identity with Western civilization, its religious and moral values, and its desire for democracy and capitalism (Davies, 1981; Samsonowicz, 1995). In other words, distance was close to zero, as catching up with the West seemed so close. Although the constant reference in Poland to the superiority of the West intimates a subjective perception of backwardness, the double-bind situation is reinforced by an assumed confidence that it can be part of the West and can catch up quickly. Hence, distance has two interlinked 'functions', one of asymmetry and another one of symmetry. The balance sheet of the objective, institutional first reality highlights the great distance between Poland and the West, while the strong identification with the West points to only a small distance.

The standard arguments see the post-1989 discontinuities almost entirely in terms of a convergence of both realities of distance, assuming that the progress through modernization in post-1989 institution-building has shortened distances. Yet the evidence on some general trends in Poland's transition strongly suggests that the distance between East and West has remained quite high. So far, democratic institutions in Poland are afflicted by volatile and unstable landscape of political parties. With eight governments in seven years, Poland has seen more governmental instability than other East European countries. Trust and confidence in democratic and market institutions is particularly low. Liberalism in Poland has widely failed in its missionary attempt, both politically and economically (Szacki, 1995). Despite positive macroeconomic indicators, the big dilemma of the state's large-scale involvement in the economy has not been resolved. Poverty rates doubled between 1989 and 1993 in Poland and all over the region.[3] The high incidence of ideological and identity-based conflict in politics and society renders the rationalization of politics more difficult.

Compared with post-1945 Poland, the distance to bridge appears to be considerably smaller in post-1989 Poland, as the country does not have to cope with war devastation, big migration waves, high loss of population, or a foreign invasion. However, if the Poland of 1990 is compared to the pre-war Poland, say of 1939, the picture looks strikingly different.

Then, the heritage of the PRL in the economic sphere would be a technological backwardness that had been increasing throughout 40 years. There has been a drastic underdevelopment of infrastructure, inadequate industry structures, low mobility of the labour force partly due to a particular habitus but especially caused by the housing situation. Furthermore, managerial skills are as backward as is agriculture. Finally many billions of debts were inherited as a result of Gierek's artificial boom. The environment is destroyed. In the mental sphere, we are confronted with devastated work ethics, dwindled spirits of initiative, and taught helplessness, which have all led to demanding attitudes. This is accompanied by the retention of a traditional model of Polishness, maintaining xenophobia and nationalist drives. For part of society, the love of country, preparedness for service and a feeling of responsibility for their country do not count for much. Moreover, the degradation of law and the reduction of legal culture have arisen.[4]

As one of the few authors problematizing distance theoretically, Claus Offe recognized that 'the designing of new institutions occurs through the replication of old or spatially distant ones'.[5] In a comparison between the transitions to democracy in post-1945 West Germany and in post-1989 East Germany, he argued that the latter case is a more difficult and complex one, although it looks less dramatic and catastrophic in its initial moral, economic, and military conditions (Offe, 1997:162–88).

> There are two cases of transition, one (1945) over a long distance and the other (1989) over a comparatively short distance in terms of the effort needed to bring about full economic recovery and political normalization. What needs to be substantiated and explained is that the long distance was bridged much more smoothly, more successfully and faster than has so far been the case with the short distance.[6]

Post-1945 West Germany had huge losses in hardware (machinery, war losses in the economy), but could draw upon cultural, personal, and ideological software resources. In post-1989 East Germany, the hardware has remained substantially intact, but the software resources such as mentalities, routines, habits, and cognitive frameworks render the bridging of distance difficult.

This chapter aims to reassess some of the assumed views on backwardness. In particular it aims to problematize the role of knowledge and identity in a situation of the collapse of order. In Offe's approach small or great distances are measured with regard to a hypothetically normal situation in a working political and economic system. In pre-1989 Poland, distances in the first reality, such as economic development or political rights, appeared to be much smaller, due to a pervasive reliance on the part both of elites and the populace on the second reality, that of identification with the West. While after 1989 the objective institutional distance between Poland and Western models decreased, the small distance with second realities has not helped dissipate feelings of backwardness.

I will examine the continuity of backwardness by looking at the role of elites and the modalities of identity-politics during the transition. I will argue that, in the liminality of Poland's transition, political and economic modernization lacked fully fledged elites. As a consequence, institution-building largely hinged on images rather than rational strategies. In many respects, the return to Europe as a project of modernization has reinforced backwardness. In this vein, Poland's distance from its own past – epitomized by the settlement of accounts, the politics of memory, and lustration – has become smaller. At the same time the small distance from the past reinforces and protracts a wide distance from the West in terms of knowledge and innovative strategies. Hence political and economic modernization, to a considerable extent, have become a utopian endeavour which has partly provoked Poland's disenchantment with the West and has, in some aspects, exacerbated a pervasive feeling of backwardness. Despite a myriad of discontinuities from 1989, the Polish elites have remained backward, but there has been a considerable shift in the meaning of their realities. While the objective institutional distance has been shortened, the subjective perception of distance has been widened.

Reducing distances before 1989

The debate on backwardness has almost entirely focused on systemic differences and asymmetries. The reasoning of mainstream Western sovietology followed the ideology of modernization programmes and neglected the deepening of backwardness (Bence and Lipset, 1994). 'The discrepancy of voluntaristic objectives and actual social processes enhanced the importance of ideology, which had the function of demonstrating the scientific correctness of these programmes and of legitimating the leading role of these parties.'[7] Given this unofficial encounter of the East with the constituents of the West, theories of modernization operated on the assumption that communism could be overcome by a change or institutional reshuffling of the mix between government/state and market. In a similar vein, in much of the sovietological thinking the 'only difference between capitalism and socialism boiled down to different proportions of the same components'.[8]

Distance from market principles and commodities was constitutive to the existence of a communist system. Several studies of state socialist economies unanimously stressed the fundamental otherness of market economies to centrally planned ones (Kamiński, 1991; Dembiński, 1991; Kornai, 1992). On the other hand, quite a few empirical analyses suggested that the introduction of market principles was desired by an increasing number of people throughout the 1980s (Morawski, 1994; Borkowski, 1994; Kolarska-Bobińska, 1990, 1994). In addition, under conditions of economic crisis

(Poznański, 1996) the traditionally tight links between Poles and their Western neighbours in terms of temporary work activities in Western countries translated into a high rate of willingness to take up a job in the West.[9]

There is good reason to assume that the systemic differences between West and East did not exclude any impact of Western models on political and economic reality. Zygmunt Bauman has pointed to Eastern Europe's dependence on the West which was primarily induced by a stimulus that travelled from the West to the East (Bauman, 1992a:84). Stimulus diffusion was characterized as a 'process in which an idea of a "superior" social form travels on its own, unaccompanied by the socio-economic conditions which gave it birth, having thus acquired the status of utopia – of a dream to be reforged into reality by conscious human effort'.[10] Although such a perspective implies the bridging function of a stimulus between two systems, it denies that stimulus diffusion is more than an idea. Although socio-economic conditions such as those of the Western welfare state were not available, the utopian expectations that developed in a state of permanent liminality in Poland underpinned the impact of principles of democratic and capitalist order. To put it the other way, a market economy and democracy were not entirely absent, but they sustained a hypothetical second reality, even if in rudimentary or incomplete form. In this vein, the division into a first and second society proved the co-existence of ideological, political, social, and organizational principles of different kinds. Second economies, second public spheres, second cultures, and second consciousnesses provided for the hypothetical availability of a still-distant goal (Hankiss, 1990:82–111). This applies also to the Polish counter-public, or to bourgeoisfied life-styles in Hungary (Szelényi and Szelényi, 1994:229).

A brief review of the career of capitalism and democracy in the Polish context of the 1970s and the 1980s shows that the attraction of Western models could be sensed in a twofold way. First, there was Edward Gierek's bid for building a second Poland in the early 1970s. Gierek's economic policy[11] opened Poland towards the West in order to profit from the blessings of the market system by means of a credits-financed consumerist boom. The drive towards another, possibly better, organization of the economy was also urged by the crisis-ridden conditions and the ficticious character of central planning in the Polish economy (Landau and Roszkowski, 1995:262). Second, after the proclamation of martial law in 1981 and under conditions of deep economic crisis, economic policy became a central instrument in restoring the party's damaged legitimacy. In a two-stage reform (the first part in 1982, the second in 1987) it was hoped to regulate a competitive market by central planning. It is important to bear in mind that 'the overall objective of the second stage reform was the introduction of a viable combination of planning and an effective self-regulatory market mechanism'.[12]

On the whole, the purpose of market reforms in the understanding of the communist regime lay in the corrective capacity the market could have on the havoc caused by a centrally planned economy. A communist state aims to control directly all economic activities, the process of economic growth, and the allocation of assets (Kornai, 1992). It aspires to extend its rule over all domains of public life and to suppress group and individual interests. The catch-all aspect of modernization played an important part in the task of the communist elites. 'Everything is politicized, except politics, which is almost completely depoliticized' . . . and 'under state socialism, everything focuses on the economy except economics, which is utterly de-economized, and as a result, is fully politicized'.[13] In turn, 'fusion determines the political and economic logic of state socialism' (Kamiński, B., 1991:24). As can be deduced from this, the communist elites took pains to regain political legitimacy by their attempt at economic modernization.

By the same token, throughout the 1980s a variety of foreign models were addressed in political and economic discourse (Kozłowski, 1995:125–34). The Spanish model should be imitated, it was said, to leave real socialism in an ordered and peaceful way. Finland was often referred to as a possible solution that would give Poland a limited sovereignty and a certain independence from the Soviet Union.[14] As early as 1980, Lech Wałęsa had equated Poland to a 'second Japan'. This model was associated with quick industrialization and economic growth, but also stressed the role of the state in steering and shaping the economy. The reference to the Swedish or Scandinavian model, rather popular around 1989, paid heed to state intervention in markets and social welfare (Kowalik, 1993). While these models belonged to the 1980s, a model for Poland in the 1990s could be Turkey. Its model-function has been buttressed by several factors. First, Turkey's situation at the crossing between East and West conforms to Poland's situation. Second, Poland's political stability and its membership of NATO are desirable objectives.

Third, despite deep religious traditions Turkey has become a secular state. As can be derived from this incomplete sample, the revolutions in Eastern Europe – with Poland as the trailblazer – addressed a virtually infinite number of models.

> Although there are many submodels within Western Europe, with distinct versions of the modern welfare state, the Western European economies share a common core of capitalist institutions. It is that common core that should be the aim of the Eastern European reforms. The finer points of choosing between different submodels – the Scandinavian social welfare state, Thatcherism, the German social market – can be put off until later, once the core institutions are firmly in place.[15]

It is safe to say that the modernization of post-1989 Poland relied mainly on economic modernization which was conceived as a political project.

These tendencies to shorten distances in the objective-institutional reality of economic reform were thwarted by liminal tendencies in the socio-economic reality. Like several countries, such as the GDR, Czechoslovakia, Bulgaria, and Hungary, Poland had been catching up with the West in terms of economic growth and industrial production until the mid-1970s. Progress in industrialization came to a reversal in mid-1975 and then started to decline rapidly. Between 1975 and 1989 the growth of all these countries slowed and the gap between capitalist and socialist countries widened again (Szelényi/Szelényi, 1994:216ff.). Similarly, the demographic profile of Poland was becoming increasingly distant from the course of demographic growth in Western countries. Under conditions of substantial increments of economic output, between 1965 and 1985 age-standardized mortality rates were rising in Warsaw Pact countries, while they considerably dropped in OECD Europe.[16] With the breaking-point of 1989 a net decrease of the population confirmed the trend of lower fertility in the whole region, which was also accompanied by a considerable increase in crude death rates.[17] Furthermore, growing rates of outward migration in the last years of communism testified to the collapse of the economy and the decline of faith in the reformability of the system.[18] Finally, there is clear evidence that the distance of Poland's economy from other European countries and the United States grew steadily throughout post-1945.[19] A comparison between Poland's international position in the inter-war period and in 1989 is striking in this respect. Polish national income in 1938 was approximately seven times lower than in the US, six times lower than in Great Britain, five times lower than in Germany, about 50 per cent lower than in Italy and Finland, and oscillated around the value of Spanish national income. It was somewhat higher than that of Portugal and Greece. Despite the 'socialist' progress under communism, a juxtaposition with Poland's economic situation in 1989 shows that the distance between the economic performance of Poland and that of the West increased considerably. In terms of gross national product per capita Poland had further fallen behind the richest countries (the GNP in the US was 12 times, in Germany 11 times and in France 10 times higher). Most tangible, however, was the distance between the Polish and other formerly peripheral economies. While Finland, Spain, and Italy had nearly been at the Polish level in 1938, in 1989 GNP in Finland was 12 times higher, in Italy 8 times, in Spain 5 times, in Greece 3 times, and in Portugal 2.5 times higher than in Poland.

In the liminal situation of 1989, the elite-negotiated revolution of 1989 displayed anew crucial characteristics of elite-induced political and economic modernization. Political capitalism (Staniszkis, 1991b) guaranteed the guiding role of the *nomenklatura* in the construction of Polish market socialism and in the fledgling process of privatization in the late 1980s. Taking power in late 1989, Solidarity elites aimed to reduce political backwardness by shortening distances with models existing elsewhere. To a considerable extent, the leap out of backwardness was to be tackled under conditions that had been the traditional tools of modernization in Eastern Europe. 'Except for a romantic fringe, the recipes for social renewal all agreed on at least one point; that the enlightenment of the people should stem from the reform of state power, and not the other way around. Reform should be accomplished for the people, but hardly by the people.'[20]

Reducing distances after 1989

The Eastern project to leave the liminal state was based on two pillars, a model-image and the elites that set out to approach this model image. I assume that regardless of systemic characteristics, Polish political elites took pains to reduce backwardness through the appeal of foreign models in order to discontinue the unsatisfactory first reality. This capacity for redress through distant models attributed by Polish elites can be characterized as the primary way out of backwardness. What is commonly labelled as modernization can be portrayed as a conscious educational effort to catch up with what was held to be Western or superior. Reducing backwardness in Eastern Europe was from the very outset a conscious endeavour pursued by a small educated elite that aimed to cushion the effects of backwardness, lessen dependence, and enhance modernization. The intelligentsia[21] played a fundamentally different role from the one we are used to in Western Europe. As a social group it was cut off from the bulk of the nation, not only from the masses but even from the traditionally minded majority of the upper class (Seton-Watson, 1967:479).

Thus, modernization in Eastern Europe was not only traditionally elite-initiated, but also implied a distance between elites and people. Eastern European elites played a frontrunner role not only in terms of modernizing the state as the central authority to provide universal literacy and specialized knowledge, but also in terms of creating a modern society. While the educated intelligentsia played the role of mediators or 'liasion officers' (Bauman, 1993) between backward Eastern countries and the progressive West, it was deprived of national independence and of a modern state bureaucracy. What is more, the intellectuals as a core element of Polish elites lacked the extra-territoriality of intellectual activity, its essential independence from social determination, or its ability to raise themselves above the level of social pressures and necessities.[22] Simplifying a complex situation, one can argue that from the nineteenth century on, the Polish intelligentsia was dedicated to the political liberation of the Polish nation. 'The people were the inert clay to the intelligentsia's active zeal, the slothful against the energetic, the superstitious against the educated, the benighted against the enlightened, the ignorant against the knowledgeable; in short the backward against the progressive.'[23] Furthermore, the better educated the privileged classes or groups were, the stronger the gap between the intelligentsia and the masses of their compatriots became.

In social science research on East European transitions, the ability of the political elites to reduce backwardness is hardly ever examined. Commonly, it is taken for granted that the elites are there and fulfil their leading function in politics and society. Thus, elite research in post-1989 Eastern Europe is guided by a central controversy. The elite reproduction theory argues that revolutionary changes in Eastern Europe did not affect the social composition of elites. The elite circulation theory claims that the transition to postcommunist regimes resulted in a structural change in the elites.[24] While in 1989 the communist party elites failed, the Polish counter-elites managed to seize hold of their opportunity only to a very limited degree. Poland seems to be a case where a convergence between elites and society was crucial for the success of mass mobilization and the emergence of Solidarity. Thus, it was argued that the Polish transition is anchored in an elite consensus about democratic procedures and strategic goals such as the free market and integration with the European Union (Higley *et al.*, 1998:8f.; Wasilewski, 1998). As already shown in Chapter 1, there is evidence that even oppositional elites were not considered as representatives of society (Gross, 1990). There was an interest vacuum in Poland, where elites represent not existing interests but, rather, the interests they wish to create by virtue of systemic transformation slated for the future. A remark of a later minister of industry, Tadeusz Syryjczyk, gives evidence for the liminal condition of the elites. He declared before the *Sejm* in September 1989: 'I represent subjects that do not yet exist.'[25]

The undifferentiated vision of the West by Easterners is mirrored by a somewhat blurred vision of the East through Western eyes. Modernization as a central task to be realized by elites and the intelligentsia is perhaps the most outstanding political project in Eastern Europe. Lacking initiation in new structures, it seems as if political elites continue to use communist-like mentalities of attaching to everything a political value. According to the fusion principle (Kamiński, 1991:7), both politics and economics in communism lose the distinctive features characteristic of Western societies. This intertwining became pathological in the Poland of the 1980s. Such a state of affairs vindicates the claim that 'the introduction of a market economy in the postsocialist countries is a "political" project which has prospect only if it rests on a strong democratic legitimation'.[26] It is quite easy to show that distinguished representatives of former 'anti-politics' succumbed to the continuity of communist-type mentalities sustaining the political value of decisions. This became clear from the electoral programme of the civic committee.[27] Similarly, Jacek Kuroń's statement on the political value of a radical economic reform is a remarkable document.

> When Jeffrey Sachs spoke in the OKP (. . .) Rysiek Bugaj, sitting next to me, said: what rubbish is this guy saying! And I said: I don't know much of what he is talking about, but listening to him I know that this solution has a political value. The programme

could be economically worse, or better. But it must have a political value, i.e. you present this programme to the people and they understand what you say and support it. When you get their support and are able to maintain it you can do wonderful things.[28]

This comes close to what Ekes deplored as the lack of political elites in post-1989 Poland. Not responding to the exigencies of the definition of a real political elite, but posing as it and trying to imitate its attitude, the Polish political establishment of the 1990s disavows – in the opinion of society – the very necessity of existence of authoritative and credible leading groups (Ekes, 1994:56). In a similar vein, Adam Michnik highlighted the imitative reproduction of communist practices. Discussing the McCarthy era in the United States and its repressive intolerance, Adam Michnik concluded, in reference to Polish lustration:

We have to do with an anti-communism that is the imitation of communist practices. What essentially did minister Macierewicz want? Unaware of this, he exactly copied the bolshevik mechanism of the functioning of a security apparatus. We remember that in 1949 in the Ministry of State Security a special department was created in order to screen party members, i.e. themselves, not the adversaries. This commission, that minister Macierewicz set up, is exactly of a type of the X Department for matters of the democratic opposition. He could not have rendered a better service to the communists.[29]

A further indication for the absence of elites is found in the very modality of the demise of communism. Social consensus and political legitimacy in communist societies were not only based on political and military power or industrial production. They were mainly backed by a broad-scale educational project of Marxism-Leninism, rendering professional formation and education one of the central pillars of communism. The emergence of Solidarity's large-scale opposition in 1980 and the mass manifestations in various Eastern European countries in 1989 strongly suggest the absolute failure of the communist educational project. The loss of faith and limited farsightedness were crucial characteristics of the elites in a situation of the irreality of the real (Tocqueville 1981; Engler, 1992; Maier, 1997).

Classical elite theorists such as Mosca or Pareto have emphasized the importance of emotional bonds inside the elites of political systems. 'The best way to convince others, is to be deeply convinced oneself and the art of arousing passions is rooted in the ability to feel passionately onself.'[30] In post-1989 Poland, social ties between the masses and the elites are weak, while creativity as a central features of the elites is doubtful. This links up with arguments according to which Polish communism prevented a political elite from rising in post-war Poland. What developed was a societal elite (*elita społeczna*) made up of two categories of beneficiaries of the system. The first category included those who identified their own private interest with the interests of the system. The second category consisted of those who in the name of realism were allowed by the system to keep a certain distance in relation to power monopoly and ideology (Ekes, 1994:53–4). Moreover, the legitimacy of the new ruling elites was still charged with a high level of political apathy. It is crucial that trust in institutions and elites was very low throughout the first half of the 1990s.

> Once more, things have been falling in line with the logic of life in the limen and are normal again: intellectuals, whether in or out of ministerial office are fast returning to their usual complaints against the witless and mindless 'masses' unable to see what is good for them, while the 'masses' are back to their habitual half-wary, half derisive view of 'those men with briefcases in the capital' who do not know and would not care anyway what real life is truly like.[31]

Elites remain distanced from society's trust, as they continue to imitate the political project of modernization typical of pre-1989. In this respect, they have been rightly equated with institutional nomads. 'The new elites replaced just a few elements leaving the rest intact. . . . In their arrogance, they have copied the communist elites they replaced.'[32] Most importantly, however, Polish political elites have remained caught up in the continuity of images that have been fundamental for pre-1989 Poland. The elites were seen as undeveloped, bare of good selections mechanisms, as cliques, corrupt, inefficient and pathological (Pańków, 1998:192). They continue to lack a political formula (Kolankiewicz, 1994). Based on data from 1990 and 1993, one can argue that the Polish political elite did not see itself as a cohesive formation or as a coherent player in the drama of the regime transition. Referring to trade union leaders, Vilfredo Pareto defined as central characteristics for the success of the new elite a practical mind, clear and precise, a realistic approach, high moral standards and education (Pareto, 1968:77–8). As the above analysis has shown, there is a negative bond that separates elites from society.

> Overall, the Polish political elite emerges in this early 1990s as fraught with ambivalence and lacking confidence. It had only a weak collective identity, and its consciousness of a common task, so strong in 1990, appears to have been waning. The elite neither trusted its own capabilities nor did it believe that the society would confirm its virtues.[33]

On these grounds, it seems safe to argue that a socio-genetic and relational approach to elites in Eastern Europe must eschew the standard perspective on elites. According to István Bibó, the calm and creative activity of the elite requires two things. First, the existence of a social consensus behind the elite selection mechanisms, and second, the actual assignment of members of the elite to the proper places in the social classes (Szakolczai, 1998). The quality of political elites in post-1989 Poland raises serious doubts on the existence of such conditions whether in pre- or post-1989 Poland. As slogans like 'revolution from above' or 'transformation as an elite-bargain' indicate, the idea of liaison officers touches upon a further central issue in Eastern Europe, namely the wide gap, the 'enormous distance between elites and publics, politics and economics, on the one hand, and the social base, on the other'.[34]

On the ground of the above analysis of lack of elites, I will argue that backwardness has remained a crucial characteristic in post-1989 Polish politics and society. To this purpose, the second part of this chapter deals with the conditions under which political and economic modernization was to be tackled. In this regard, the hypothetical second reality with reference to a better or more successful model image is crucial. 'The entire history of liberalism in the post-communist countries is nothing else but a number of attempts to transplant solutions that supposedly had been "tested" elsewhere to local soil.'[35] There is good reason to assume that in spite of great efforts the distances have not been reduced to a satisfactory degree and 'elsewhere' remains distant. 'Elsewhere' means 'distant', be it in geographical, temporal or mental terms.[36] First, 'elsewhere' was mystified because a better life was systematically withheld from the people. Second, imitation provided for the identification with this distant 'elsewhere', which was believed to be infinitely better than the bleak reality of communism. The distance was significant in that it considerably blurred any clear idea on a sustained long-term project of political and economic modernization. As Adam Michnik put it:

> I think that we know precisely what we do not want, but none of us knows precisely what we do want. There is no language which could correctly describe our aspirations – that, too is one of the peculiarities of this time. None of the known languages synthesizes our experiences. The language of political analyses and sociological forecasts, the language of historical reflection and religious meditation does not suffice. The values whose presence we sense intuitively – and to which we want to be faithful – are values existing at the meeting point of different spheres of our human condition, and hence the language in which they could be described cannot be internally homogeneous. Hence we are looking for another language which would pinpoint the inexpressible![37]

The East–West divide was a major paradigm long before communism deepened the distance between the two (Schöpflin, 1993). Modernization in Eastern Europe was historically tightly linked to the creation or enhancement of knowledge, as epitomized in the great educational project of Soviet communism. By contrast, elite-initiated modernization in post-1989 emphasized the importance of political crafting and elite-driven transformation. In these lines, it was considered to be 'best for the responsible elites . . . in Eastern Europe to "shop around" for models and implementation of modernization that seem optimal for particular institutions'.[38] In a similar vein, concepts such as lesson-drawing suggested a relatively smooth process of adaptation. 'The process of lesson-drawing starts with scanning programmes in effect elsewhere, and ends with the prospective evaluation of what would happen if a programme already in effect elsewhere were transferred here in future.' A lesson was defined as 'knowledge that is instructive, a conclusion about a subject drawn after the fact from observation or experiences. In its most primitive form, a lesson is the assertion of "what everyone knows".'[39] One can sense an almost intrinsic linkage between 'what everyone knows' and 'the only game in town' (Linz and Stepan, 1996a) as a symbol for a consolidated democracy. The foregoing examples underline to what extent Western-based political practices and systemic devices were assumed to shape modes of organization and patterns of behaviour.

Action at a distance

The foregoing discussion has focused on the conditions under which Polish elites set out to shorten Poland's economic and political backwardness. I have argued that Polish elites themselves were in a liminal condition, as the permanent crisis in pre-1989 Poland weakened a social consensus on the representativeness of elites and deprived them of farsightedness and confidence. In what follows I will show how the project of modernization as undertaken by economic shock therapy can be read as an attempt to reduce distances by reference to blurred images. In this regard, the con-tinuity of backwardness is less a question of comparative assessment of the quality of the democratic system, institutional pluralism, or economic wealth. It rather implies a habitus of political elites that is characterized by a zeal to overcome the transitoriness of political and social order, but is prevented from achieving this goal by a double obstacle: first, by the deeply rooted but vague mental and spiritual bonds with the image of the West; second, by the identity-creating experiences of communities in their own past. In both regards, the overcoming of distance plays a crucial role. Leaving one state and setting out to arrive at another state involves entering a liminal situation. Liminality embraces 'new ways of acting, new combinations of symbols are tried out, to be discarded or accepted'.[40]

While volumes have been written about the implementation of democractic and capitalist institutions, hardly any study deals with the experiential conditions of learning. A noteworthy exception is Jankowicz's remarkable study of the translatability of five key words in the business and management vocabulary from English into Polish, which concludes that 'the transition to a market economy is less a matter of knowledge transfer, but more one of meaning transfer, and that the western side has grossly underestimated the difficulties involved'.[41] Following up the problems of translatability, I propose to examine the problem of distance in Poland's transition by applying Bruno Latour's concept of action at a distance. The French sociologist and philosopher of science developed this concept in a study on the knowledge transfer in the wake of eighteenth-century explorations of distant regions. Latour claimed that knowledge cannot be defined without understanding what gaining knowledge means. In other words, knowledge is not something that could be described by itself or by opposition to 'ignorance' or to 'belief', but only by considering a whole cycle of accumulation.[42] At the centre of Latour's interest stands the search for the mechanism that allows for the feeding of 'centres of calculation' that pile up information in order to seize control of the world that is being discovered. Initially, there is the disorientation of navigators who, when landing on an unknown island, lack any knowledge or familiarity with it.[43] The repeated effort of going there would be in vain, if it was not backed up by the accumulation of reliable information and knowledge. Only organized and channelled communication to centres of calculation enabled science to draw reliable knowledge from these explorations. This becomes particularly clear when one looks at how the cartographer came to dominate the world as a consequence of a cycle of accumulating and providing information.

According to Latour (1987:223) the distance must be overcome if the knowledge gained in the exploration of a distant island is to be successfully translated into the actual space or situation in which it is supposed to be used. He elaborates three key elements that reply to the question of 'how to act at a distance on unfamiliar events, places and people. Answer: by somehow bringing home these events, places and people.' This means first: 'Mobility' is achieved by inventing means that render events, places and people mobile so that they can be brought back; Second: 'Stability', to keep them stable so that they can be moved back and forth without. . . . additional distortion, corruption or decay; Third, 'Combinability', so that whatever stuff they are made of, they can be accumulated, aggregated, or shuffled like a pack of cards.[44] Distant places were mobilized, brought home to centres of calculation in the form of maps, drawings, and readings. The reliability of these mobiles made them stable and allowed for combinations with further knowledge that had been collected elsewhere (on different islands) and by different explorers.

This chapter makes use of Latour's framework for an analysis of the continuity of backwardness in Poland's transition. In the language of action at a distance, democracy and market economy as distant configurations of rules and institutions must be brought and translated into the Polish reality. A translation in Latour's understanding is a situation or process 'in which one actor or force is able to require or count upon a particular way of thinking and acting from another, hence assembling them together into a network not because of legal or institutional ties or dependencies, but because they have come to construe their problem in allied ways and their fate as in some way bound up with one another'.[45]

The affinity between action at a distance, liminality and mimetic conflict can be sensed here. Explorers are in permanently liminal conditions as they are uprooted from normal stable conditions. Exploration, however, is inherently a mimetic learning process, as imitation is a primordial means of communication and institutional innovation. The common fate of East and West was bound up with one another, as the reciprocity of imitation processes indicates. In 1989 this common fate which bound up East and West became overwhelming. In this context it is doubtful whether there was a cognitive certainty about well-defined systemic features or universes of democracy or capitalism. Liminality is about experimental behaviour in the sense of 'any action or process undertaken to discover something not yet known'.[46] If the socio-economic reality and political elites are liminal, then political and economic modernization of pillars of systemic change such as democracy and capitalism is likely to be based on hazy images rather than stable and reliable knowledge.

I will now proceed to attempt an explanatory account of the interrelated problem of missing elites and persistent backwardness. Before undertaking this, one remark on methodology is timely here. It might be objected that the jump from eighteenth-century explorations to recent East European transformations that implicate the reconstruction of complex institutions and a whole social order is too audacious. Indeed, such an analogy dares to juxtapose the gaining of knowledge in a structurally simple process with complex relations in a whole society. Yet the crucial conditions, namely distance and lack of knowledge, are met in the void of the communist collapse. The undefined, diffuse and blurred character of assumed systemic models such as democracy and capitalism points to the utopian features of the desired community with the West.[47] Finally, postcommunist societies did not have a real prospect of returning to liberal Western democracies. Before 1945 they were already hopelessly distanced, a gap that was not caused but only deepened by the rise of communism (Szacki, 1995:208).

Distance from Western modernity ruled Eastern European reality, as 'for the last several decades these countries have lived in rather deep isolation, which without completely destroying the feeling of ties with the West nevertheless did rupture many real ties'.[48] In turn, the West instinctively feared the East, a consequence of misunderstandings and lack of knowledge which preceded the World War and the imposition of Soviet communism, as Norman Davies has argued. Evoking the Czech crisis in 1938, the author of the most authoritative book on Polish history related the attitude of the British Prime Minister Neville Chamberlain, who referred to Czechoslovakia, Poland's neighbour, as a 'distant country about which we know nothing'. The word 'distant' signified not a geographical but an emotional distance.[49] 'The Pole, Czech, or Hungarian of average education knows quite a lot about France, Belgium, or the Netherlands. The Frenchman, the Belgian or Dutch of average education knows nothing about Poland, Czechoslovakia, or Hungary.'[50] Furthermore, the reciprocal isolation between East and West pervades the tradition of Western historiography which has taken civilization as synonymous with Western and tends to summarize European history under the West. Neglecting the significance of interdependencies between East and West, a set of assumptions recurs time and again. As Davies has shown (Davies, 1996:16–25), it is thus maintained that West and East, however defined, have little or nothing in common. Moreover, the division of Europe is justified by natural, unbridgeable differences, taking the West as superior. Finally, it is argued that the West alone deserves the name of Europe.

Throughout the 1980s the economic depression in Poland played an important role in advocating radical economic solutions with which to replace the crisis-ridden centrally planned economy. In this vein, a common claim held that neo-liberal ideology coined the reasoning of the Solidarity trade union (Adam, 1993:189). The modernizing and democratizing strategy of Solidarity has been stressed by different authors (Ekiert, 1996; Glasman, 1996). 'The idea of the reconstitution of civil society on the basis of the rule of law and the guarantee of civil rights and expressed through a free public sphere and a plurality of independent movements and associations was present in all the opposition documents.'[51] Yet in the East European context also, oppositional elites had serious problems in overcoming the prevailing distance: 'In most countries, practically all modern specialization came into being during the communist rule and the specialists have no collective, institutionalized memory of professional life under any other conditions.'[52] In turn, the common characteristics of the new political elite in communist Poland led to a double isolation. On the one hand, Solidarity elites were isolated from real life in society; on the other hand, they were isolated from the intellectual memory of the outside world. 'This double isolation of societal elites had to influence the shape of its ideas about society and about directions of world development. In a similar vein, it had an impact on the quality of its achievements, first in the professional domain, later in the political realm.'[53]

A closer look allows us to detect that, on the contrary, the lack of concepts and strategies in Solidarity at the end of the 1980s was blatant. As early as 1980 and 1981 Solidarity had been prevented from accumulating knowledge and social learning by its proper mentality.

> The inability to generalize the movement's experience and to put it into an abstract formula created a barrier to the accumulation of knowledge and social learning in Solidarity. In such a situation the personal experience of the movement's leaders has a double value; the fact that the knowledge gained by the movement's activists cannot be transferred is a useful rationalization and a half-conscious self-justification for leaders who want to retain their positions as long as possible.[54]

While this inability was conspicuous before the round table, it became acute after Solidarity's triumph in the June elections of 1989.[55] The very same day Jacek Kuroń declared on TV the reason why Solidarity could not possibly take over power: 'We were unprepared, without leadership, without any concept.'[56] Similarly, the supposedly well-established neo-liberal ideology did not stretch over more than a very few specialists. In an evaluation of the situation in June 1989, the knowledge about proposed models appeared to be rather imaginary.

> The neo-liberals are very active and popular in Poland. They intend to abolish socialism and take recourse to capitalism in order to cope with the crisis. They come up with solutions *à la* Friedman and with the example of Chile. One has to take stock of the fact that no analysis of what really happened in Chile has been published either in the press of the liberals, of Solidarity or in the official press.[57]

This lack of information went along with the hazy meaning of economic liberalism before and after 1989. Ignorance, naive beliefs in profits without losses and in immediate results was characteristic for the protagonists of economic change (Szacki, 1995:211). One can sense their hazy conception of market economy in the degree of the suspicion which it evoked among Solidarity-elites: 'The project of shock-therapy, introduced half a year later by the first Solidarity-government, was still at the outset of 1989 ideologically and politically unacceptable for the usual trade unionists as well as for their leaders.'[58]

In summer 1989 the Solidarity elites were comparable to explorers searching for the island of utopia. 'For the time being, everybody in Poland is alone on earth, nobody has seen, has read nothing. We start from scratch.'[59] Contrary to common belief, Leszek Balcerowicz did not seek the mandate so as to apply 'neo-liberal ideology' to the Polish economy. After an exhaustive search for candidates he had to be persuaded painstakingly to assume the portfolio of Minister of Finance (Kuczyński, 1992:55). In addition, his own account casts doubts about the conditions for policy-learning and prospective evaluation: 'I did not have – and nobody had – experience in guiding a post-socialist economy in the period of transformation.'[60] On the whole, the common denominator for political elites in 1989 was the identification with a catch-all model. 'Poland wants to be like the states of the European Community.'[61] Given the ascendancy of distance, Poland under communism had itself become an 'island' where the 'transmission of ideas had been completely blocked' and many things had to be (re-) invented anew.[62] Such an isolation in terms of knowledge resembles what Karl Mannheim called 'docility' in aristocratic-authoritarian regimes and 'self-neutralization' in democracies. 'The former consists in the mass of people being prevented from learning, from acquiring new knowledge.' [In the latter] 'we often observe a failure to think and learn, due to the fact that the people let some organization or machinery do their thinking for them.'[63] While adequate for democracies, this assertion seems to fit even better when it is inserted into the context of the so-called Peoples' Democracies that were pervaded with an omniscient ruling party machinery.

In all that, the island effect in the Polish context was not confined to geographical, mental or cognitive distance. It also included the recapturing of the past. Accordingly also, the past is full of islands, prone to be addressed by action at a distance. A variety of myths that were constructed after the Second World War on both sides of the Iron Curtain influence the post-1989 Polish reality. In Eastern Europe, nothing could 'make burst the past that had been frozen into ice' by the Soviet-driven mythologization of liberation from Nazi Germany by the Soviets in the name of equality, fraternity, and liberty (Judt, 1993:103). In relation to the post-war order of 1945, Norman Davies highlighted the reign of a distant past: 'The 1945 settlement. . . . was a colossal feat of political engineering. However, in almost every East European country, it is interpreted as the culmination of a natural historical process, and is constantly rationalized by reference to distant historical events, real or imagined.'[64] These various distant reference-points bring about the situation that 'for East Europeans the past is not simply a different country, but a whole archipel of vulnerable historical territories that must be protected from attacks and distortions by the inhabitants of the neighbouring island of memory.'[65] Accordingly, action at a distance also points to different 'islands in the past'. Contrary to Western Europe, the Eastern part of Europe owns too many pasts, among which Tony Judt enumerates the following reference-points: 1918–21, 1938, 1939, 1941, 1944, 1945–48, 1956, 1968, and 1989. It is striking that Judt omitted the emergence of the Solidarity trade union in 1980 as perhaps the most incisive crisis both for an Eastern European society and for a communist regime. It was in the Poland of this epoch where hope soared highest and where, 16 months later, despair was deepest. Most import-antly, it is in this island of the past that the germs of democratization in the Polish case are located. In Part II of this book I will examine two islands of the past under the headings of the 'image of the West' and 'the image of Solidarity'. A third island of the past will be examined under the heading of 'the image of 1989', which actually stands for the non-achieved rupture with its own past.

How influence of any sort can be effective over a distance has already been thematized by such contrasting figures as Max Weber and Gabriel Tarde. In his Sociology of Religion Max Weber argued that, traditionally, the quality of local deities did not lead to monotheism but rather reinforced religious particularism. On the contrary, the Jewish Yahweh evolved as the universal and omnipotent God, given his specificity as a God that ruled 'as a God from afar' and who approached 'only when the military need of his people required his presence and participation'.[66] It is this 'effective influence from afar' (*Fernwirkung*) which presumably was a factor that participated in the evolution of the concept of Yahweh as the universal and omnipotent God. In this connection, the influence of Western models on Poland and other parts of Eastern Europe can be compared to a worshipped divinity.[67] Not only the economic crisis but also the socio-genetically rooted desires harboured by political elites in pre-1989 Poland forged 'a new dream of a utopian leap out of history, this time through worship of the "market"'.[68] Such worship over time and space had also been thematized by the French sociologist Gabriel Tarde, who defined imitation as action at a distance. According to Tarde, this mechanism enables imitations across geographical and temporal distances.

> Imitation happens, not only from very far away but also over great intervals of time. It establishes a fruitful relationship between an innovator and an imitator which may be separated by thousands of years, between Lycurg and a deputy of the national convention, between a Roman painter who painted a fresco in Pompei and a modern designer who takes his inspiration from it.[69]

Imitation through action at a distance is thus one of the most important mechanisms of political innovation. Innovation research in organizations has defined innovation as 'an idea, practice, or object perceived as new by an individual or other relevant unit of adoption ... If the idea is perceived as new and different to the adopting unit, it is an innovation.'[70] According to another definition, innovation 'is the work of many people and is related to the adoption of some new invention or discovery on the level of behavior, of action. Innovation involves new behavior, new habits, new interlocking expectations'.[71] What matters in these approaches to learning and knowledge transfer are the sources of knowledge and their points of destination. The separating space, the distance, is not considered to be a major problem. Yet spatially or temporally distant points, as Poland and the West in our case, suggest a basic contextual difference between the original setting and the point of destination. Pareto regarded human actions as motivated by several types of residues. The first two referred to the 'instinct of combination' and the 'preservation of aggregates'. Concentrated in persons, one can speak of 'innovators' and 'consolidators'. One is out to get, the other to hang on to what he has. Pareto argues that the history of man is the history of the continuous replacements of elites; as one ascends, another declines (Pareto, 1968:36). The more an elite consists of innovators alone, or consolidators alone, the less it is able to meet normal exigencies (Pareto, 1968:9). The Polish case strongly suggests a clear penchant of elites to fulfil the task of consolidators, as a lack of confidence and an isolation in terms of experience and knowledge refer them to utopian images as the source of innovation.

To sum up, one can safely argue that 1989 can be analysed as having a double impact of the island-effect. On the one hand, the post-1989 political elites in Poland were equivalent to explorers searching for an isolated island. Lacking experience with distant models, the Solidarity elites in 1989 were comparable to explorers just landed or having been thrown on the unknown and alien territory of democratization and marketization, largely ignorant of its measures, its dangers, and the tasks to be tackled. The sudden discovery of this island in 1989 came along with the desire to adopt unconditionally all the things that had been witheld from it earlier, such as knowledge, ideas, and information. On the other hand, the strategic disarray in the liminal condition of the end of communism led to a renewed focus on islands in the past. As political and economic modernization did not enhance confidence in the state and society, widening the social distance between elites and the people, the identification with the islands of the past increased. Strategies were sustained by myths drawn from scattered islands representing different conceptions of the West and of their own past.

The continuity of distance

This chapter has argued that the continuity of backwardness can be attributed to the lack of a fully fledged political elite in Poland's transition. The ideal scenario for the end of backwardness would have consisted of the narrowing-down of institutional distances with Western models by rational and knowledge-based political innovation. This chapter has examined why elites were quite distant from the West in terms of knowledge, and how they re-established identities with their own Polish past. While the reconciliatory round-table community and the policy of the thick line promised good conditions for modernization, the emotional appeal of the return to Europe and the indiscriminate adoption of Western economic and political models actually showed that the political elites in Poland were rather ill-prepared. The recapturing of the past and the continuing distance from the West in Poland are consequences of permanent liminality and imitation at a distance. The constant transitoriness and the dependence on utopian images have raised expectations of discontinuities to a high degree. At the same time, no coherent and experienced political elite is able to unfold.

As the socio-economic classes have remained widely unstructured and political electorates and identities largely malleable, political elites have oriented modernization efforts largely to utopian islands in the West and in their own past. Political and economic modernization through imitation has succeeded in shortening distances in the first reality, as is shown by undeniable progress in democratic institution-building and by the achievements in economic reforms. Yet the perception of a non-achieved modernization at the exclusion of Poland's active and creative participation is widespread in Poland. Before 1989 the subjective distance towards Western models was rather small, while the objective-institutional distance from the West was quite high. In post-1989, the objective-institutional distance has substantially decreased, whereas subjective assessments of distance have substantially increased. A reading in the lines of action at a distance shows how reference-points for Polish elites remained imaginary. Most importantly, however, the link between the people and elites was further loosened in a state of permanent liminality. This has all culminated in an eliteless society (Szakolczai, 1998).

The continuity of backwardness has been made explicit by having recourse to the second reality of distance as a non-contingent given in Poland's transition. Distance prevails in so far as several island-effects have not been removed. The islands of the past still exert a disproportionately high influence on politics and on society. This applies not only to the unresolved question of retribution for communist crimes or lustration for the political and administrative elites. It is also valid for the unconscious cleavage-lines of political decision-making and the recruitment of political elites.

Part II

The second part of this book includes three chapters that examine the continuity of the second reality with regard to the three central images that have played an essential role in Poland's permanent transition. These images are that of the West, that of Solidarity, and that of 1989. I will argue that the socio-genesis of these images and their continuity are central to identity politics in Poland's transition. This second track of analysis assumes that the second realities of liminality, mimetic conflict, and distance have reinforced the recurrent strengthening and institutional impact of these images. To this purpose, I will analyse the constitution, crisis, and reconstitution of these images in pre- and post-1989 Poland. By focusing on these three images, I do not claim to create a complete and exhaustive treatment of Poland's transition. Yet these images may include or cover other crucial reference points that have come to rule Polish history, such as nationalism or Romantic patriotism.

Chapter 5 examines the continuity of the image of the West which has been a central reference-point for Poland before 1989 and has, if anything, increased its influence since 1989. The struggle for national independence, attempts at political liberty, and the pursuit of economic growth have all hinged on the expectation of Polish elites to leave behind their own backwardness and to catch up with the West.

Chapter 6 probes into the continuity of the image of Solidarity which came into being as a result of the events in August 1980. I will argue that the fundamental experience of the self-limiting revolution of 1980 and 1981 allowed for the re-emergence of Solidarity as a political force at the end of the 1980s. Solidarity's revival, and its disintegration in the aftermath of 1989, can be explained by the continuities developed in Part I of this book. The liminal experience of the underground, coupled with mimetic conflict over the identity of Solidarity, led to its institutional disintegration. The war at the top, as the differentiation process in the Solidarity movement throughout 1989 and 1990 became known, opposed several strands of Solidarity that were, to different degrees, in double-binds with an idealized image of Solidarity.

Finally, Chapter 7 provides an analysis of the image of 1989 and its consequences for post-1989 politics. It will examine three dynamics that show the obsessive identification in Polish politics with the presumed rupture-point of 1989. The politics of lustration, the politics of permanent reform, and the desire to return to the start focus on the image of 1989 as the symbol for an absent rupture-point. By contrast to the other two images examined in Part II, the experiential basis of the image of 1989 generated the round-table community. Yet it had existed beforehand as a collective desire to discontinue communist rule which represented foreign oppression and the alienation of society.

These images differ considerably as regards their historical range, experiential basis, and perception. Despite these apparent differences, they share some core attributes which draw on the continuities examined in Chapters 2, 3, and 4. It is crucial to recognize that the images are not well-established and defined systems or clear-cut models. While the expected community with the West after 1945 was withheld from Poland, the post-1989 project of return to Europe has turned into a lengthy process of permanent transition. Similarly, the political round-table community in 1989 only temporarily suspended historical antagonisms. The nationwide Solidarity community of 1980 has become a recurrent element in Polish politics, epitomized in the parallel processes of disintegration and reconstitution of political alliances such as the Solidarity-governments between 1989 and 1993, or the reconstitution of the post-August community under Solidarity Electoral Action (AWS) as of 1996.

Most importantly, this book conceives of these images in a relational perspective. In this regard, images in the Polish transition do not constitute collective representations or social facts that would be reference-points for society as a whole. On the contrary, the images are contested among antagonistic groups in Polish politics. Thus, the image of the West was espoused by the communists and by the Polish opposition, although on a very different basis. The image of Solidarity has exerted both integrative and conflictual influences, as can be seen in such opposite movements of conflict and integration as the war at the top in the early 1990s and the reconstitution of AWS in the second half of the 1990s. In a similar vein, these images are mimetic as both antagonists share their commitment to pursue inherently utopian projects. It will be argued that the genesis and development of these images and their impact on society and politics justify their being seen as the pillars of the second reality in two regards. One of their common attributes is their significance for the passions of equality and liberty in Poland's transition. As such, the image of the West is based on Poland's common religious and cultural heritage with Western Europe. On one hand, these have been sources of inspiration for concepts, principles, and expectations for equality in a liminal society. On the other hand, they have become the destination points of expectations of liberty. I will argue that post-1989 Polish politics and society have remained very much dependent on these images, and that many of the paradoxes in post-1989 Poland can be at least rendered more understandable by such a view.

5
The Continuity of the Image of the West

The image of the West was frequently evoked both in pre- and post-1989 Poland. Unsettled by recurrent crises, Poland had to 'turn towards the West, because otherwise a complete catastrophe menaced'.[1] The jump to the market economy was induced by the 'economic spirit' that wanted a 'return to Europe'.[2] A standard definition of the image of the West is based on two main constituents. The first is the emergence of the co-existence of three logics: capitalism, industrialization, and democracy (Feher, 1995:56–8). These logics are conceived as dynamic on the basis of distinct institutions and institutional networks which presuppose a relatively independent learning process in each case. These logics are more or less independent. The second constituent is supposed to be the West's inherent universalizing project. Western ideology and the social organization implicit in its project managed to learn and assimilate the competing civilization in the East, while retaining its identity and claim to superiority.

In Feher's reading, the image of the West appears as a model of universalizing quality. On these grounds, communist modernity set out to become universal by competing successfully in the field of industrialization, while it excluded the development of both democratic and capitalist logics (Feher, 1995:57). Such an argument emphasizes the autonomy of the Eastern path. It conceives of the image of the West as a competitor which will be combated by a rationally induced version of modernity of its own. For Feher, the West as the combination of three logics, those of capitalism, industrialization, and democracy, is not a geographical concept, because many countries in the geographical East belong to the socio-cultural West (Feher, 1995:66).

Linking up with such a view, the end of communism in 1989 was seen as a systemic change which attracted attention on behalf of the crafting of a new system. Contrary to a historically grown pool of values and ethics, modernization in Eastern Europe on the basis of Western models was conceived as an operation from scratch. Western patterns of the growth of capitalism and prosperity were largely by-products of moral and ideological initiatives by early entrepreneurial and commercial protagonists. On the contrary, the rise of capitalism in post-1989 Eastern Europe was widely perceived as a spontaneous and outcome-oriented leap towards the market. Thus 'privatization and marketization' were 'not rights-driven but outcome-oriented; not class-based but elite-initiated; not creeping and halting but sudden and highly visible; not supported by moral and ideological arguments or rights and freedom but defended in the name of vehemently and universally desired economic prosperity'.[3] The terms 'sudden' and 'universally' seem to point to an autonomous decision seeking a satisfying outcome. Going even further, Ralf Dahrendorf has denied such a fixation on the West, claiming that the countries of East-Central Europe have not shed their communist system in order to embrace the capitalist system, whatever it is, but have shed a closed system in order to create an open society (Dahrendorf, 1990:39).

In any of the above approaches, the means and modalities of catching up with the West are understood in realistic terms, weighing the perspectives of successful imitation of models. Feher acknowledged that 'while Soviet societies compete, at the same time they parasitically co-exist, especially in a technological sense, with "the West" and develop certain functions in imitation of, and in response to, Western societies. "Imitation" and "response" should be taken seriously'.[4] The fascination for Western achievements and the longing to join the core structures of Western civilization and politics are portrayed as perceptions of the independent logics of capitalism, democracy, and industrialization combined with the universal appeal of the Western project of modernity and its diffusion. In this vein, adaptation to the West is induced by the rational pursuit of these logics.

As pointed out by Jadwiga Staniszkis, 'revolution from above has allowed the negotiated establishment of a new generative grammar based on private ownership and parliamentary democracy'.[5] She has further argued that this revolution is incapable of filling the potential space thus created. On the contrary, this space is filled by 'two mechanisms that are no longer subject to central coordination and are largely spontaneous. These are: "revolution from the past" (i.e. the dynamic of "political capitalism", already initiated by the communist *nomenklatura* prior to the turning point) and "revolution from the side" (i.e., the impact exerted by the world capitalist system, currently in the throes of recession and readily viewing the former communist bloc as a cushion against its own tensions)'.[6] Yet Staniszkis' claim for the spontaneity of these mechanisms does not seem fully convincing. When she speaks about the spontaneous power of the two mechanisms of 'revolution from the past' and 'revolution from the side', an important aspect is neglected. For East Europeans, the past is 'an archipelago of vulnerable historical territories' (Judt, 1993). Thus, the revolution from the past can hardly be confined to most recent events before the collapse of communism.

The image of the West is commonly seen from a dyadic systemic perspective. As studies in political economy or democratization studies are mainly interested in the discontinuities of institutionalized logics or systems such as capitalism or democracy, their line of thought is focused on the mechanisms of substitution. Essentially it is assumed that Western models started to exert a decisive influence on politics and society only as of 1989. This chapter examines the influence of the image of the West in Poland's transition from a different perspective. It accepts that neither democracy nor capitalism were institutionalized logics and that they had no institutional network in the first reality, although they existed in various forms in the second reality. The second reality of the image of the West embraced a set of politically and socially relevant processes that sustained permanent liminality. In this context one can speak of a counter-public, independent trade unions, and the self-organization of society. Furthermore, the democratizing thrust of civil society, the second economy, and half-hearted market reforms were inspired by the endeavour of the political elites to draw distant Western models closer. In this vein, economic reforms and democratic institution-building in the late 1980s and early 1990s can be understood as generated in Poland through a figurational dependence on the image of the West.

To this purpose, this chapter presents a socio-genetic analysis of the quality of the image of the West as provider of models for institutional innovation. I will argue that the image of the West has been a central element of imitation in Poland's permanent transition before 1989 and long before the end of the Second World

War. Several rupture-points in political and economic moderniza-tion throughout the modern period alienated and distanced Poland from the track of Western modernity. In turn, its increasing insti-tutional and ideological isolation reinforced its mental and spiritual allegiances with the image of the West. This image, however, showed essential features of a second reality. In liminal situations, the image of the West embodied an imaginary community on the basis of Western values and principles. There was also a double-edged meaning to the image, as not only admiration but also criticism and suspicion defined Polish stances towards the West. The longer there endured liminal conditions such as the social contestation of communist power endured in post-1945 Poland, the stronger grew the appeal of the image of the West.

There is evidence for the continuity of the image of the West in Poland's transition on at least two accounts. First, it continued as a promised or expected community with a more developed civiliza-tion to which Poland had belonged before the loss of statehood. Second, the image of the West counter-balanced the dependence on the Eastern option in the shape of Soviet communism.

The emergence of the image of the West before 1945

The double-bind with the image of the West not only points to the project of reducing backwardness through modernization, but implies features of a long-term habitus in Eastern Europe. The work of Norbert Elias has focused on the stamping of social habitus and identity-formation. In his studies on the Germans, Elias (1992) traced back causes for the decivilizing turn in Germany through Nazism and the Holocaust to socio-genetic particularities of German history. He argued that large-scale disruptions such as the Thirty Years War caused permanent marks in the national habitus of the Germans. Germany's catching up in the context of the European powers required violent military action through internal and external wars. In this regard, its defeat of 1918 was a traumatic event. A second characteristic was that Germany's development as a state was ridden with many more disruptions and discontinuities of political and social order than that of France or England. If we transpose this picture to Eastern Europe, we perceive an even higher impact of disruptions. Boundaries, governments, nation-states, bureaucracy, and elites there have been precarious throughout modern Eastern European history (Bibó, 1992; Okey, 1992; Schöpflin, 1993). After the divisions in the late eighteenth century, Poland remained in a permanent state of transitoriness, as it was deprived of the status of an independent nation state and remained under foreign occupation.[7]

The underdevelopment of modern social structures was paralleled by a psychological unpreparedness for the requirements of modernity. Poland had not passed through the school of liberal individualism and had not developed such bourgeois values as economic capacity and industriousness, self-reliance in economic life, thrift, and so forth.[8]

Fraught with historical discontinuities, social and national habitus in East Central Europe became stamped with the political psychology of collective fear (Bibó, 1992). In this regard, East Central Europe formed a fraught community of fate, ruled by a sense of grievance, of European destiny denied and merit unperceived (Okey, 1992:130).

In his book *Three Europes* the Hungarian historian Jenö Szücs came up with the thesis that Central Europe makes up a transitional stage between the West and the East, always prone to imitations of Western models because of its (pretended) geographical and socio-cultural closeness (Szücs, 1988). At the outset, from the ninth to the eleventh century, the lands of Central Europe adopted the Western model of organization of relations between noblemen and vassals. The late Middle Ages were characterized by particular efforts to join Western civilization. A unified peasantry, the development of towns and cities, the unfolding of a nobility, a knightly culture and the advent of universities nurtured this process. On the other hand, the negative effects of a numerous nobility, endowed with far-reaching political rights, the weak development of towns, and not least, the Mongolian raids, deepened the civilizational differences between East Central Europe and the West. Thus, the unfolding of a civil society after a Western model was hampered. This line of thought joins up with István Bibó's divison of Hungary's history into three parts. While across the first 500 years of this millennium Hungary shared its fundamental roots of social structure with the West, Bibó argued, the sixteenth century brought about a split with Western tradition and forced Hungary to develop in conformance with the Eastern European model. This was the time of a 'stagnation in the relations of power', a time of 'deadlocks' and hopeless attempts to return to the Western model. As Bibó saw it, in 1945 there was an opportunity to leave the impasse and to jump on the 'Western way of societal development'.[9]

In the Polish case, the attraction of the image of the West became particularly strong under liminal conditions such as those of insur-rections or war. There is a powerful link between the Polish inferiority complex and the integrative strength of Romantic thinking that consisted of principles, ideals, and images of the West, and which has lasted up to now. A central characteristic of Polish backward-ness has been the fear of not obtaining sources of identity that had been withheld for a long time. This can be shown by a look at two different types of nationalizing policies in inter-war Poland. Prolonged statelessness, which prevented the development of a state-oriented, state-framed, 'civic' or 'territorial' understanding of nationhood, had reinforced ethno-national self-understanding (Brubaker, 1996:85). Nationalizing policies and practices varied sharply between the Western and the Eastern borderlands.[10] If the trend since the 1880s had been towards a sharper crystallization of bounda-ries between ethno-national groups (Brubaker, 1996:89), this tendency reflected the high insecurity of identities and national borders as well as state unity in Poland and the eastern borderlands.[11]

Coupled with the inferiority complex so typical of Central European countries and specifically Poland and Hungary,[12] the assumed superiority of the West crystallized in the Polish and Hungarian desire to join the Western community. Such a desire was central to the Polish resistance movement at the end of the Second World War. A document of early 1944 addressed political and economic measures for reconstruction:

> The Polish nation . . . unanimously and decidedly opposes all attempts to impose on us a model of government from the East. Our distinctiveness from the Russian East and German barbarity is characterized by a thousand-year tradition of freedom and Christian culture. Our present spiritual fortitude has its source also in the thousand-year struggle in defence of the freedom and culture of Western Europe.[13]

Summing up, one can argue that the image of the West is neither adequately understood as an absence of rationally induced institu-tionalized logics, nor as a mere myth. A series of disruptions in the form of insurrections and wars opened up perspectives of community with the West. 'Virtually all forms of nationalism that have developed since the eighteenth-century English, American, and French version have been based largely on a desire to imitate the successful European nation-states, combined with fear and resentment of the West'.[14]

The attempts to achieve modernization or allegiance with the West were reinforced in liminal situations. Yet both in 1918 and in 1945, for different reasons, a community with Western civilization was not possible. However, the image of the West remained crucial. In this vein, one can argue that communism prevented Eastern Europe from catching up with the West after the Second World War, but it did not cause the split with the West (Szacki, 1995:208).

The image of the West after 1945

After 1945 the attitude of Poles towards the West was a mixed one at best.

> The Eastern intellectual's attitude towards the West is therefore complicated, and not reducible to formulas of sympathy or antipathy. It is somewhat like disappointed love, and as we know, such deception often leaves a sediment of sarcasm. It took such a calamity to enable the new system, entirely contrary to the prediction of Marx, to have been born in backward Russia, and for the Revolution to have become an enterprise directed by the bureaucrats of the Center, and it took such a calamity to bring matters to the point where Europeans seeking to change the obsolete order of their countries must agree to submit to a nation which has never known prosperity or freedom.[15]

As shown extensively in Chapter 4, the superiority of Western models always strongly attracted Poland and Eastern Europe as a whole. The imperative of modernization implied imitative or alternative strategies of catching up with the West (Arnason, 1993:101). In post-1945 liminality, national patriotism, demands for social justice, and pervasive attempts to establish democratic culture were considerably influenced by Western models.

The desire to shorten the distance with the West had a tangible experiential impact. While in terms of knowledge and social or political learning the distance has remained considerable, in terms of identity there has hardly been any distance. East and West have regarded each other mutually as model and rival. Their fate was bound up with one another.

> The worse the position as regards those examples with which a person or a nation draws comparisons, the greater the need to

raise one's consciousness and cease the pulling of stupid, pre-
tentious faces. These Polish faces and complexes appear most
often when a Pole is confronted by the West. For then he feels
towards the West, with its wonders, its prosperity and contented
calm, admiration and rejection, humility and pride, when he
considers that he has endured more and has achieved less than
is due to him.[16]

A double-bind assumes that the admired model is also bound by
the presumed imitator. Indeed, the East also fascinates the West.
Since 1956 'the "Polish Road" appeared as the destined path for
that "third force" of which European socialists had dreamed for so
long.'[17] In fact, 'in many areas state socialism formed the
"exoskeleton" of Western democracies: its presence enabled them
to process challenges to social and technological policy productively
and in so doing to demonstrate that they were economically, militarily
and, moreover, morally "better" than the only operative counter-
model for industrial society, namely the state socialist variant'.[18]

A general interest in and admiration of the West by Eastern
Europeans met with ignorance by Westerners regarding Eastern
Europe. Conversely, the universalizing project of socialism by pro-
moting social, economic, and technological modernization was
destined to accelerate the prospective decline of the culturally decadent West. In this respect, it is hardly surprising that after the
Second World War the Soviet bloc's self-image rejected the option
of being Eastern and, rather, regarded itself as 'the most developed . . .
Western stage of our civilization'.[19] This could justify a check of
their 'idolatry of Western models which was so prevalent among
the cultivated circles of the "Eastern Marches"'.[20] This upsurge of
enthusiasm for their own cultural heritage should 'break that habit
of imitation which was inevitable as long as French, English, or
Belgian capital, investing in the mines, railroads, and factories of
the "Eastern Marches", pushed its books, films, and styles upon
them (. . .) Unhappily, in freeing themselves from the spell of the
West, the literature, science, and art of the Marches became totally
dependent on the new metropolis. Once imitation was spontaneous
and voluntary, but now it is obligatory.'[21] After 1945, 'any attempt
to find one's own way is denounced as Titoism. Any attempt to
reach into one's own national past is possible only to the extent
that this past parallels the development of the Russian nation.'[22]

After the disappointment with the West and the leaning towards Russia, Polish history after 1956 was driven by the endeavour to extricate its own destiny from backward Russia and to 'return to Europe'. This catchword of 1989 has not yet been fulfilled as – despite great steps towards integration into the European Union – Poland has yet a long way to go to be accepted as a peer.

The image of the West was neither exclusively a myth or dream, nor was it a set of independent logics such as democracy or capitalism. Emotional bonds and mental dependencies with the West increased as a result of utopian images of equality and of liberty. The national road to socialism in the wake of 1956 or Gierek's second Poland were not only attempts to gain more independence from Soviet Russia but also stressed Poland's Western option.[23] On the one hand, the effects of the Polish opposition, counter-public, second society, work emigration, and commodities were much too real to be myths or dreams.

> The emergence of an alternative society was a slow and long process. In spite of serious setbacks, it yielded important results not only in Hungary but, to a smaller degree, also in Poland and Czechoslovakia. This was a slow process in the course of which people could regenerate their dignity; they could achieve a certain degree of economic independence; they had the opportunity to re-create their communities and their social networks. ... The success of this process, the emergence of independent, autonomous alternative societies within the official, first societies, with the potential of ultimately transforming and democratizing these first societies, was the only hope for Eastern Europe.[24]

On the other hand, Poles lingered on between official prohibition and unofficial permissiveness. When Western principles and practices were introduced in the first efforts of privatization, the results were largely negative. Private agriculture, Gierek's credit-bought miracle in the 1970s and the reality of the 'second economy' can be described as 'invisible' or indirect effects of Western influence. Built up with an import-led strategy to induce consumption, Gierek's second Poland was guided by the image of the West. The failure of this strategy not only reinforced the liminal situation in Polish politics by boosting its opposition movements, but also made Poland relapse into the double-bind with Soviet Russia. As a consequence, a forced eastward reorientation in trade made Poland's economy more subordinate to the CMEA.[25]

During the 1980s a reversal took place, as the image of the West became more dominant once more. At the individual level, a high degree of Polish emigration for work on the eve of 1989 was maintained also after 1989. Trade with CMEA countries was in decline throughout the second half of the 1980s.[26] From 1989 onwards, trade with Western European countries has considerably increased. In terms of export and import to and from countries like Germany, France, Italy, and the United Kingdom, between 1991 and 1995 Poland approximately doubled its share in millions of dollars. At the same time, trade with Eastern Europe (in particular with Central European countries) diminished considerably.[27]

On the whole, it appears that the second reality of the image of the West was based on distant images, and thus the realization of Western models favoured blurred conceptions of democracy or capitalism. The logic of capitalism and democracy was reflected in the attempts at marketization and democratization in the Poland of the 1970s and 1980s. Yet under conditions of distance in both ideological and communicative terms, both projects were undifferentiated and hazy. They escaped critical evaluation and lacked a clear meaning. 'Democracy was the primordial catchword written on the flags of the Solidarity movement and as such it constituted an unquestioned good.'[28] The notions 'democracy' and 'democratic' were already imaginary and overstretched in the early eighties, as

> they become synonymous with all which is good and absent from the world governed by the system. Under conditions of lack of democracy every thing of value that would have been perceived as the desired element of social life would be fitted in the meaning of democracy. As a slogan of political emancipation, the term democracy becomes too broad, absorbing the whole of collective aspiration and desire. The differentiation of conscious and justifed usages of the term from ritualistic and masked usages can thus be sometimes made difficult.[29]

As illustrated in inquiries among the delegates to the Second National Congress of Solidarity in April 1990, the first priority was to 'realize democracy, because there is too little', while the second priority was 'to combat communism, because there is too much'.[30]

Although Solidarity envisaged objectives such as 'liberty' or an 'anti-crisis pact' (later on becoming free elections), these objectives were subordinated to the overarching desire to resuscitate Solidarity as a trade union. In terms of a clear-cut policy option, the meaning of democracy is problematic at best. If there is a theoretical limbo in the case of democracies such as Japan, Italy, or India (O'Donnell, 1996:41–2), it is likely to be considerably broader in Eastern Europe.

In this regard, 'the point is precisely what is meant in operational terms by the only seemingly unequivocal concept of "capitalism" or "market economy"'.[31] An important point that puzzles the observer in this respect is the incoherence of statements in public opinion polls before and after 1989. While market-type solutions[32] encountered increasing support, a high proportion of Polish society declared its loyalty to the achievements of state socialism, highlighting employment security, state price controls and social services.[33] In other words, the desire for the market arose in Polish society in close combination with the crucial characteristics of a centrally planned economy. Incoherence of expectations about the market economy points to the existence of a myth of the market in the Poland of the 1980s (Kolarska-Bobińska, 1990:161). Thus, 'the market' could amount to a garbage can, that blurred any concrete meaning:

> We agree that a market is necessary, but which market? A market according to Milton Friedman and the Chicago school, or a market with a human face whose ideological consequences will not be an apology of egoism, brutality and the Roman maxim *homo homini lupus*? A market, where recklessness will be more profitable than generosity, or a market of a type which allows for the redistribution of goods that is necessary in order to save our country from violent outbursts of discontent in society?[34]

While democracy was synonymous with non-communism, capitalism was largely synonymous with non-socialism. Switzerland and Sweden, simultaneously with Haiti, Iran, and Madagascar, were put 'into the bag called "capitalist world" which was both eighteenth-century England and present-day Germany' (Zieliński, 1994:34). If such an approach is, as Zieliński asserts, a popular simplification and a fundamental error, then this only underlines its widespread usage and its diffusion. Rather than starting the rational imitation of the logic of capitalism, elites and the normal population were prey to the image of the West.

A study of the translatability of five key words (among which is *market*-ing) in the business and management vocabulary from English into the Polish language called attention to the deep differences between the meanings, current usages, and associates that key terms such as 'market' could imply. Thus, 'the transition to a market economy is less a matter of knowledge transfer, but more one of meaning transfer, and that the western side has grossly underestimated the difficulties involved'.[35] Accordingly, market as a concept was distant as an fully-fledged institution, but very close as a mental and emotional category. This double-edged meaning sustained the paradox according to which the market became the most articulate and perhaps most definite category for institutional innovation to be detected in pre-1989 Poland. Furthermore, the meaning of economic liberalism before and after 1989 was rather hazy, since its propagation was ruled by ignorance, naive beliefs in profits without losses and in immediate results (Szacki, 1995:211). In this vein, the project of shock-therapy, introduced half a year after the round-table pacts, had been ideologically and politically unacceptable not only to the usual trade unionists but also to their leaders (Skórzyński, 1995:223).

There is ample evidence that the ascendancy of the image of the West across ideological camps in pre-1989 Poland was a reciprocal process. Both political antagonists converged in their proclaimed belief in the market as a panacea. Throughout the 1980s, the communist regime was keen on boosting its legitimacy through market reforms. Similarly, the meaning of market was double-edged, and so were the expectations associated with it. Under market socialism, it was hoped to shift some of the caring responsibilities of the state onto the market (Bauman, 1994:20–1). In communist reasoning, the mobilization of market principles was directed to remedy the crisis of state socialism. In this vein, it was the Rakowski-government from mid-1988 onward which dismantled crucial pillars of the centrally planned economy in Poland.[36] Unprepared economic reforms in a liminal situation of political uncertainty led to high budgetary deficits as a result of tax evasions, excessive wage increases, and high inflation (Poznański, 1996:110–11). Conversely, for non-communist economic reformers, the introduction of the market aimed to dismantle state socialism as much and as quickly as possible. This tendency reached its peak in the adoption of economic shock-therapy in late 1989, most notably reflected in a zeal for profound stabilization, liberalization, and broad-scale privatization.

It is no surprise that between the plan of reform, proposed by the last communist prime minister Rakowski, and the Balcerowicz plan, 'there was little difference the eye of an economist could spot'.[37] Rakowski's government shifted radically in the state's attitude towards the well-being of workers. 'The necessity of open unemployment as a disciplining force was pronounced as an official line, and subsidies for many essentials were removed. The government indicated that it was not going to protect enterprises against bankruptcy, even though very many of them ran deficits.'[38] Whether for the purpose of market socialism, for political capitalism, or for shock-therapy, it was always the market that was mobilized in the first place. While material goods, as well as privatization, freedom, and economic reform, played an important role, all these dynamics hinged on the magic attraction exerted by market. The market was used as a panacea by all political currents, while its meaning was, to speak in Latour's terms, arbitrarily 'shuffled like a pack of cards'.

Being more sceptical in the beginning, and defending egalitarian values such as social justice, wages and other such matters, Solidarity increasingly voiced proposals for economic reform. The set-up of the anti-crisis pact in 1987 speaks clearly for such an assumption. Taking the failed referendum on the economic reform in 1987 as a starting-point, the Solidarity opposition saw potential for negotiations only in the economic field (Skórzyński, 1995:202). By contrast, moves towards democratic liberalization, that is, political agreements, were excluded until the very eve of the round-table negotiations. After the end of the round table it was widely taken as a surprise that – against all expectations – substantial progress had been achieved in democratic institution-building rather than in economic matters (Skórzyński, 1995:203).

Furthermore, the image of the West also meant to escape the double-bind situation with Soviet Russia. One can rightly assume, following Jenö Szücs's thesis, that the drive towards the West was also motivated, perhaps even boosted, by the zeal to become detached from the East, in particular from Soviet Russia. As early as 1971, Leszek Kołakowski drew attention to Poland's desire to leave the forced community with Soviet Russia.

Fear of fraternal guns from the East is, of course, not unjustified, but it is consciously exaggerated as a 'patriotic device' for stifling the smallest demands and as a means of convincing the nation of the absolute hopelessness of all its efforts. In reality, the goal of Poland, as of the other nations of the Soviet zone, is not to provoke an armed conflict, but to exert ceaseless pressure aimed at diminishing Polish dependence on the USSR, a dependence which can only be weakened through pressure.[39]

At the end of the 1980s this interlacement was all the more binding. 'Paradoxically, although Eastern Europe finds itself in a situation of countries that are dependent and enter capitalism and international divison of labour with delay, its sees itself and its problems in categories of Europe.'[40] This argument points to the so-called international constraint of Poland. Commonly it is argued that in summer 1989 Solidarity held to the round-table agreements at least partly, because of the lasting menace of a Soviet intervention. Similarly, the shock-therapy was intended to establish radical *faits accomplis* so as to distance Poland economically as much as possible from Soviet Russia. This apparent paradox peters out once a mere economic understanding of periphery and centre is replaced.

The desire for unity in a community with Western Europe was not limited to the spontaneous shock-therapy of 1989, but had been an integral part of Polish identity-politics.

> Poland's uncomfortable position within the Soviet bloc is aggravated by the strength of her traditional bonds with the West. After four decades of Soviet supremacy, there are no signs that these bonds are weakening. People's Poland earns a greater proportion of its GNP from trade with Western countries than any other member of the Warsaw Pact. The Polish Emigration in Europe and America surpasses that of all of its neighbours. The flow of Polish visitors to the West, both private and official, outstrips comparable figures from anywhere else in the bloc. The percentage of practising Catholics in the population exceeds that of anywhere else in Europe. In the arts and the sciences, Poland keeps in closer touch with developments in the West than in the USSR. . . . In spite of many official pressures, most Poles remain more consciously 'western' in their tastes and attitudes than do the citizens of most western countries.[41]

As the pillars of the first reality of command politics and a centrally planned economy dissolved, the power of the image of the West increased, signifying both a saving anchor and a promised land. Poland's state of permanent liminality thus boosted the mimetic engagement with a utopian image crystallized in its overall depend-ence on the image of the West.[42] 'The "return to Europe" was a really courageous, multi-layered and provocative demand... what it really implies is: We want what Western European societies have (now with material goods palpably mixed in).'[43] In other words, the desires of Western people are the desires of the Polish people. Standing proxy for many, the Polish dramatist Sławomir Mrożek expressed how liberty was equivalent to a double-bind with the West: 'You are a Pole, an intellectual. You feel in the highest degree a Westerner, a European. If Poland was only free, it would be a Western country. If it was only Western, everything would be fine.'[44] Poland's envisaged community with the West was reinforced by the election of Cardinal Karol Wojtyła as Pope in 1978. 'There is little doubt that it has already done more to reinforce Poland's Catholic and western identity, than any other event in living memory.'[45] On the whole, Poland has regarded itself – due to its Catholic heritage and its recurrent integration into Europe – as (Western) Europe's equal, endowed with a necessary self-assertiveness al-though being driven towards Western models. 'A nation that is self-confident does not fear indebtedness, it can draw on foreign models with full hands, without losing its unprecedented personality and beauty.'[46] In a mimetic perspective, the end of communism would exacerbate the rivalry for the same objects, that is material welfare and institutional integration.

The image of the West after 1989

While the first reality of communist institutions and values dissolved, the expectations of politicians and Poles crystallized around the image of the West. It is timely to point out that the image of the West is not identical with the European Union or any other institution. Nor can it be properly summarized under the expecta-tion of achieving institutionalized logics such as democracy or capitalism. The image of the West can perhaps be grasped best by a mental and emotional dependence on utopia which is permeated by a sense of community. Dependence does not only apply to objective or measurable terms, but is also important in terms of cultural equity and identification. While the effects of being 'Western' might be conscious in first-reality outcomes, the driving forces to becoming so are mainly unconscious and hidden in a second reality. Thus, Eastern Europe's dependence on the West includes the complementarity of both the individual-psychological and the collective-institutional levels. 'On the left as on the right, the West is not just a place on the map where democracy and industrial capitalism emerged, it is also an empire of the mind, imposing belief in an essential form of human society emerging from a progressive pattern of history, including the modern tradition of revolutionary democracy.'[47] The image of the West implied both passions that ruled the events of 1989. As it embodied the zeal to equality through community on behalf of markets and democratic institutions, it also crystallized the craving for liberty.

'The West shone in the distance, the light of hope in a world of defeat and despair.'[48] The passion for liberty did not imply a return to an idealized state of happiness, but was essentially relational and mimetic. 'People yearned for Western political institutions, a Western standard of living, Western freedom, etc. but not for capitalism.'[49] This applied also to foreign policy options, as 'Poland feels vulnerable because it has an incomplete sense of belonging to the Western community of nations. It is a fundamental issue of national identity and self-esteem, a declaration that the Polish nation belongs to the Western civilization and has contributed to the development and security of the Western world.'[50] In the second reality, the Poles had come to cherish desires of becoming a double of this image of the West. Thus, the revolutionary passion for liberty was complemented by a prospective community between Poland and the West as equals.

On the grounds of such a prospective community with the West, this second part of the chapter will give some clues about disillusionment with the image of the West. Initially, identification with the West could be sensed both for economic and for political models. In this vein, 'Solidarity ... did not develop any serious model or system in politics, in law, and, above all, in economics that was substantially different from one already known in the West.'[51] The essential attraction that Western civilization exerted on Solidarity-elites was tangible in the recurrent references to Western models such as Finland, Austria, Spain or Sweden. In July 1990, Lech Wałęsa's adversaries announced the foundation of a party movement that would stand in opposition to the Centre Alliance. It was no accident that the article in the daily *Gazeta Wyborcza* announcing the foundation of *ROAD* (Civic Movement-Democratic Action) was entitled 'West of the Centre' (*Na Zachód od Centrum*).

Such tendencies towards the introduction of Western principles as a 'technique of Westernization' created 'a lot of political tension and attacks from below' (Staniszkis, 1991a:128–9). One can sense how the presumed improvement of living conditions (although coupled with a natural interest in the preservation of power positions by pre-1989 elites) had a counter-productive effect. Above all, starting economic competition with the West on the basis of command industrialization deepened Western perception of Eastern economic backwardness. The high competitiveness in heavy and military industries and in economic growth as the primary fields for systemic rivalry before 1989 had largely contributed to the breakdown of the Polish economy. After 1989, due to the negative effects of communist-led industrialization, this carrier of the pre-1989 rivalry with the West penalized post-1989 economic adaptation to the West. Gierek's project of a second Poland led to the progressive increase of hard-currency debts.[52] Similarly,

> Eastern Europe's long-standing technological lag behind not only the major OECD countries but also the group of newly industrializing countries expanded. This poor technological capability also reflects Eastern Europe's failure to adopt advanced technologies imported from the West, due to a highly inefficient system of intra- and inter-sector technological diffusion.[53]

Consequently, the major ideological and organizational principles that embodied the image of the West before 1989 have been seriously questioned since. Such trends are palpable in the fickle career of liberalism, the ideological and programmatic lever that was most tightly associated with the West's victory in Eastern Europe and in Poland in particular. Liberal ideas under communism had not resulted from a liberal tradition but, rather, had originated in the negation of real socialism (Szacki, 1995:174). In turn, the notion of liberalism was subjected to a huge extension of meaning which entailed a diffused illusion that there had been a unanimous 'triumph of liberalism' (Szacki, 1995:175). Accordingly, the appeal of liberalism as a political and ideological source of modernization can be regarded as widely coterminous with the image of the West. Although more recent economic indicators bear witness to a positive development, the pillar of this success story, namely liberalism, has fallen into shambles. The crumbling of the liberal dream in Eastern Europe intimated a serious crack in the solid appearance of the image of the West. Liberalism 'rather quickly lost its initial popularity and, rightly or wrongly, is blamed for the high social costs of the economic and social transformation'.[54] The harshest attacks against Western liberalism were driven by the Catholic Church. As a letter of the Polish Bishops put it:

> Yesterday it was the East, but today the West will insist that Poland fully accept social, political and also whole-hearted religious liberalism. So we are confronted with a new form of totalitarianism, that is, intolerance of the good, of God's laws, so that with impunity we may propagate evil and in effect once again wrong the weakest.[55]

If liberty was the original inspiration, then the 1989 revolution has temporarily lost its bearings.[56] The only genuine liberal party in Polish politics, the Freedom Union – also the most influential representative of the Solidarity-legacy in party politics – has been progressively weakened by inner tensions and by the polarization of the political landscape.[57] Although it rose to power in the wake of the parliamentary elections of September 1997, the Freedom Union won fewer votes than its constituting parts – the Democratic Union and KLD – had won together in 1993.[58]

Liberalism shares many features with the development of civil society after the demise of communism. Before 1989 civil society stood for the sphere of activity independent from and opposed to communist state power. The pursuit of anti-politics and the increasing scope of individual and collective autonomy engendered new forms of public life and political pluralism. Based on such a development, it was argued that in post-1989 Poland civil society 'is becoming the strongest, most rapidly developing realm of the polity'.[59] Yet some care seems to be needed, since the very impressive quantitative growth of associations renders the structures of fledgling civil society questionable. The atomization of the opposition and the demobilization of elites (Smolar, 1996c) is accompanied by a protracted political and social apathy and persistent lack of trust in public institutions. In a similar vein, the destruction of normativeness gives broad leeway for the atrophy of norms which are substituted by 'particularism, immediacy, and fortuitousness' (Kojder, 1998:258). In this regard, 'post-totalitarian civil society is "shallow"' (Grabowska, 1997:32). Confronting the relatively successful expansion of a public political realm before 1989 with what prevailed afterwards, Daniel Nelson summarized what could be seen as the parallel existence of two realities.

A discomfiting dichotomy, however, is present. Where civil society began earliest, developed furthest while communists still ruled, and exhibited the most extensive activity – namely, Poland and Hungary – voting participation is proportionately lower, public cynicism higher, and trust (or confidence) in the president, parliament, and political parties is far less than in the military or church. These results. ... have been in sharp contrast to relatively positive economic news from Poland, ample foreign investment in Hungary, and considerable diplomatic attention to both countries from the West.[60]

The partial reversal of the image of the West is also tangible in the criticism of the Polish constitution. Critics argued that the constitution was too universalistic and does not pay tribute to Polish national identity. Such a critique is based on the assumption that the West is ridden with a crisis in values (Graczyk, 1997:237).

A further example for the failed implementation of policies on the grounds of a blurred image of the West can be shown in the short-term career of corporatism in the Polish context. Corporatism or neo-corporatism were considered to be modernizing patterns in the relationship between the state and the economy which would help to redefine democratization and marketization in a situation of economic and political transformation (Ost, 1989; Tatur, 1994). Quite a few authors have seen in the pact on the state enterprise of February 1993 an equivalent of 'corporatism,' and have emphasized its potentially stabilizing effects on the nascent social order.[61] Yet its results have widely been assessed as a miscarried imitation of Western models. In this context it was argued that the copying of models rather generates and complicates problems which, in the case of corporatist solutions in contemporary Poland, can be assessed as incoherent, inadequate, and defective (Hausner, 1994:46).

As of 1989, all Solidarity governments, despite varying degrees of commitment and adverse declarations, have pursued a line of economic liberalism. This is also true for the conservative Olszewski government which, initially, had contrasted programmatically with the economic policy of its predecessor, the liberal Bielecki government. Despite some slowdown of privatization efforts, 'during Olszewski's tenure no large-scale retreat from the liberalization of prices and business activity engineered in 1990–1991 occurred, the tax burden on the private sector was not significantly increased, and the government's rhetoric on privatization warmed considerably'.[62] To a considerable extent, Solidarity governments were seen as defenders of pro-Western attitudes. Such an assessment was confirmed for the micro-level, as a recent study on Polish youth and its perceptions of Westernization argues. 'In Poland, . . . the reforms were the outcome of sustained pressure from popular movements, particularly Solidarity.'[63] One of the central policy aims of the last Solidarity government in 1992/3 was the 'pact on the state enterprise' which represented an attempt 'at combining pragmatic liberalism with what might be called participatory syndicalism'.[64]

Politically, the watershed came in 1993, when the last Solidarity government was replaced by a post-communist coalition between the SLD and the PSL. In its wake a status reversal occurred. Since early 1996, Polish politics had increasingly oscillated around a polarization. On the one hand, the post-Solidarity right-wing coalition[65] highlighted national and religious issues and thus came to delineate a genuine anti-Western profile. On the other hand, the post-communist coalition SLD had developed a pro-Western profile only in the course of post-1989 politics. Although not a front-runner of Westernism, it used to be considered as a guarantor of pro-Westernism in Poland. After Poland joined the Council of Europe in 1991, three major events of Poland's allegiance to the West occurred under post-communist governments. Since autumn 1996 Poland has been a member of the OECD, while NATO membership was prepared by the invitation to negotiations in summer 1997. Also in summer 1997 Poland entered the first round of EU-enlargement candidates (Wągrowska, 1997).

Conflicts in economic and political areas have contributed to a fragmentation of the worshipped image of the West. In economic areas where the East is highly competitive (steel products, textiles, and agriculture) and thus would be able to 'unite' with the West in terms of market access, conflicts very soon sharpened. 'Both left- and right-wing political groupings within Poland attempted to capitalize on this constituency during 1991 and 1992 to oppose ratification of the treaty on associate EC membership.'[66] Rivalry soon became tangible in various conflicts on economic goods. The European Union (EU) banned Polish animal and meat imports on behalf of alleged – and not proven – foot-and-mouth disease in April 1993, a move that provoked a retaliatory ban on EU imports of these products into Poland. 'This incident illustrated both the intensely political nature of agricultural trade with the EC and Poland's growing frustration with the Community's unwillingness to live up to its promises of market access.'[67] Similarly, the West's reserves crystallized in a 'tariff war' and restrictions against the expansion of Eastern steel products to European markets (Berend, 1995:143). Moreover, Poland's performance in attracting foreign capital in the early 1990s was disappointing.[68] 'The limited measures of the European Community did not lead to results until now. Western Europe, in reality, is building up a new kind of Maginot line.'[69] A good example is provided by its status as a low-wage economy.[70] Low labour costs are usually considered by economists to be a competitive asset, while in the Polish perspective they only underline the feeling of being second-class Europeans.

This iron curtain in a velvet disguise has caused a notable mutilation of the Polish project of return to Europe. 'More generally, the disarray into which the post-Maastricht EC had fallen in mid-1992, as well as rising protectionist trends within the EC *vis-à-vis* the Central European countries, implied that Poland, Hungary, the Czech Republic, and Slovakia were likely to remain in the EC's "waiting room" indefinitely, with many promises of increased market access going unfulfilled.'[71] Such an 'enlargement' was made when Poland was included in Western Europe's sphere of safe countries in order to cut the constant inflow from Germany's eastern neighbour countries. From 1988 on there had been a considerable rise in immigration from Eastern European countries (in particular Poland, Yugoslavia, and Romania) into Germany. As a result, EU member states refused to receive both natives from these countries and immigrants who wanted to enter the EU taking these countries as first hosts. This inclusion of the Visegrad countries into 'Europe' was vehemently opposed by the Polish government, which resented this 'export' of the EC's immigration problem (Lavenex, 1997:16). The conflictual implication of this stop-gap Westernization may threaten a destabilization of Eastern Europe. 'By moving the fence eastward, not only has Western Europe chosen to ignore the economic instability in the eastern part of the continent; it has added to the East's problems by forcing societies ill-equipped both culturally and economically for the task to deal with refugees and immigrants who are there more or less by accident and whose final destination remains the West.'[72]

On the whole, in the first reality of a community with the West, Poland and Eastern Europe have to learn to cope with wide-ranging burdens of a social, economic and political kind.[73] Mimesis is reciprocal, and its effects are likely to affect both the imitator and the model. As Ken Jowitt remarked: 'Nor can we expect the "clearing away" effect of the Leninist extinction to be self-contained, to be a political storm that considerably loses its force as it approaches Western and "Third World" coasts.'[74] The effects of the double-bind with the image of the West can be felt in the stakes for the West and the East. In Offe's view, the implications of 1989 are not only about 'catching up' but also about the 'merger of the Second and First Worlds'. What is primarily at stake is whether Western democracies 'will be able to avoid becoming infected.... by the structural and moral shortcomings of the collapsed system'.[75] And what is secondly at stake is whether Western principles and concepts are 'adopted by the post-communist societies as an attractive goal for their own further development or whether they reject it'.[76]

The threat of becoming infected is all the more understandable in the framework of mimetic conflict, since 'acquisitive mimesis is contagious, and if the number of individuals polarized around a single object increases, other members of the community, as yet not implicated, will tend to follow the example of those who are; conflictual mimesis necessarily follows the same course because the same force is involved.'[77] This picture of single or exclusive objects involves a myriad of themes, ranging from economic and social welfare over institutional and military stability up to citizenship and the sharing of a common cultural identity. On the other hand, peace and stability are not simply exportable to the East. As Claus Offe put it: 'Despite the universalistic principles proclaimed there (and presumably also institutionalized), principles that can be viewed by all human beings and implemented, the institutional system underlying this social order is possibly incapable of grounding and founding itself or even of assisting with any attempts to imitate it elsewhere.'[78]

In the post-1989 reality, political and economic co-operation in the Visegrad triangle (Poland, the former Czechoslovakia, and Hungary) has rather quickly turned out to be conflictual. The cohesive influences in the shaping of the Visegrad triangle were a common determination to join the West by integration into Western economic and political institutions; external security against the destabilizing Soviet Union was crucially important too. After a short honeymoon, however, centrifugal forces have become dominant. 'Striving jointly to rejoin Western institutions, each country has not only adopted different strategies of economic development but has also energetically competed against the other two in securing Western investments and contact while neglecting trade possibilities with the triangle.'[79] The 'spring of nations' in 1989 has entailed a rise in nationalism and rivalry among former Eastern bloc countries. Concrete co-operation in the Visegrad triangle has failed, leaving the field to rivalry for meeting the criteria to join Western institutions. Thus, unity had to be imposed from outside. 'The competition among the three states to be the first to enter Europe is held in check by the Western political community's inclination to treat the new democracies of Central Europe as a unit.'[80] The community of Eastern European countries has become questionable on a different account, too. In order to extricate Eastern Europe from Soviet-dominated Eastern Europe, Eastern European intellectuals such as Vaclav Havel, Milan Kundera, György Konrad, and Adam Michnik coined the concept of Central Europe (Ash, 1990:186–226). This concept was grounded in a desired fusion between East Central Europe and Western Europe, with the concomitant exclusion of Russia. Nowadays, this concept of Central Europe has become a major semantic tool for exclusion from Eastern Europe. While Central Europe stands for civilized, democratic, co-operative, and therefore having a better chance of joining NATO and the EU, this concept has come to partially exclude Slovakia, let alone Ukraine, Belarus, and European Russia (Ash, 1999).

On several accounts, Poland finds itself in a situation similar to that after 1945. Endowed with a genuine sympathy for and a high identification with the West, it has embarked upon the endeavour to return to Europe. The desire for a community with the West as peer was at its peak in 1989. However, the image of the West has exerted a double-edged influence on post-1989 Poland. The image of community with the West was a central factor of identity politics in Poland before 1989. In the wake of 1989, however, it has been flawed on several accounts, as Polish politics and society have experienced the strong impact of Western models in the first reality of institutional politics. In this vein,

from the outset, the Eastern candidates were put in a position of inferi-ority and periphery. They were not given a chance to discuss the future Europe. They have first to comply, to respect the norms, to integrate *the acquis communautaire* and to make efforts to successfully pass the exam. They must continually prove their aptitudes to form part of the European Union. Therefore, they suffer from not being considered as countries endowed with a certain personality, capable of contributing something to the European debate.[81]

Rather than Poland's institutional adherence to the West, there is something like the institutionalization of postponement[82] of EU-enlargement. Accordingly, public approval of integration into the European Union, while being constantly high throughout most of the 1990s, has declined considerably since 1997.[83] As subjective perceptions assess a growing distance with the West, disillusionment and a feeling of being second-class Europeans is increasing.

Of course the danger of a new dependence is not rooted in a Russification or resovietization of Poland. Paradoxically, it is the lack of vision, of specific ambitions for Poland, the fight against the Church, the derising of tradition, the kitsch-like modernity of supermarkets of Western small towns (. . . .) that converts us into a caricature of the West that we are acquainted with from worried sermons in the Church. We will obtain a Poland of vulgar, not noble liberalism.[84]

The continuity of the image of the West

This chapter has argued that the continuity of the image of the West constitutes a non-contingent given in the second reality of Poland's transition. Generated as a result of disruptions in Polish state and society, the image of the West is tightly linked to permanent liminality and mimetic conflict. As a result of its liminal position as an in-between country and a long-standing mimetic desire for identification with the West, Polish intellectuals had been under the spell of the West before 1945. The image of the West embodied the central destination point of utopian desires and expectations of a better future. Soviet coercion sealed Poland's distance with the West most from 1945 onwards.

In crucial moments of rupture-points in institutional politics, different kinds of images of the West have been fundamental to Polish identity-politics. By virtue of its institutional and ideological isolation, Poland's mental dependencies and identification with the image of the West increased considerably. Modernization approaches constructed the perception of the West as distinguishing political, economic, or social variables. By contrast, evidence shows that it was rather the uniform image of the West that provided for a quasi-infinitude of desired objects.

People living in the East had hopes for a new and authentic life, an earthly paradise beyond the Wall. For them Western freedom and prosperity was not only a goal to emulate but also invincible proof that life was worth living, that it was not devoid of value and meaning, that oppression, humiliating compromises, and an existence without dignity were only a transitory episode in their lives.[85]

From 1945 onwards, distance from the Western first reality in terms of economic achievements and political liberty increased. At the same time, the appeal of the image of the West enhanced the longing for manifestations of the second reality. The Polish road to socialism as of 1956, Gierek's second Poland in the 1970s, or Solidarity's revolution in the 1980s reflect the utopian aspects of this second reality. Furthermore, the image of the West induced the desire to discontinue the dependence on Soviet Russia and to come back to Western civilization.

Hence, the second reality of the image of the West had a great share in the breakdown of communism. It has proved to be a non-contingent given also since 1989. The image of the West was crucial for the Poles' desire to establish a community with the West as peers. Essentially, this involved putting an end to the image of the West as a second reality, by making Poland a Western country and by merging first and second realities. However, post-1989 Polish politics makes clear on several accounts that 1989 has not discontinued the second reality of the image of the West. While disillusionment, apathy, and the perception of being second-class Europeans are widespread, the West still remains central to Polish politics. The political goal of integration into Western institutions (including security issues *vis-à-vis* Russia) still enjoys relatively high but decreasing public approval and is sustained by the recent return of a government of the Solidarity tradition.

On the whole, the assumed return to Europe – the essential expectation of discontinuity – has become a long-term endeavour which is economically and socially burdensome and, politically, increasingly contested. Poland's desire to reach equality and liberty in a prospective community with the West is menaced with serious distortions. Poland thus has become a victim of its own ambitions.

Several decades ago, there was a real threat of turning Poland into an additional Soviet republic. Today, without any political interference, our country is assuming the attire of some kind of American state. The visible effects resemble an image in a distorting mirror (. . .) The point is that Poland – which within the last two centuries has been so cruelly afflicted with partitions, wars, and occupations – has always manifested its vitality and independence first of all through its culture. The present stage of the systemic transformation seriously jeopardizes the maintenance of this tradition.[86]

While Poland's allegiance to the West since 1999 has become anchored in NATO membership and prospective EU-adhesion, the second reality of the image of the West is likely to persist. In this regard, the parallels between post-1945 and post-1989 are striking. Czesław Miłosz spoke of the disappointed love of the West that pervaded Polish elites. By the same token, in 1992 Hungarian prime minister József Antall deplored the West's unrequited love *vis-à-vis* the East.

We are not the backyard of Europe. . . . I hope . . . that they will at last pay more attention to our region and that they will be sensitive to the fact that the nations of this area, from the Poles to the Hungarians and others, have viewed the Western world with unrequited love for centuries. This unrequited love must end because we stuck to our posts, we fought our own fights without firing one shot and we won the third world war for them.[87]

6
The Continuity of the Image of Solidarity

While many volumes have been written about the trade union Solidarity, two central themes have guided research on this topic. They either deal with Solidarity's unity or with its splitting apart.[1] Before December 1981 the contrast between us (Solidarity/society) and them (the communist state) had been constitutive. Despite the complex political situation, the one-dimensionality of Solidarity's self-image in 1980 and 1981 took into account only two forces: 'us 'and 'them' (Staniszkis, 1984:145–6). In order to highlight the refusal of the communist regime, and inspired by experiences of the Gdańsk community (Kubik, 1994a), unity became the catchword after the August strikes of 1980 had finished. Against currents that favoured a decentralized union organization, a unified Solidarity with its core in Gdańsk became essential to streng then Solidarity's collective identity (Ost, 1990:101–2). To a large extent, it was the claim of total representation of society against and outside the communist system that sustained Solidarity's unity before the proclamation of martial law.

This dichotomy vanished in the wake of martial law. The fall into illegality as a result of the trade union law of 8 October 1982 and the emergence of the communist trade union OPZZ became an obstacle to Solidarity's enterprise activities.[2] The underground situation of Solidarity between 1981 and 1989 entailed a virtual suspension of experiences of collective identity. The huge strike potential vanished away and the myth of the general strike crumbled (Smolar and Kende, 1989:15f.). As a survey among workers in Lublin and Warsaw during 1983 and 1984 showed, the we-image of we-society, we-workers or we-Solidarity evaporated into a broad image of generalizations such as the slogan 'we the Poles'.[3] Although the lifting of martial law in the mid-1980s opened up spaces of a parallel culture, the backlash after 1981 entailed a considerable loss of oppositional consciousness in society. Consequently, 'because of mild measures instituted during martial law, the fear quickly vanished while the humiliation persisted. This was the result of the society's perception being forcefully transformed from a subject to object of politics.'[4]

Yet a persistent myth of unity kept the underground Solidarity together as a 'monolithic collective subject' (Szacki, 1991:718). For this reason the unity of Solidarity throughout the period 1980 to 1989 is assumed despite the fundamentally liminal experience of the underground. To my knowledge, practically no writings on Solidarity distinguish conceptually the original Solidarity of 1980–1 from that organization which renewed its official activities in 1989. Admittedly, some authors distinguished between an 'old' and a 'new' Solidarity (Ost, 1990:208–9) or between a first and a second Solidarity (Modzelewski, 1995). Yet in both contexts the relationship between the two Solidarities is understood as historical and evolutionary. They are seen as drifting apart, as not having very much in common. Such a viewpoint is at variance with the prevailing sentiment of unity among Solidarity elites and members who perceived the trade union as a continuum without any rupture. Most strikingly, this perception became manifest when the trade union was re-legalized on 17 April 1989. Despite long-term and arduous efforts by which Solidarity leaders overcame the initial resistance of the communists, they did not celebrate this achievement effusively. In their view, Solidarity had existed without rupture since 1980, the renewed registration being a mere 'negotiated concession without great meaning'.[5] Although, to my knowledge, no monograph has been written on post-1989 Solidarity, the existing literature concurs that Solidarity's unity disintegrated, both ideologically and institutionally, in the early 1990s at the latest. Accordingly, the list of political parties and alliances that emanated from Solidarity's fold has been considerable.[6] As a consequence, it was argued that the myth of Solidarity as a movement for reform and for modernization is 'definitely coming to an end'.[7]

Contrary to evolutionary accounts of Solidarity's disintegration, this chapter will examine the hypothesis according to which it was the myth of Solidarity's unity that made the movement break apart in the 'wars at the top' in the early 1990s. To this purpose, I will argue that the story of Solidarity is not one of progressive disintegration. Throughout liminal conditions in the underground, the loss of its institutional and organizational basis led to the creation of the image of Solidarity, and Solidarity activists and its leading circles became increasingly dependent on the second reality of the memory of the nationwide community that it had generated. In order to elaborate upon Solidarity's impact on institutional politics in the early 1990s, this chapter will conceptualize the image of Solidarity from its constitution as a trade union in 1980 to its reconstitution as the non-communist power centre in 1989. In 1989 the expectations of discontinuity in Polish society focused anew on Solidarity. Yet while in 1980 it built its institutional basis in the factories and society on an anti-image of the communist regime, in 1989 the image of Solidarity was based on the memory of its own profound experience of nationwide community. Despite several discontinuities of an ideological, institutional, and personal type, this image of the Solidarity community was carried throughout the underground and came to constitute the basis for mimetic conflict in 1990.

Thus, this chapter draws on Solidarity's disintegration both in 1981 and during the 'wars at the top' in 1989 and 1990. Finally, the reconstitution of the image through AWS in 1996 will be sketched out. What is postulated here is not the continuity of Solidarity in institutional terms, nor in programmatic or ideological orientations. The continuity of the image of Solidarity shall give solid indicators for the second realities of liminality, mimetic conflict, and backwardness. In 1980 Solidarity created a short-lived second reality, in terms of an alternative consciousness and organizational principle, to the communist regime. This second reality crystallized in a short-lived pluralism of political and social life, supported by the independence of trade unions and mass manifestations. On the eve of 1989, the desires of the different trade union organizations of the Solidarity tradition concurred in considering themselves as identical with the original Solidarity. The mainstream current of post-1989 Solidarity claimed to represent the whole of Polish opposition, while splinter-groups such as Solidarity 80, Fighting Solidarity and others contended to be the real successors of the first Solidarity. Yet the point of attack was different. Now, the different camps unanimously strove for the totality of their representation. The political antagonism between communism and society had been withering away already in 1988, while a quasi-pluralism brought a myriad of new political associations to the scene. After the dissolution of communist power, the image of Solidarity became a stumbling-block for the institutional and ideological unity of post-1989 Solidarity. The image had two characteristics that were at odds with each other. On the one hand, it insinuated a re-emergence of the community of 1980. On the other hand, due to a variety of post-Solidarity organizations and a political agenda radically different from that of 1980, the visions of community were contested. In turn, the image of Solidarity underpinned the mimetic conflict that was to break out over its heritage.

The constitution of the image of Solidarity

There is a widespread conviction that Poland's unique role in East European transitions relied upon a coherent, fully fledged elite of Solidarity. Thus, Grzegorz Ekiert argued that the demobilization policies pursued by the Jaruzelski regime failed because of Solidarity's particular strength, which was not fundamentally affected by martial law and the underground period (Ekiert, 1966:286–9). In line with this scholars and activists have emphasized the modernizing strength of the underground Solidarity that seemed to be sufficiently prepared in terms of strategy and staff to tackle the task of democratization. According to such a viewpoint, Solidarity 'by 1986 . . . was almost entirely a movement for systemic reform'.[8] It was also characterized as an 'elite that cohered, and even in its current divided and divisive state offers Poland something more important than either marketization or civil society: an "established" leadership'.[9] In a summary of the underground period Janusz Pałubicki, the Solidarity chairman in Poznań, held that Solidarity union leaders had been sufficiently retrained before 1989 in order to tackle the tasks that they were expected to fulfill.[10]

In contrast to such assumptions, the underground Solidarity was in liminal conditions on several accounts, as argued extensively in Chapter 2. The number of people who identified themselves as having belonged to Solidarity dropped considerably, from 37 per cent in 1981 to 22 per cent in autumn 1985.[11] During 1980 and 1981 the collective identity of the Solidarity opposition had become manifest through mass protests, strike actions, and activity in a broad range of enterprises. Under martial law and also after the general amnesty of 1986, however, its persistence was rendered virtually impossible. While in its heyday Solidarity had had its stronghold in the big factories, by 1989 its basis there had vanished. Hence the underground period deprived Solidarity of its constituting attributes. 'And so, Solidarity's dirty little secret: it was not a union at all, it was a myth.'[12] By the same token, the presumed preparedness of the underground Solidarity as an organization for democratic reform was questioned by the Paris-based periodical of the opposition, *Kultura*, that drew a bleak picture: 'Without organizational projects, without a programme that could replace the nostalgic reclamation of the Gdańsk accords, the national executive board of Solidarity in its current shape has become a rudimentary remainder from another epoch, incapable of elaborating a policy that would be adequate for the present and directed towards the future.'[13] In 1989 Solidarity was indeed surprised by the communist party's sudden readiness to negotiate. 'Despite the many years they had passed dreaming of this chance, the opposition-leaders were not – either as regards expert knowledge or psychologically – at all ready to tackle this game.'[14] Moreover, events anticipated strategic options. Before the communists signalled their willingness to sit down at the round table, the programmatic guidelines of the underground period (the 'long march' and the general strike) were superseded. The first document since 1981 – by which Solidarity in August 1988 addressed the communist regime – spoke about Solidarity's support for economic reforms in exchange for its legalization. The draft declaration on behalf of the inaugural agreement with the regime still contained the proposal of 'establishing relations towards approaching elections on the basis of a constructive relationship of broad societal support, including Solidarity'. During the three following days Solidarity's declarations were considerably softened. The final version, apart from omitting to mention the 'anti-crisis pact', just limited itself to the formula of 'co-operation for the democratic concern'. This could mean everything and nothing (Skórzyński, 1995:87–8).

And yet the myth of Solidarity remained so powerful as to constitute a solid claim for a collective monolithic subject in 1989. At the end of the 1980s Solidarity managed to raise its rate of approval from less than 25 per cent in May 1988 to over 75 per cent in March 1989. In the same time span the perception of Solidarity as an institution beneficial to society rose from 18 to 67 per cent.[15] The elections in June 1989 amounted to an anti-communist referendum, elevating the Solidarity opposition to the height of public approval. How could the image of a monolithic collective subject be maintained in liminal conditions? How could the myth of unity be nourished and, finally, reactivated? A look at the bonds between the social and individual dimensions of the underground Solidarity may elucidate this point. In what follows I will examine the connection between Poles and the collective subject of Solidarity with some central concepts developed in the works of Norbert Elias and Max Weber. Throughout his work Elias has emphasized the multi-layered character of habitus and identification. In this view, mentalities in collective groups must be conceived by paying attention to the complementarity of individual and collective identities. Following on that, one can claim that individual self-images and group we-images are not separate things. Or, as Elias put it, 'the individual bears in himself or herself the habitus of the group, and . . . it is this habitus that he or she individualizes to a greater or lesser extent'.[16] Hence the processes of habitus- and identity-formation over long periods must be seen as 'changes in the We–I balance' (Mennell, 1992:194).

The question of the modalities of social composition in Solidarity was one of the central themes of research on the topic. Some prominent studies conceived of Solidarity as rooted in a socioeconomic class (Laba, 1991; Goodwyn, 1991). This class was seen as mainly formed by workers. Indeed, the centrality of workers in constituting Solidarity and contributing to the end of communism is beyond doubt.[17] However, the concept of class seems hardly to be applicable to a communist system, as more than 40 years of communist rule have made a class structure on the scale of society disappear (Pakulski 1993; Bauman, 1994; Ost 1995:192). First, this was because economic criteria that usually account for class cleavages were insignificant; second, it was because Solidarity was much too heterogeneous an organization to draw clear distinctions other than between generalized social groups such as the workers, the intelligentsia, or the farmers. Kubik later tried to revise Laba's and Goodwyn's assumptions by characterizing Solidarity as an outcome of a cultural-political class. In his view, 'this cultural political class was made up not of workers or intellectuals but of all those who subscribed to a system of principles and values . . . who visualized the social structure as strongly polarized between "us" (society, people) and "them" (the authorities, communists)'.[18] Moreover, taking the cue from Max Weber, Kubik and Staniszkis refer to 'Solidarity' as a status (or cultural) group (Kubik, 1994:447; Staniszkis 1984:146).

The definition proposed by Kubik, although pointing in the right direction, is not fully convincing. In Weber's definition, *Stand*[19] is determined by the social estimation of honour.[20] Life conduct (*Lebensführung*) played a crucial role during the legal activities of Solidarity, but it grew in importance in the underground. This should be briefly illustrated. First, the underground Solidarity essentially continued its ethic of non-violence. Despite some temptations to strike back against martial law by violent action,[21] such a reaction was clearly refused by the underground leader Zbigniew Bujak. The most significant symbol of the self-limiting opposition in the underground was perhaps the award of the Nobel Peace Prize to Lech Wałęsa in 1983. Second, a central experience of martial law was the arrest of Solidarity activists and its leaders.[22] Practically all the central figures who played an important role in 1980/81 and would resume a leading position in 1988/9 served a sentence of several months. Third, the Catholic Church acquired crucial importance as the spiritual and material source of oppositional life-conduct in the underground. While the Church had been an ally of Solidarity before martial law was proclaimed, it became its shelter in the underground. The manifestation of the oppositional ethos was to a large extent limited to the experiences of small communities under the safeguard of the Church. Thus, the individual profession of sharing common, collective values was promoted. During the two visits of Pope John Paul II to Poland in 1983 and 1987, Solidarity displayed its presence and was able to keep alive its symbolic repertory. 'One cannot fail to notice the symbolic presence of the trade union movement: the relics of Solidarity, the memorial tablets, banners, slogans, the crosses of flowers, and stylized cribs as symbols of suffering, death, and the expected resurrection of Solidarity.'[23] Moreover, the Church's tutelary function extended from religious welfare for workers to the provision of places for seminars, lectures, and sales of underground publications.

Let us finally come back to Elias's claim for a change in the we–I balance. By the concept of life-conduct one can show how Solidarity survived as a we-image even though it had temporarily lost the central attributes of its organizational apparatus and coherence. Accordingly, the we-image was preserved as identity-forming life-conduct, shifted to the level of small-scale communities. It was the I-image – dispersed among individuals sticking to Solidarity ideals which were permanently maintained by small-scale communities – that accounted for the survival of Solidarity. The link between individual destiny and collective identity was clearly expressed by Adam Michnik, whose letter to General Kiszczak – responsible for the implementation of martial law – said: 'For me, General, prison is not such a painful punishment. On that December night it was not I who was condemned, but freedom: it is not I who am being held prisoner, but Poland.'[24]

This complementarity between we- and I-images played a crucial role in Solidarity's mobilization in the late 1980s. Solidarity survived with the support of decentralized underground structures, the active help in small communities sheltered by the Catholic Church, and due to a largely functioning counter-public as the 'most durable and safest structure of the underground'.[25] While the young generation of workers was to make the first step towards Solidarity's public survival by staging nationwide strikes in spring and summer 1988, this collective mobilization was sustained by the continuity of Solidarity leaders from the generation of 1980. This linkage over a temporal distance is supported by a comparison of data from the two National Congresses of Solidarity in 1981 and in 1990.[26] The data provided indicate two apparently opposite developments. At the end of the 1980s, Solidarity, at least in its leading circles, was an ageing organization. On the one hand, the continuity of Solidarity's National Commission between 1981 and 1990 was relatively low, which indicates a high loss of union leaders during the underground. On the other hand, more than 50 per cent of participants at the Congress belonged to the National Commission. As a consequence, there was a generational leap with a relatively high stability of a core of leading figures. The top ranks of Solidarity in 1988/89 were practically the same as in 1980/81, whereas the active basis at the shop-floor level was made up by the new generation. Essentially, there were relatively few central individual figures to serve as a link between Solidarity I and Solidarity II.[27]

This continuity of leading figures is connected with the power of Solidarity's image. Three events in 1988 and 1989 intimate to what extent its influence in society hinged on the power of images. First, when the preparatory talks for the round-table negotiations seemed to be in a deadlock, a television debate between the OPZZ chairman, Alfred Miodowicz, and the Solidarity chairman Lech Wałęsa changed things entirely. To see the mythical leader of Solidarity on TV screens literally revived the image of Solidarity and pulled it closer from a distant but not forgotten past. 'For the first time a mass of spectators could hear and see the chairman of the subversive underground organization – until not long ago a 10-million-strong trade union – which for the huge majority was nothing but a distant memory.'[28] The semi-free elections in June 1989 proved for a second time the importance of the image of the charismatic Solidarity leader. Every candidate running for Solidarity under the auspices of the civic committees had a photo with Wałęsa that was diffused on thousands of posters across the country. 'Wałęsa , next to the symbol of Solidarity, became our sign of identification.'[29] It seems to be only conclusive that the only Solidarity candidate not to be elected had not had a photo taken with Wałęsa (Kuro ń and Żakowski, 1995:269). A third example extends the power of images to the scrupulously imitative repetition of a symbolical event. During the May strikes in 1988 the Catholic Church, with the consent of the communists, assumed the mediation of the conflict. To this purpose, three mediators were chosen: Andrzej Stelmachowski, Tadeusz Mazowiecki, and Andrzej Wielowieyski. These three intellectuals were those who had mediated between the fledgling Solidarity trade union and the communist regime in August 1980. One can perceive the zeal for turning back time and transplanting a distant event into the present. Being an anachronism, 'it essentially was a step backwards, a significant setback'.[30]

Solidarity's backwardness in the underground aimed at identification with an image of Solidarity which came to dominate the intentions and strategies of negotiations at the end of the 1980s. The mental bonds that linked many activists with a mythical Solidarity were based on the appeal of a utopian second reality. As a consequence, formerly programmatic key points or strategies were subjected to distorted meanings. It is well known, for example, that Solidarity pursued trade union concerns both in 1980–1 and in 1989. Different groups linked up with Solidarity's tradition as a trade union, in particular the spontaneous strike waves of young workers in May and August 1988 that prepared Solidarity's re-emergence from the underground. These strikes were staged by young union leaders of the new generation whose first concern was expressed in the demands of the inter-enterprise strike committees: trade union pluralism, and the legalization of Solidarity.[31] To a large extent, the absolute preference for the re-legalization of Solidarity as a trade union also reflected the mood at the broad shop-floor level. Thus the establishment of an independent, self-governing trade union in 1980 in connection with the programme for a self-governing republic amounted to the 'identity-card' of Solidarity in 1980/81. Consequently, in 1989 'only the recognition of Solidarity's right to legal existence would lead to cancellation of the military dictatorship and the opening of a political path to democratic transformation'.[32] While the political strategy of the Solidarity opposition was shaping 'according to on-going events . . . the stable point in it. . . . was the postulate of the relegalization of the union'.[33] This postulate was the only clearly formulated and steadfastily pursued demand for negotiations at the round table.

The central reference-point for the trade union, however, was at a distance for most of the Solidarity explorers in the round-table negotiations. Each of the two – the striking new generation and the old generation assembled in the civic committee under Lech Wałęsa[34] – conceived of trade union in a different way. Starting from its relegalization in 1989 throughout the 1990s, Solidarity has claimed to be a trade union in defence of workers' interests. For the new generation a trade union meant, most generally, the defence of workers' interests in enterprises and the workplace. The trade unionist tendency grew stronger, while the majority of workers did not intend to sacrifice their interests and wage demands in the name of an illusory political victory (Kuczyński and Nowotny, 1994:249–50).[35]

As outlined in the above analysis, the image of Solidarity emerged as a consequence of a complex process. Created as a spontaneous *communitas* among workers in the Gdańsk shipyard, it soon came to represent a nationwide movement endowed with the mythical imagery of national liberation. Under liminal conditions, the desire for identification with Solidarity led to the creation of an all-encompassing image based on persistent myths. As a consequence, in terms of action at a distance, the combinability of programmatic and ideological issues became practically boundless. By aspiring to the whole of the image, the acutal object was lost from sight. Adam Michnik's assessment of the immediate post-1989 period elucidates this fact:

> Solidarity continually lived at this time by the myth of its power. It wanted to take over power everywhere, where it was possible, wanted to dictate government personnel politics. . . . One thing the leaders of Solidarity did not want to do: to reflect upon what the formula of a trade union should be in a democratic state of law in an epoch of transformation to the market.[36]

In fact, the trade-union aspect of Solidarity became increasingly blurred. Originally, belief in the power of the 'general strike' had been its most powerful instrument. At the end of the 1980s, how-ever, this instrument had completely vanished (Smolar and Kende, 1989:16–18). Solidarity's leading circles around Lech Wałęsa regarded the revival of the trade union as synonymous with reclaiming its role as the only opposition force in Poland.

Lech Wałęsa's speech before the Second National Congress of Solid-arity in April 1990 was telling in this respect. Voicing harsh criticism against the deviating 'trade-unionist' trade union Solidarity 80, he scorned the strictly trade-unionist model of a trade union – espoused by Solidarity 80 – because in that case 'we must proclaim a general strike immediately'.[37] What is more, Solidarity's relegalization in the wake of the round-table pact was achieved in exchange for recognition of the Law on Trade Unions of 1982, by which strike activity was made practically impossible. A further blow against core trade union interests came in the form of the protective um-brella for the Mazowiecki government proposed by Wałęsa in autumn 1989. This measure suspended Solidarity's strike activities and trade-union demands as much as possible in order to support the rigid economic programme introduced by the Mazowiecki government. As such, it implied an indirect negation of and opposition to the model of a trade union. Despite the growing importance of the Solidarity trade union as a representative of workers' state enter-prises, survey data from 1991 and 1993 show that trade unions have remained weak in post-1989 Poland (Gąciarz, 1994:272).

The constitution of the image of Solidarity can be read in the lines of the continuities analysed in Chapters 2 to 4. It essentially consisted of a twofold process. Solidarity as an institution was de-prived of the key attributes which had underpinned its success in 1980. Its mass character waned away with the weakening of its organizational basis. Central objectives of Solidarity's strategy, such as core trade-unionist demands, became increasingly contested or blurred, while the imperative of the general strike was obsolete by the end of the 1980s. Although its capacities for collective mobili-zation were maintained to a certain extent, society's identification with Solidarity remained largely on the level of images. In other words, this shift in preferences jettisoned the central strategic aims of the first Solidarity, such as trade union demands and egalitarian claims for social justice. The image of Solidarity as experienced in 1980 stamped the mentalities of many Poles, and generated a spir-itual attachment to the continuity of small communities mainly under the protection of the Catholic Church. It was essentially these mental and emotional bonds with this image that helped to revive Solidarity as a relevant social movement and restore its relevance for politics.

In the wake of the round table, this image of Solidarity became subject to a mimetic conflict among contestants which all claimed their attachment to the original Solidarity. Although political parameters and society's support had changed considerably, post-1989 Solidarity organizations identified with the utopian image of Solidarity. In this vein, Solidarity II was essentially confronted with the image of Solidarity I as a double. There are striking parallels with the totalizing aspects of the image of Solidarity, aiming at the identification with a national and societal community.

The image of Solidarity after 1989

In the aftermath of the round-table community, the history of Solidarity after 1989 very soon became one of its disunity and rapid disintegration. In the wake of the semi-free elections of 1989, Solidarity succumbed to a process of accelerated institutional differentiation. After its relegalization in April 1989 and its victory in the elections of June 1989, it formed a parliamentary representation and came into power in autumn 1989. All of a sudden trade-unionist tasks had to be combined with parliamentary activity and, some months later, with governmental responsibility. In 1989 and 1990, two major camps emanated from Solidarity's institutional differentiation that were distinguished as the Wałęsa camp and the Mazowiecki camp.[38] The government camp assembled Solidarity intellectuals with a supposedly leftist past. Prime Minister Mazowiecki and the OKP chairman Geremek were regarded as the political leaders, while Adam Michnik, editor-in chief of *Gazeta Wyborcza*, was considered the ideological leader. On the other side, Lech Wałęsa, who had renounced both a *Sejm* mandate and the prime ministership in 1989, aimed to overcome his growing distance and marginalization from the centre of politics. Under the pretext of defending pluralism, he dissolved the civic committees in June 1990 and promoted the foundation of a political party, the Centre Alliance. The confrontation between both camps came to a head during the presidential campaign in autumn 1990. Mazowiecki surprisingly dropped out at the first ballot against the unknown businessman Stanisław Tymiński who, in turn, was beaten by Wałęsa in the runoff election.

It is held to be paradoxical that the establishment of the Solidarity government accelerated the disintegration of Solidarity (Wnuk-Lipiński, 1996:146). Likewise, it is assumed to be a paradox that the presidency of Wałęsa contributed to the weakening of Solidarity and the strengthening of post-communist parties (Kwiecień, 1996:11). The old order was removed by a peaceful consensus between former contestants in the round-table community. Shortly afterwards, the human and institutional source of democratization was driven into a self-lacerating war at the top. The war of all against all opened up the way to the attack against the Solidarity governments of Mazowiecki and Balcerowicz, and was followed by a second war at the top when the Wałęsa camp dissolved (Michnik, 1995:295–301). 'The communist regime had not achieved in ten years what the war at the top managed in only one and a half years: namely the destruction of Solidarity.'[39]

I surmise that Solidarity's disintegration can be explained by the unity of the image of Solidarity, which became the central model for its elites after 1989. Commonly, models are conceived as the reference-points for political strategies in order to shape outcomes in the institutional first reality. One early model was Finland – a model implying escape from direct Soviet domination. Once martial law was lifted, the model was Austria – a model for neutrality between East and West. After the landslide victory in the June 1989 elections, the model became Spain – a model of political and economic reform.[40] Similarly, Adam Michnik depicted in February 1989 three ideal-typical ways to follow, of which the first two were implicitly excluded: the Afghani, the Iranian, and the Spanish way. In 1990 he warned what would follow the Lebanese way, the war of brothers: Balkanization. Michnik fervently espoused the Spanish way, 'To avoid violence and thoughts of revenge in the context of a compromise between the former regime and the democratic opposition.'[41] Although a great deal of care is needed, if a complex configuration such as Solidarity's role in Polish politics is adapted to a theoretical framework, there seems to be good evidence for the protracted impact of the image of Solidarity on post-1989 politics and society. In turn, Solidarity's disintegration happened as a result of an inherently self-referential process.

> Let us remember that in 1989 nobody, no expert could foresee which course the path from communism to democracy would take.... The Solidarity elites.... numbered, how many, some two thousand people all over the country? These two thousand

people made the revolution, and all the rest, acclaimed but only watched. Thinking that all would go by itself. That the introduction of democracy meant immediate welfare. Because Western democracies are rich. And suddenly it became clear that although democracy worked, the margin of poverty was growing. And who then is guilty? The ones who introduced democracy.[42]

However, the deconstruction of the myth of Solidarity was more short-lived than most analysts expected.

As argued throughout this book, in liminal conditions the second reality of utopian images acquires a predominant role in the mentality of collective groups in society. Subsequently, I will argue that the second reality of the image of Solidarity can explain the paradoxical war at the top. I will argue that, as in 1980, the desire of Solidarity's leading circles was directed towards the maintenance of the unity of its image. As different groups wanted to appropriate the identity of Solidarity I, the relationship between Solidarity II and the image of Solidarity can be considered as a relationship between doubles. The institutional disintegration of Solidarity and the emergence of party pluralism very much relied upon the totalizing character of the desires of Solidarity II aiming at identity with the image of Solidarity. The hypothesis of a mimetic conflict among various groups in Solidarity II over the image of Solidarity I can be shown by an analysis of clear tendencies to avoid doubles.

A first tendency to avoid competitors was intimated in Solidarity's claim to represent society exclusively as of the mid-1980s. The reconstitution of a guiding board of Solidarity in 1987 and 1988 was driven by the ambition to represent the entire opposition, notwithstanding the rising quasi-pluralism in Polish society. Between 1987 and 1989 Solidarity sought to reclaim the image according to which 'Solidarity was the only opposition-force in the country' (Mazowiecki, 1989:17). Yet this second subjectivization of society was grounded more in the desire for unity than in real unity. As the wars at the top indicate, in terms of identity-politics the transitional period after 1989 was one of deep crisis. In this vein the end of Solidarity was equated both to a collective parricide and to an infanticide (Bauman, 1994:14–18; Wnuk-Lipiński, 1996:147). This moment of crisis set the basis of a mimetic conflict which, in Girard's terms, testifies to a threat to cohesion in a collective group or society. 'Ideas of parricide . . . and infanticide always crop up when cultural cohesion is threatened, when a society is in danger of disintegration.'[43]

This disintegration was prefigured in the liminal underground which had stamped the organizational features of Solidarity II. While Solidarity I had assembled nearly 10 million Poles, the unofficial numbers for early 1989 oscillated around 700 000 members. Furthermore, in 1980 the irreconcilable dichotomy between the communist regime and Solidarity accorded an exclusive function of society's representation to the latter. In 1989, Solidarity's position as the only representative of society was seriously questioned. Before 1989 the envisaged deal with the regime was accompanied by the proposal of a societal coalition of the main political forces. Solidarity II managed to become – next to the Catholic Church – the only representative of opposition to the regime at the round table.[44] However, the liminal condition of both antagonists, and of the Polish political environment in general, casts serious doubts about the actual representativeness of Solidarity or of the communist regime. As Jan Gross argued,

> both the Magdalenka and the round-table talks were an ad-hoc gremium which, on the one hand, embodied the authorities . . ., and on the other, society. I use 'embodied' rather than 'represented' because just as there was no delegation of authority from the state/party governing institutions to the group of the government side negotiators . . . so their interlocutors were not, strictly speaking, representatives of society.[45]

Between the closure of the round table in April and the elections in June 1989 lay barely two months. All over Poland, local and regional civic committees were spontaneously set up so as to assure a sufficient number of Solidarity candidates. These committees ran under the common banner of Solidarity. Their overwhelming victory in the June elections was followed by the first harsh conflict inside Solidarity II. Soon thereafter, Lech Wałęsa and many other members of the National Executive Commission wanted to dissolve the committees. One could argue that this move against the committees came down to a shift in paradigms for Solidarity II. Whereas it had pursued the common goal of re-legalization of the trade union at the round table, after the June elections the image of Solidarity dwindled in importance and gave way to particularism. Understandably, research on party politics focused on the differentiation of Solidarity and on the paricularization of the party spectrum.[46] Yet one could easily argue the opposite. The development of party pluralism in Poland bears attributes of undifferentiation, since political parties have tended to avoid clear-cut identifications as factions, but rather, have tried to convey an image of broad unitary alliances. With the exception of the Peasants Party, PSL, all the major parties rejected identification as 'faction'. In particular, parties in the heritage of Solidarity have espoused broad-ranging electoral alliances such as the Catholic Electoral Action in 1991, or the Catholic Electoral Committee 'Homeland' in 1993, grouped around the Christian National Alliance (ZChN). In a similar vein, this tendency to avoid a clear-cut programmatic orientation in favour of a broad appeal for national community was characteristic of Lech Wałęsa's Non-Party Bloc for the Support of Reforms (BBWR) in 1993, of Jan Olszewski's Movement for Poland's Reconstruction (ROP), and, in particular, of Solidarity Electoral Action (AWS) as of 1996.

It can be safely argued that Solidarity's disintegration in the aftermath of 1989 is tightly linked to the obsessive desire to maintain the unity of its image. Apparently, Solidarity as a unified power should be preserved. Furthermore, this move was underpinned by the intent to avoid 'double power' in Solidarity (Kuroń and Żakowski, 1995:273). The rivalry between Wałęsa and the civic committees indicates a mental and spiritual dependence on the image of a Solidarity-*communitas* in both the two camps. As I showed at the outset of this chapter, the image of Solidarity conformed to unity which as an object of desire was exclusive. Both Solidarity's National Executive Commission and the civic committees aimed to appropriate its image. Such an assumption is reinforced by Wałęsa's decision to forbid the committees the use of the word Solidarity (Kuroń and Żakowski, 1995:273).

Despite martial rhetorics between the camps, and the dominant tendency to launch factions and parties, evidence suggests that the real obsession in Solidarity II was to avoid splits and divisions. In this vein, Wałęsa's opponents advocated a further existence of the civic committees. They were also keen to avoid the rise of a double power centre. In particular, Solidarity activists belonging to the intelligentsia espoused the idea of Solidarity as a continual common and unitary movement. On behalf of the foundation of ROAD in July 1990, Zbigniew Bujak and Adam Michnik stressed the importance of keeping Solidarity together, rather than split into parties. Michnik entreated a solemn unification of people of different currents and social origins, tied together by the bond of the 'ethos of Solidarity'. By underlining the unique Solidarity experience, they wanted to abandon a political tradition based on parties. As Zbigniew Bujak declared: 'The word party means "part", therefore if we have to divide into parts one has to think of: how? We want to flee from a tradition we do not accept. However, we reflect upon which of Europe's current phenomena could influence the criteria of our divisions. Today Europe is uniting.'[47]

This statement points to a unifying zeal in the name of the image of Solidarity. Party pluralism and a diversification of the political landscape were eschewed on behalf of a desire for unity. A situation of undifferentiation is characterized by two features. First, the immediacy of time indicates the opposite of temporization. Second, the lack of spacing evinces a blurring of borders and an immediacy of contacts and exchange.[48] In this respect, Adam Michnik's appeal to 'put off divisions' had a programmatic character (Michnik, 1995:241–2). It deliberately aimed to overlook differences of political convictions and traditions. The image of Solidarity as the focal point of the drive towards unity is explicit here. 'I belong to those for whom the political formula of a movement Solidarity is enough. I think that it better describes my preferences than entreating the spirit of the left and the right, the spirit of Christian democracy or Social democracy that are evoked by some of my colleagues.'[49]

One might object that the appeal to put off divisions is certainly an attempt to temporize. Yet the hint about temporization seems to be merely rhetorical. Rather, Michnik's remark corroborated the leap back in time that wanted to fix the image of Solidarity as a model for the early 1990s. In this regard he advocated a recurrent experience of *communitas* in post-1989 politics. His appeal to unity with reference to Solidarity espouses undifferentiation in ideology and social structure. 'In my conviction this is the great chance for ROAD; this unity of different generations and professions, different conditions and worldviews, of workers, peasants and members of the intelligentsia that is emerging out of the ethos of Solidarity.'[50] A careful reading will discover substantial parallels with Michnik's writings in the 1970s, where the New Evolutionism emphasized the great convergence of different currents in Poland's opposition. Thus, Solidarity's backwardness in relation to its image implies a persistent desire to undo time. Such a zeal materialized in the endeavour to detach the post-1989 Solidarity from the Polish party tradition. Advocates of this trend aimed to suspend the pluralization of political life and to avoid the emergence of further doubles. Bujak and Michnik, but also intellectuals such as Bronisław Geremek and

Tadeusz Mazowiecki, inveighed against the disintegration of the new Solidarity. As the mainstream strand of the second Solidarity was to be kept united, such a unity implicitly excluded the establishment of competitive organizations from splinter-groups that shared Solidarity tradition. Exclusion is inherent in the mimetic conflict which is focused on unity. There was a desire to oust the adversary from the Solidarity circle precisely because both sides identified with its image.

Lech Wałęsa supposedly favoured the opposite scenario. While the govern- ment camp argued in favour of one political and social movement, Solidarity, the Wałęsa camp subscribed to party pluralism. He called upon Solidarity to provide the staff and organizational skills for nascent parties. Eventually the Centre Alliance, founded in May 1990, not only emanated from Wałęsa's efforts but also supported him politically. Yet Wałęsa's explicit espousal of party pluralism and, by that, differentiation, makes up only half of the story. Most strikingly, the importance of the image of Solidarity for the identity of post-1989 Solidarity became apparent when Wałęsa prohibited *Gazeta Wyborcza*[51] from continuing to use the symbol of Solidarity. Confiscating the symbol, he replied to direct attacks against his person. By withdrawing this badge it became clear that Wałęsa, just like his adversaries, stuck to the idea of unity that was embodied by the image of Solidarity. A plausible interpretation of this move cannot overlook the appropriation of the image of the Solidarity *communitas* for Wałęsa's own cause. To appropriate the symbol of Solidarity for his trade union branch meant to establish the identity between the Wałęsa camp both in the new Solidarity and the image of Solidarity. At the same time, the other camp was excluded and thus a double was prevented. In this case, the conflict between opposed camps in post-1989 Solidarity was essentially a struggle for identity which was led through the appropriation of commonly respected and desired symbols. To be deprived of Solidarity's symbol was perceived as being 'the sign of the end of Solidarity'.[52] To use the power of the symbol of Solidarity that had a 'high emotional value'[53] in order to cut off ties with another part of Solidarity went beyond a simple attempt at differentiation. Wałęsa's desire very much resembled that of his opponents, who were heavily hit by the withdrawal of the symbol, as Michnik's remark proves: 'Solidarity was the most important element of my life'.[54] As has been illustrated, this tendency to prohibit or eschew hypothetical doubles speaks for the cherishing of the real double, the image of Solidarity itself.

The emergence of dissident trade unions at the end of the 1980s and their conflicts with mainstream Solidarity can give some further hints about a mimetic conflict on behalf of Solidarity's image. Commonly, these split-off groupings, like the Working Group (*Grupa robocza*), Fighting Solidarity (*Solidarność Walcząca*) or, most importantly, Solidarity 80, are seen as a natural result of the incipient process of differentiation at the end of the 1980s. These trade unions rigorously stuck to the trade union tradition of the Gdańsk Accords of August 1980, and rejected any political deal with the communists. Solidarity 80 referred 'to the roots, to the ideas of 1980 to that kind of understanding with society as well as to the expression of its aspiration.'[55] In the words of its chairman, Marian Jurczyk: 'We decisively refuse that trade unions should take up activities of political nature, since this always menaces a loss of their authenticity and identity. The fundamental function of a trade union is the defense of workers' interests' (Jurczyk, 1990). To grasp the essential point here, one has to look beyond the outcome-level of anti-politics and the will to pursue trade-unionist demands. In the case of Solidarity 80, the desire for identification with the trade unionist core of Solidarity I made up the core link.

The conflicts between mainstream Solidarity II and Solidarity 80 indicate to what extent the image of Solidarity had become the major reference-point for both. Basically, the desire of mainstream Solidarity was to avoid the emergence of doubles. Once again, one can elucidate this mechanism by pointing to the mutual efforts to stick to unity and avoid at any cost the appearance of a double. Girard stressed the power of prohibitions in curbing mimetic desire: 'Not to repeat any action associated with the crisis, to abstain from all mimicry, from all contact with the former antagonists, from any acquisitive gesture toward objects that have stood as causes or pretexts for rivalry. This is the imperative of prohibition.'[56] In notable equivalence with this assessment, Solidarity fought for two years against the legalization of Solidarity 80, whose registration was refused by the decision of a court because the trade union did not accept the clauses of the Law on Trade Unions of 1982. An interpretation along the lines of mimetic conflict indicates why mainstream Solidarity contested Solidarity 80's identification with origins at the Gdańsk shipyard. To fight against its registration meant to avoid the legal emergence and consolidation of another contestant for the 'true' image of Solidarity.

Given the unanimous conviction in either camp about representing the true image of Solidarity and pursuing the right track for unity, hatred and resentment against each other increased. Most of the reciprocal accusations were of the following kind, with inter-changeable names. 'The idea of Solidarity entered into a phase of agony. This agony is Lech Wałęsa's responsibility.'[57] On their part, Wałęsa and his changing allies denigrated their rivals as eggheads or Jews. This unanimity in suggesting a clear-cut separation between the good and the bad shows that 'the ideological differences between the Mazowiecki and Wałęsa camps were a sham. In fact, the divisions between the two camps stemmed from personal and social animosities.'[58] Envy and jealousy were present in at least two particular forms. Wałęsa's refusal to take over the prime ministership in summer 1989 made the trade union leader feel increasingly excluded from the political process. Solidarity's civil parliamentary club (OKP) and the Mazowiecki government had a growing influence on political decisions, while Wałęsa's voice remained strong mainly due to its personal charisma. On the other hand, intellectual leaders were becoming more and more uneasy with Wałęsa's charismatic leadership.[59]

This conflictual constellation of mirror images points to the unanimity of contestants which aimed to avoid the appearance of doubles. Adam Michnik spoke about the lasting division lines that separated him from Marian Jurczyk, the leader of Solidarity 80. 'What do I have in common with Marian Jurczyk who is crying out his nonsense?'[60] To put it bluntly, both Michnik and Wałęsa, both Jurczyk and Jankowski were convinced they would not only represent rightly and properly their Solidarity, but that they would be the one and only Solidarity. They were equal in their unconscious double-bind with their image of one Solidarity. As Girard put it,

> the faster the blows rain down, the clearer it becomes that there is no difference between those who deliver the blows and those who receive them. On both sides everything is equal; not only the desire, the violence, the strategy, but also the alternation of victory and defeat, of exaltation and despair.[61]

In this mimetic conflict, 'it is not that one wants the object but that one does not want to see it in someone's else's hand'.[62] The antagonist should be prevented from using symbols that are supposed to belong only to one side. Although during 1989 and 1990 the leaders of both camps in Solidarity II had shifted their attention from trade union activities to the political realm, the conflict with Solidarity 80 concerned the exclusive representation of the Solidarity trade union. Solidarity II considered itself to be the true preserver of the trade union tradition, as Solidarity 80 did.

To recapitulate, the identification of leading circles in Solidarity II with the image of Solidarity can be put forward as an important cause of Solidarity's disintegration in the wake of 1989. While Solidarity II differentiated in institutional and programmatic terms, the mimetic image, Solidarity I, was subject to the opposite tendency: it embodied the unity of a memorable nationwide community in 1980. In other words, while Solidarity II split apart as a movement, the core of its identity remained indivisible. All the main currents in Solidarity II made an effort to save the indivisibility of the image of the Solidarity *communitas*. Such behaviour expressed the fundamental desire of Solidarity II, which wanted to reclaim its lost identity. 'The need to define one's own position and to opt for a political path of one's own is the actual reason for Solidarity's identity crisis.'[63] Each of its currents (camps in Solidarity II, civic committees, Solidarity 80) aspired to become its own imagined version of Solidarity I. These were the desire for total representation and for the unity of the movement. To become equal with an imagined double comes down to cherishing the second reality of a nationwide community. Hence, attempts to achieve an exclusive representation of Solidarity was a central cause of Solidarity's disintegration in the wars at the top. The two Solidarities, I and II, can thus be regarded as twins in Girard's definition. He takes up the point that in some primitive societies twins and mirrors inspired a particular fear.

> Twins invariably share a cultural identity, and they often have a striking physical resemblance to each other. Wherever differences are lacking, violence threatens. Between biological twins and sociological twins there arises a confusion that grows more troubled as the question of differences reaches a crisis. It is only natural that twins should awaken fear, for they are harbingers of indiscriminate violence.[64]

In this regard, 'twins offer a symbolic representation, sometimes remarkably eloquent, of the symmetrical conflict and identity crisis that characterize the sacrificial crisis'.[65]

The transition literature argued that given their high degree of indeterminacy, social and political processes in transition are asymmetric and irreversible. 'The main reason for this asymmetry springs from ... the high degree of indeterminacy of social and political actions and the inordinate degrees of freedom that collective and even individual action may have at some momentous junctures of the transition.'[66] As the above analysis has suggested, the continuity of the image of Solidarity depends heavily on the second reality, which is expected to provide identity and thus to discontinue the state of disorder and confusion. Although the thrust for identity triggered the destruction of Solidarity, these processes, as argued in this chapter, were neither asymmetrical nor irreversible. In this vein, the reciprocity of contestants which all cherished a common image of Solidarity comes close to reciprocity in the process of symmetrical differentiation. Gregory Bateson defined this process as a behaviour pattern whereby the behaviour of two groups follows an exchange of symmetrical responses. Inside both group A and group B, the behaviour patterns are A, B, and C. In the mutual relationship, the behaviour patterns between the two groups are X, Y, and Z. Each group will drive the other into excessive emphasis of the pattern, which, if not restrained, can only lead to more and more extreme rivalry and ultimately to hostility and the breakdown of the whole system (Bateson, 1972:68). In the case of Poland, the differentiation of post-1989 Solidarity was symmetrical as it drew heavily on the identification with the community of 1980, epitomized in the image of Solidarity. The stress was laid on the unity of what either side identified as its own Solidarity I. In Girard's terms this would sound as follows: 'The more desire aspires to difference, the more it generates identity.... Mimetic Desire is always more self-defeating. As it progresses, its consequences become more aggravated.'[67]

Although post-1989 Solidarity has not renounced its organizational core as a trade union, so far it has lingered over a clear definition of its identity. The Second National Congress in April 1990 failed in this respect, when it declared Solidarity to be 'both a trade union and a social movement' which wants to participate 'in the transformation of political and economic order'.[68] While the foundation of a political party was explicitly rejected, the 'creation of an own trade-unionist representation in parliament and in the organs of territorial self-administration'[69] was not excluded. In the mean time, Solidarity spawned more than a dozen political parties or movements. This notwithstanding, the union leadership has stuck to maintaining an outstanding political role. Most clamorously, it did so in spring 1993, when the parliamentary group of the Solidarity union initiated a successful vote of non-confidence against the last Solidarity government of the then prime minister, Hanna Suchocka.

The liminal condition of Solidarity's identity crisis was commonly interpreted as the deconstruction of the myth and the ethos of Solidarity (Frybes and Michel, 1996a and 1996b). In the wake of 1993, Solidarity's extra-parliamentary opposition and the crisis of the Polish right, however, helped to revive the cohesive power of the image of Solidarity. The totality of the image of communists[70] was fundamental to the cohesive effort of the Polish right, which assembled some 40 party groupings under the umbrella of Solidarity Electoral Action. As of 1995, a new drive for unity has been perceived around the spirit of Solidarity. During the presidential campaign of 1995, in public discourse . . . a 'new imperative of unity of the "August people" emerged as well as the idea of a return to a certain version of the civic committees'.[71] The result was unexpectedly high electoral support for Lech Wałęsa in the presidential elections of October 1995. Solidarity's forced distancing from official party politics after the electoral defeat in September 1993 resulted in nothing less than a 'replica of the Solidarity camp of 1989'.[72] In its wake, the VII National Congress in June 1996 decided that 'the trade union participates in the forthcoming elections to the *Sejm* and the Senate in the frame of the "Solidarity Electoral Action"'.[73] Thus, seven years after 1989, the Solidarity trade union has become the hinge of a broad coalition of centre-right parties. On the whole, however, Solidarity Electoral Action has not contributed to a normalization of the party system. 'Solidarity Electoral Action ended many years of disarray and chaos that ruled the former Solidarity camp. It partly managed to reconstruct it, but it did not contribute to the shaping of a normal party system.'[74]

The continuity of the image of Solidarity

This chapter has conceptualized the image of Solidarity as a non-contingent given in the second reality of Poland's transition. Since its emergence in 1980, the image of the Solidarity *communitas* has kept a central role as the provider of identity for political elites. This image experienced two different kinds of decomposition of its organizational, ideological, and identity attributes: the fall into the underground in 1981, and into institutional differentiation from 1989 onwards. Each time, the following liminal period bruised

Solidarity as an institution but kept its spirit and its image alive. The wars at the top in 1989 and 1990 can be characterized as a fully fledged mimetic conflict of symmetrical differentiation between several currents in Solidarity II. As shown in this chapter, Solidarity's legitimacy and continuity must be sought after in its mythical appeal as an image that perpetuates the Polish tradition of recreating and desiring existential communities.

At least three times during Poland's transition the image of Solidarity has embodied the major reference point for the expectation of discontinuities. In 1980 the convergence of Polish opposition forces from different intellectual and social contexts such as workers, intellectuals, and the Catholic Church led to the subjectivization of Polish society. The anti-structure of the 1980 community was simultaneously a mirror image and mimetic double to the negated communist regime. In 1989, Solidarity could repeat its role as the representative of Polish society and the Polish nation. The roundtable community temporarily discontinued the political antagonism between the communist regime and Polish society. Despite the end of the Solidarity governments in 1993, and the extra-parliamentary opposition between 1993 and 1997, the image of Solidarity has continued to exert powerful influence as a major source of identification for considerable parts of the population. It was also a source of political legitimacy which came to restructure the political landscape in the second half of the 1990s. Before 1989, the image of Solidarity embodied the expectation of its revival as a trade union and a political force. In the wars of the top, its image was at the centre of conflicts inside Solidarity. While many analysts proclaimed the end of the myth of Solidarity in the mid-1990s, the image of Solidarity has revived the post-August-1980 community.

7
The Continuity of the Image of 1989

In a political environment of national reconciliation and community, prime minister Tadeusz Mazowiecki's first address to the *Sejm* declared that his government would not assume responsibility for the heritage of communism and would draw a thick line under the past. He wanted to limit the responsibility of his government to its own actions.[1] The thick line (*gruba kreska*) soon came to stand for a policy of prosecuting the former authorities only for crimes that could be fully documented and were legally prosecuted at the time they were committed. Although such a meaning diverged from Mazowiecki's original intention, Poland was a semi-democratic island among communist countries at that time, and the participation of communist ministers in his government made the sacking of civil servants impossible. Thus, the thick-line policy envisaged an abstention from purges in ministerial bureaucracy as well as in the secret services (Kozłowski, 1991:18–20).

The suggestion to refrain from prosecution of former communist authorities in the government and in the administration was not made for pragmatic reasons alone. In particular, Adam Michnik's writings and actions have supported a conciliatory stance towards the former communist regime (Michnik, 1990; Michnik and Cimoszewicz, 1995). The thick line amounted to an unprecedented move to create distance, to install a radical rupture with the past. Let bygones be bygones, no trials, no recrimination was the motto (Ash, 1998). This distancing from the polluting past by the thick line aimed to back up the post-1989 normalization in Polish politics. Thus, in the early 1990s it was alleged that de-communization had come to an end as a result of public disinterest in purges, induced by a rational quiescence and inaction. The driving force behind the tendency was 'not only an abysmal breakdown of historical memory, but partly a reasonable assessment of the unprecedented moral and practical dilemmas of the present'.[2] Thus, by the declaration of the thick line and its implementation, 'the past was – as an act of political will – isolated from the present'.[3]

The positive effects of the round-table community should be stressed in this connection. The absence of revenge in 1989 in a spirit of *communitas* assured the non-violent demise of communism. At the same time, the communist past exerted a steady influence on post-1989 politics, not only epitomized in the return of post-communists to power but also in the division of the political landscape and heated political debates on themes such as the constitution, economic transformation, abortion, or decentralization. Although the institutional framework of communist Poland was dismantled, the 1989 community has not brought about a rupture with the communist past. 'Many more Poles (...) still find that the lack of a dramatic break between old and new, the legal continuity, delegitimizes the new regime.'[4]

Several authors have thematized the necessary return to normality in post-1989 Poland. In this vein it was argued that Poland's way to normality requires the deconstruction of three myths that had been crucial for pre-1989 (Frybes and Michel, 1996a, 1996b). In such a reading, the myth of Solidarity and the myth of enchanted politics became deconstructed in the first half of the 1990s. During the emergence of political democracy the disappearance of these two myths could help to weaken the romantic myth of the Polish nation (Frybes and Michel, 1996b:79–82). Constant changes in Polish politics have confronted analysts with new scenarios. As I argued in Chapter 6, post-1989 Solidarity did not simply disintegrate in the wake of the wars at the top. The mimetic engagement of Solidarity leading circles with its image played a crucial role in the reconstitution of a political force under the heading of Solidarity. Since 1996 Solidarity Electoral Action has assembled 40 political parties of the conservative type and has achieved something like a new community of a third Solidarity.[5] Moreover, the arrival of the post-communist coalition to power in 1993 induced commentators to assume that Polish society was subject anew to a meta-reality (*nadrzeczywistość*) (Ekes, 1994:142–6).

This chapter examines some of the most pervasive themes in post-1989 politics and society under the aspect of the continuity of second realities. I will argue that the anti-structure of the round-table community generated a new image that has stamped politics in post-1989 Poland ever since. This image of 1989 is of double-edged significance. On the one hand, this experience of *communitas* achieved a peaceful and consensus-based institutional change. On the other hand, the anti-structure of *communitas* has prevented the establishment of new, stable political and social structures, due to the lack of a decisive rupture-point and a missing cathartic moment in Poland's transition.

These continuities stand for the assumption that the expected discontinuity with communist rule has failed so far. The image of 1989 stands for the identification with liberty and equality as the central but contradicting passions of Poland's revolutions. As the new start after the revolution of 1989 was made in the name of liberty, the round-table community and the ensuing short period of plasticity and effervescence in politics and the economy represented the equality of all Poles. I will argue that this extraordinary period of 1989 raised high expectations but has basically put off decisions on the identity of collective actors and their relationship with their own past. Various developments in post-1989 Poland suggest that 1989 was not the rupture-point, as cleavage-lines and unresolved problems of the pre-1989 past have continued to exert a crucial influence on collective groups, electoral results, and political decisions.

While 1989 has been the yardstick of discontinuity with communism, it has simultaneously kept Polish politics and society in a circle of expecting discontinuities that were actually missed in 1989. I will examine this image of 1989 by looking at a threefold dynamics that shows the centrality of recapturing of the past: first, in the contested assessment of the communist past and ensuing attempts to decide political guilt by the zeal for cleansing; second, the politics of permanent reform's underpinning of the revival of political conflict alongside historical antagonisms between post-communists and post-Solidarity; and third, I will focus on intimations of *communitas* in post-1989 Poland which have embodied a persistent desire for a return to the start.

The emergence of the round-table community was examined at length in Chapter 2. Due to the reinforcement of expecting discontinuities, a second reality has built up in post-1989 Polish politics and society. Political mentalities do not correspond to actual needs or interests, but keep on living in the pre-1989 past. This past does not influence post-1989 in an evolutionary way, such as the post-Solidarity antagonism (1989–93) or post-communism (1993–7) would have it. The image of 1989 must be understood as a relational category in which the image of a non-achieved but highly desirable *communitas* is constantly evoked. Post-1989 Polish politics has been like a roller-coaster in this respect. References to experiences of *communitas* or solidarity have alternated with tendencies of high contesta-tion and political conflict.

The Politics of Lustration

The reconciliatory environment of the round-table *communitas* soon waned away. As Adam Michnik put it:

> I was always hostile to decommunization and to furious anti-communist rhetorics. I always regarded the menace of a return of communism to power as fairy tales for naive people, written for the refreshment of politicians from the Belvedere camp. To-day, however, I ask myself whether the obstinacy and consequent destruction of the ethos of Solidarity could not lead to a violent about-face of public opinion in favour of the post-communists?[6]

Complying with claims of rightist parties in 1991, the Olszewski government made the first step to a settlement with the past. On the grounds of moral necessity and national probity, rather than of revenge, Jan Olszewski postulated the settlement of accounts with past guilt. For there to be forgiveness one must know who is guilty and who is forgiven.[7] In June 1992, the Minister of the Interior, Antoni Macierewicz, presented a list of 64 putative collaborators of the former Intelligence Service. The 'dossier affair' accused rivals of the ruling right-wing coalition, among them a series of former opposition leaders. This included also president Lech Wałęsa, who could not entirely disperse allegations about his collaboration with the Intelligence Services. While the first charges could be inter-preted in terms of manipulation and blackmail due to political motives,[8] lustration soon became a major issue in the activities of various political forces. Six political parties presented draft laws on lustration in summer 1992. Although lustration did not play a major role in the parliamentary elections of 1993, it was relaunched in 1994, when four new projects for legislation were tackled. One project was presented by the new president of the Polish Republic, the post-communist Aleksander Kwaśniewski (Grajewski, 1996).

Far from being confined to symbolic acts or rhetorics, the politics of lustration have had strong effects on domestic political stability. In 1992, the Olszewski government was toppled in the aftermath of the lustration crisis it had instigated. In December 1995 prime minister Józef Oleksy was charged for co-operation with the Soviet Intelligence Service and resigned under public pressure in January 1996. With the return to power of the post-Solidarity coalition in 1997 and the adoption of the lustration law in 1998, the settlement with the past has become politically more heated than ever since 1989 (Grabowski 1998).

> The problem of lustration links up several elements: the question of settlement of accounts, the cleaning of public life of particularly degenerate remainders of the communist system, the problem of state security, whose higher functionaries should not be at the mercy of possible blackmail arising from their unclear past. Finally, it means also the natural necessity in European conditions to introduce moral order in politics. During the last five years none of these questions has been resolved. This has had a fatal effect on Polish political life.[9]

Yet it seems that concrete steps towards political accountability are not to be expected. A comparison with Germany should help to elucidate this point. Three options for coming to terms with the past were proposed by Claus Offe and analysed for the German case: disqualification, retribution, and restitution (Offe, 1997:82–104). Disqualification 'consists either of the withdrawal of special status rights or privileges or of some curtailment of general status rights of categories of people or corporate entities'.[10] In post-1990 Germany, many dismissals from jobs or non-admission to jobs often disguised political purging as economic or technical disqualification (Offe, 1997:94). Due to the policy of the thick line and the absence of an 'occupation'-regime, as in the German case, no legislative acts have targeted political lustration in Poland. While there have been cases of indirect 'retroactive' justice, in the most sensible area of political accountability for the communist period, neither disqualification, retribution, nor restitution have proved to be viable options in the Polish case. Rather, cases of retribution concerned singular violent acts.[11] Conversely, trials in which political accountability was at stake were either suspended or passed to a higher level. In April 1996, the Gdańsk court stopped the trial against General

Jaruzelski and Kazimierz Świtały for their responsibility in the violence against workers in December 1970. Only a few days earlier the Warsaw military court had stopped the investigation against ex-prime minister Józef Oleksy for his alleged intelligence activity.[12]

There is good reason to assume that attempts at lustration in post-1989 Poland lack a finality in terms of real retribution. A perhaps more striking example is provided by the allegations against former prime minister Józef Oleksy. After the charges for collaboration with Soviet intelligence in December 1995, Oleksy resigned as prime minister under public pressure. Although his ratings in public opinion polls dropped considerably, three days later he was elected chairman of the SdRP before legal proceedings against him were discontinued. In this vein, Kuroń and Modzelewski rightly assessed that the problem 'was not particularly the innocence or guilt of Józef Oleksy'.[13]

In Michnik's account the ritual and violent character of other moments of rupture in Polish history discard voluntary or rational action while, rather, stressing the importance of imitation. The above evidence casts doubt on arguments that see lustration as a philosophy or the result of a certain anti-communist ideology. There is almost a sequence of 'wars', replicated by imitation. The war at the top followed the logic that any participant group wanted to clean its own image of an idealized, pure and spotless Solidarity I from the dirty hands of its adversaries. These wanted to seize hold of the same image that – in their opinion – was equally pure and idealized and needed to be defended against the others' grip. This first war at the top was followed by a second, the falling asunder of Lech Wałęsa's camp in the wake of the presidential elections (Michnik, 1995:295–301). Along similar lines, two civil wars of tradition have been identified. One of them – the old war between post-communists and their former adversaries – is being fought out on a broad scale. The second is regarded as more civil or internal (*bardziej domowa*). It wages between the different currents of the former anti-communist camp (Paczkowski, 1996:19). This assessment dovetails into Girard's understanding of mimesis. Imitation is an unconscious and inevitable behaviour in a crisis situation. A good illustration of reciprocal mimesis is given by Piotr Sztompka, who described institutional distrust in economic areas by the following behaviour of investors in the stock exchange: 'Investors seem to rely on the wildest rumors and exhibit a pervasive suspicion of all official pronouncements, statistical data or economic prognoses. They are pushed and pulled by blind imitation of others and by the herd instinct which results in alternating waves of enthusiasm and despair.'[14]

The peaceful consensus at the round table and the absence of rigid lustration laws such as those in Czechoslovakia made commentators declare the demise of de-communization, induced by a rational rather than morally guided abdication of historical memory (Holmes, S. 1994). After long controversies, the *Sejm* in April 1997 passed a bill requiring all top officials and candidates for political office, including the president, to disclose their ties with the former intelligence services. Under the auspices of the new post-Solidarity coalition, de-communization has become a central policy. However, the importance of lustration is not primarily a problem of the judiciary. As the procedural aspects of justice, factual proofs, and final retributions lose importance, purges have after all a symbolic nature.

The symbolic nature of lustration is supported by the scarcity of effective proofs. A notable indication is the transparency in the Ministry of Internal Affairs up to spring 1990. For several months an unknown number of Russians bustled in the building, assisted by functionaries of the Ministry (Karpiński, 1996:9–10). Furthermore, lustration is thwarted by the destruction of documentation on pre-1989 secret service activities. Such suppositions are not only put forward by SLD members like the *Sejm* deputy, Dziewulski, who claimed that 60 to 80 per cent of dossiers were destroyed, but are shared by 'anti-communists' like former Minister of Interior Andrzej Milczanowski (Grajewski, 1996:12). The 'crime against documents' has indeed mushroomed in Poland. Many academics are convinced of the implication of corruption and the destruction of documents. Data collected from the Statistical Yearbook show a considerable upward trend in the destruction of documents. Moreover, perception of moral guilt is very high in Polish society.[15] In terms of legitimacy, perception matters more than 'reality'.[16] An example is the scepticism of public perception about the regularity of the proceedings against Józef Oleksy. More than half of the polled population did not believe that the 'Oleksy matter' had been reliably clarified.[17] Similarly, over 60 per cent of those polled believed that the proceedings against Oleksy were not free of political pressure. Advocates of this opinion were mostly close to the post-Solidarity camp.[18]

Moreover, the issue of lustration is embedded in a 'culture of distrust'. 'Trust appears to be the most rare of social resources. The culture of distrust seems to be deeply embedded. Once the decay of trust reaches this cultural level, distrust becomes contagious and self-enhancing.'[19] In this vein, the implementation of the lustration law was impeded for a long time by the distrust of the judiciary towards the lustration procedure. For over one year the lustration court could not start working, because it was not possible to find 21 judges to serve on the court. The reasons for widespread suspicion among judges to volunteer were alleged procedural vagueness, the incompleteness of files, and the fear of being associated with a political option. Despite some recent improvement, the standing of judges in Poland has traditionally been low. Such a politicized position is all the more dangerous in Poland's politically volatile environment (Patora, 1997; Grabowski, 1998; Pietkiewicz, 1998).

Yet several indicators show that Poles have moved away from the idealized image of 1989, as they are more keen on submitting state functionaries to a process of lustration. The increasing desire for de-communization is also perceptible in public opinion polls, which have marked a considerable rise in advocates of lustration in Polish society. Between June 1994 and December 1997 the number of those favouring procedures of screening for adherence to the Secret Services rose from 57 to 76 per cent.[20] A conviction of unanimous attribution of guilt is absent for lustration as a political project. On the scale of legislation or of concrete political accountability, lustration has turned out to be practically undecidable. 'The symbolic nature of such acts follows clearly from many public statements of those who are against tolerance . . . In all probability, none of those formerly in power will be jailed in Poland.'[21]

Michnik conceived of charges against presumed agents in post-1989 Poland as equivalents to anti-communism or expressions of a 'lustration philosophy' (Michnik, 1995:293–4). The sweeping and indiscriminate impact of lustration after 1992 proves that differences are blurred. Not by chance, these 'vortices of Jacobinian decommunization' targeted not so much protagonists of the former regime, but rather, putative 'agents' in Solidarity, against whom the Minister of Interior acted in the style of a Grand Inquisitor (Krzeminski, 1993:190). By contrast, an optimistic outlook on the end of de-communization has suggested that the politics of rage and irrational scapegoating had few chances to become dominant in post-1989 politics (Holmes, S., 1994:36). The unresolvable problem of guilt and retribution in the Polish de-communization makes a strong case for the continuity of sacrificial crisis in the Polish drama. Lustration means 'the performance of an expiatory sacrifice

or a purificatory rite'.[22] What matters most is the potentially contagious character of accusations of every kind, against everybody
and under a myriad of reasonings. In the wake of the lustration
law, the zeal for revenge, purging, and cleansing has become stronger,
quite in analogy to France in 1944, where reciprocal attributions
of guilt were rampant (Judt, 1993). The fear that 'governments may
become addicted to witch-hunting or scapegoating, and may resort
to ever more indiscriminate use of such practices as a solution to
all kinds of political problems'[23] has been partly fulfilled.

There is clear evidence that complicates the reading of de-
communization in post-1989 as a policy to be implemented by any
political force. The point is that the creation of normality by the
thick line actually prompted opposite results. 'The unusually characteristic trait of the Polish transformation was that the renouncement
of the communist party on responsibility was not accompanied by
any – voluntary or compulsory – attempt of settling accounts: its
judgement or its naming.'[24] Such a lack of discontinuity has reinforced the continuity of a second reality of memory which has
been quite typical of recent Polish history. In his remarkable essay
'The Shadow of Socrates', Adam Michnik claimed that at the cradle
of Polish modernity there was a murder and a scandal. The former
issue concerns the assassination of Gabriel Narutowicz, the first
president of the Second Republic, in 1922. He was shot by a fa-
natic of the Polish Right after a campaign of defamation had been
waged against him. Second, the publication of Stefan Żeromski's
novel 'Early Spring' (*Przedwiośnie*) provoked a huge scandal. In his
novel Żeromski, actually a patriot and advocate of Polish independence, disclosed the dark sides of the Second Polish Republic. After
1945 the communists defamed the memory of the Second Republic. Probably as a reaction against this de-historization, the Poles
glorified it. The collective consciousness of the Poles completely
repressed these two founding events; hence the truth about the
pillars of the new order were hidden. In Michnik's words, Poland
had a 'corpse in the basement' (Michnik, 1995:378).

The supposed rupture in 1989 would have provided a unique
occasion for a cathartic moment in the Polish drama. What is more,
this need for purging had been looming large throughout Polish
post-war history. In 1996, the Polish writer Gustaw Herling-Grudziński
related for the first time a story that had happened 40 years earlier. In 1956, shortly after the Polish October, Jerzy Sawicki, the
famous Public Prosecutor in the Nuremburg Trials, visited Herling-

Grudziński in his Italian exile. He had come on behalf of the Polish government to learn about the means by which *épuration* was achieved after the fall of Italian fascism. Sawicki's motivation was that sooner or later the communist system would break apart and one had to prepare for the settlement of accounts with the past.[25]

It seems safe to assume that clear-cut policies of retribution or disqualification are not the core of the image of 1989. Rather, it is the fervent reciprocity of accusations without clear attribution or proof of guilt which makes any permanent attempts at cleansing rather fruitless. The question for transitional justice was politicized. 'So in the absence of an agreed, public, legal procedure, Poland has not enjoyed a Spanish-style consensus but bitter, recurrent mud-slinging and crude political exploitation of the files.'[26] The politics of accountability, or lustration, are the most acute example of the inability to purify the post-1989 conditions by a cathartic purge.

> It is not enough to change street names and – in the manner of a ritual murder – to eliminate a historical personality from memory for the sake of exalting another. It is not possible to return to normality by a new (regular, continuous) ritual murder and scandal. Anyhow, as long as the first murder and scandal of modern Polish history are not deciphered, we will be slaves of history, banned into the subconsciousness.[27]

The Polish predicament is perhaps elucidated by a comparison of two ruptures which Germany experienced in the twentieth century. While Germany's basic economic and societal institutions survived after the Second World War, the trial against the main perpetrators of Nazi crimes and the purges against the main exponents of its apparatus entailed a rupture with the abnormality of pre-1945 (Herz, 1982). As argued there, West German self-blame and moral guilt was canalized into an 'acquiescent political culture' which led to a political convergence, while in East Germany nostalgia for the 'old system' keeps up a high politicization and moral ambiguity (Offe, 1997:174–5). Even if de-nazification was incomplete and the main-stays of National Socialism were continued in the form of newspapers, periodicals, and books, the German drama (Krockow, 1992) experienced a cathartic moment. Nazi followers on a broad scale withdrew from politics, a fact that left little potential for a politics of indiscriminate accusation. Continuing with the comparison with Germany, the situation in post-1989 Polish politics rather resembles post-1918 than post-1945 Germany. In the aftermath of the First World War, the stab-in-the-back legend attributed guilt to the home front that abandoned the German army and caused its final defeat. In the instability of the Weimar Republic, this legend was used not only in political discourse, but became a major mechanism of distrust towards democratic institutions and for the persecution of presumed traitors to the fatherland. 'The year 1918 meant neither an absolute rupture nor a complete regrouping of the political forces.'[28] By contrast, '1945 left very little leeway for the lie about a stab in the back' (Bracher, 1970: 469–88). Although the preconditions were quite different, post-1918 Germany and post-1989 Poland share a common feature. By accusing the home front in 1918, the attribution of guilt remained undifferentiated and could possibly concern everybody. Drawing a thick line in 1989 could hardly be effective, since the round-table community blurred roles and responsibilities and thus removed any yardstick for attribution of guilt.

Thus, to draw the line under the past entailed the opposite result, contributing to a big blur. 'People of the leftist wing of the former Solidarity opposition did not grasp how menacing it is for Poland to leave this question – the judgement of communism – undecided. This is the result of the conviction that fundamentally nothing bad had happened in the course of the 45 years and that nobody was responsible for it.'[29] In turn, lustration has become a proxy for the search for scapegoats.[30] 'But the Polish attempt to follow the Spanish example did not work as it did in Spain. Within a year, the issue of the communist past had come back to bedevil Polish politics, and continues to be used in a messy, partisan way, with ill-documented accusations being made about past collaboration with the communist authorities.'[31]

By arguing this, however, caution is necessary in two regards. The round-table community blurred accountabilities but made a peaceful end of communism in Poland possible. Furthermore, a violent end of communism is not the same as a catharsis.[32] As the Romanian case shows, the dramatic and violent events of late 1989, such as Ceauşescu's execution, did not bring about a cathartic e ffect or an acquiescent political culture (Guruita, 1998). Rather than refute our argument, the Romanian case supports the view that continuities in Poland's transition are relational and oriented towards utopian images. The predicament of the politics of lustration in Poland is located in the utopian nowhere of the rupture-point of 1989. In turn, the attribution of guilt and the identification of the guilty become unbounded.

Politics of reform and the ritual of change

Indecisive lustration links up with ritualized patterns of change which reflect the search for the initiation-point of transition. In one typical statement of Lech Wałęsa's this sounded as follows: 'Nothing has yet been done because you have not given me the chance to do anything. I promised a radical change and I will keep my promise as soon as it proves possible, as soon as I gain enough power to fulfill the nation's real intention.'[33] In the mid-1990s there was a widespread feeling in Poland that the endeavour to come to terms with the changes, to arrive at normality, had failed. In many respects, it is not the consolidation of structures but the recurrent appeal for changes and reforms that stands out. Tackling the second wave of reforms, for prime minister Jerzy Buzek, there was no doubt about the need to make up for lost time.[34]

An analysis of the emerging middle classes has argued that 'there is no doubt that there are relatively more admirers of change among the three middle classes, whether old or new: the class of skills, the class of knowledge, and the class of money'.[35] This point is particularly interesting because the Polish people's expectation of discontinuties in 1989, to a large extent, addressed the Solidarity elites. As a consequence, in post-1989 Poland it was the very reformers of 1989 who, in the following period, pushed for further reforms. They have invoked change in virtually all areas of social and political life. Perhaps most striking in this regard was Lech Wałęsa's appeal for an 'acceleration of reforms' (*przyspieszenie reform*) in early 1990. Two main political alliances with affinity to the post-Solidarity current promoted the zeal for change in their names. The first one was the 'Non-Party Bloc for the Support of Reforms' (BBWR), set up in 1993, and the second, founded by ex-prime minister Jan Olszewski in 1995, was baptized the 'Movement for Poland's Reconstruction' (ROP). In the light of the chaos in the Polish party system after 1990, 'the presidential campaign of 1995, while aggravating its sources, made evident only the need for changes'.[36] An indication for this conjecture is Jacek Kuroń's electoral campaign for the 1995 presidential elections. He presented himself under the slogan, 'It's time for a change'.

The key points of an analysis of political discourse exemplified by a speech by former prime minister Jan Olszewski and a declaration by the Catholic bishops of Poland bear common attributes (Kowalski, 1993). Both documents are 'exemplary instances of the rhetoric deployed to invoke the natural and to condemn the unnatural' . . . 'The rather violent notion of "breakthrough", another commonplace of current political discourse, is invoked in both fragments to suggest that the inauguration of the new era requires a spectacular break with the past.'[37] In turn, the Catholic Church was not at all satisfied with the changes brought about by the transition of 1989. Subsequently, the Church became the herald in criticizing the ravages of permissiveness induced by Western liberalism.

The conjecture on the missing rupture-point as the main cause for the politics of reform seems to be confirmed if the changes in post-1989 Eastern Europe are cross-checked by a look at the beliefs of the main social philosophies and their stance towards Eastern Europe (Hankiss, 1994a: 534–9). In this vein, conservatives would argue that 1989 did not bring about a real change in East Central Europe. In turn the Social Democrats warn that the lack of a social contract may abort the whole transition process. The crucial pattern, namely distribution, was ruthlessly disrupted by the invasion of the forces of the market. Since then no new rules of the game, no new distributive patterns with any charity or legitimacy have emerged. Finally, in the view of neo-Marxists, the West paralysed these societies by enforcing a neo-liberal ideology on them, making a second revolution the only solution to the impasse. The nationalists 'think that the long-expected change of regime has not taken place'.[38] It comes as no surprise that four of the five approaches presented here are to various degrees unhappy with the situation and advocate a fresh start. While only a liberal interpretation would draw a favourable picture of the transformation, one important reservation must be made. Western liberals watching the East usually produce positive accounts without being aware of the state of liberalism in Eastern Europe. Jerzy Szacki put it perhaps most clearly by defining liberalism as utopian, in so far as it is 'incongruous with the state of reality within which it occurs'.[39] In this vein, Szacki also pointed out that the catchphrase 'return to Europe' 'does not refer (except for Czechoslovakia, perhaps) to those things that today's liberals most often have in mind: rights of the individual, liberal democracy, the free market economy, etc.'[40] The continuous appeals for change seem conceivable only in a situation where no initiation of transition in Poland is being felt. 'If Poland was experiencing a postcommunist political crisis. . . . [it meant] the more things change, the more they stay the same.'[41]

Furthermore, there are those stereotypes which see Solidarity as the absolute representative of Polish society. It is assumed that it reunites stable and traditional values such as the Catholic religion and the national identity. Finally, Solidarity is considered to be the driving force behind the reconstruction of Poland's nation and society (Frybes and Michel, 1996b:78). By the same token, these stereotypes have been mirrored in certain myths about communism. Among these are the definition of communism as a totalitarian and repressive system that was imposed from outside and was alien to national and European spirit.

The politics of change and reform also apply to unfinished identities, shifting self-images, and the status-reversals of political parties. Chapter 5 has dealt with the status reversals after the shift in power in 1993. Moreover, the round-table community has allowed post-communist parties to forge an image of their own past (Roszkowski, 1997). Generally, post-communists have been disqualified for the allocation of party assets in private firms since the beginning of privatization at the end of the 1980s.[42] A law on the restitution to the state of PZPR[43] property prior to 24 August 1989 was not effective, since the assets were shifted from the post-communist Social Democracy (SdRP) to private companies. Still, several lawsuits charged the SdRP for the illegal disposal of former PZPR property. Despite a number of verdicts, the SdRP has failed to meet its obligations, also taking advantage of its government position (Roszkowski, 1997:14). A similar charge against the former communist trade unions OPZZ has not been effective either. The OPZZ are supposed to return financial assets to the Solidarity trade union that were withdrawn from the latter in the wake of martial law and assigned to the OPZZ in 1984.

In the 1990s, the return of successor organizations of the communist parties to power in different parts of Eastern Europe was initiated by the victory of the post-communist alliance between the SLD and the PSL in September 1993. This trend was continued with the victory of Aleksander Kwaśniewski in the presidential elections of November 1995. Along with this there was also a status reversal in party politics. In the wake of their victory in 1993, the post-communist parties were widely regarded as modern Westernizers. They were keen to implement rules of democracy and capitalism, adhered to market reforms and privatization and propagated the speedy integration of Poland into NATO and the European Union (Drweski, 1995:11). Accordingly, the SLD–PSL coalition was mistakenly self-labelled as a leftist one. In Marxist terms, it rather represents a 'bourgeois-proletarian-peasant' coalition which attempts to merge the 'European' rhetoric of the SLD with the national xenophobia of the PSL (Roszkowski, 1996:9). On the other hand, Solidarity has become the representative of rightist, conservative, nationalist, and Catholic values. Their shift in political subject-matter and international reputation accounted to a certain extent for a reversal of roles, which made Solidarity appear backward in comparison to the modern, Western-oriented post-communists.

The distinctive feature of the situation in Poland is therefore the existence of a larger number of parties with different combinations of policy characteristics. This has made the emergence of anything like a coherent party system a slow and uncertain process. The endeavour to establish a party system links up with the experience of Solidarity. Contrary to its high and quickly changing differentiation in party organizations, the emerging party system has not achieved any establishment of clear differences in policy terms. It is striking how parties of such a different origin as the liberal and post-Solidarity Freedom Union and the post-communist SLD have similar attitudes as regards their economic policy and their stance of institutional allegiance with the West.[44]

Such a malleability of identities comes along with the lack of normativeness, and moral confusion (Kojder, 1998; Sztompka, 1998). A good example for quickly changing identifications with symbols of the past is displayed by sympathies towards two personalities of Poland's most recent past. A former Soviet-Polish spy in the United States, General Marian Zacharski was imprisoned there for life in 1981 and was exchanged four years later. Colonel Ryszard Kukliński, at great personal risk, had provided the United States with blueprints for the imposition of martial law in 1980. This move apparently played a crucial role in averting a Soviet intervention in Poland. In Poland, Kukliński was sentenced to death in absence. This judgment was commuted to 25 years of prison in 1989. In the 1990s, public opinion polls showed that many Poles regarded Kukliński as a traitor, while they consider General Jaruzelski a patriot who vindicated the introduction of martial law by having avoided a military intervention by the Soviets (Pasek, 1997:21). After the withdrawal of the charges against Kukliński in 1997, he visited Poland in 1998 and was given a hero's reception. Interestingly, it was due to the support of president

Kwaśniewski and Leszek Miller, interior minister at the time, that Kukliński was freed from the treason charges (Michnik, 1998). Conversely, Lech Wałęsa promoted former o fficers from the Security Office (UB), while he discharged a former UB-officer who had collaborated with Solidarity and therefore was sentenced to prison before 1989. Wałęsa's argument was that he had committed treason against the Security Office and, therefore, was not trustworthy. As president, Lech Wałęsa ordered the dismissal of Adam Hodysz, a former UB officer and Solidarity collaborator, from his post as captain of the State Defence Office in Gdańsk. On the other hand, he promoted four ex-colonels of the UB to generals, of whom one had been active in anti-Solidarity investigations.[45]

The modalities of political conflict between post-communists and post-Solidarity are quite telling about the ritual of change and the continuous effort for reform. As the rupture-point in 1989 is missing, the image of 1989 opens up with shifting identities of the characters on the political scene. Second realities remain the central anchor-points for the expectation of discontinuities. However, discontinuities are mainly expressed in images, while self-images or roles are constantly being changed or readjusted. Like the initiation of transition, its desired end is missing. Two examples should be sufficient to cast some light on this point. For almost eight years after the collapse of communism, Poland was governed according to a legal framework derived from an amended and revised constitution that dated back to the Stalin era. 'The shock-therapy of 1990 was clearly unaccompanied by a similar therapy in the legal-constitutional realm.'[46] Similarly, the affair of Oleksy – regardless of his guilt or innocence – made clear to the Polish public that the People's Republic has not definitely finished (Marciniak, 1996:121). 'This problem of categories is especially acute in Eastern Europe, where for nearly fifty years collective national identity was in large measure determined by the nature of one's relations with the Soviet Union . . . since 1989 all that is gone (and consigned to a limbo between history and memory whence it will only be retrieved with difficulty).'[47] A reversal of the Polish drama would have introduced the *dénouement*, it would have unravelled the good from the bad, the right from the wrong. In post-1989 Poland, the reversal is only one of roles[48] abolishing degrees and differences. As Gustaw Herling-Grudziński put it: 'The blur was the fruit of the round table. It is unquestionable that the round table was necessary as an instrument to avoid bloodshed. However, a normal procedure of negotiations, respect for mutual distance, was converted into an orgy of fondling, an atmosphere of "we love each other" or "Pole with Pole".[49]

As can be derived from the foregoing considerations, many attempts at normalization in post-1989 Poland intimate the continuity of a considerable gap between the first and second reality. It would thus be too shortsighted to limit the continuity between pre-1989 and post-1989 Poland to one of former elites in key positions in state and economy. 'Not only the emerging political system, but also the emerging political culture are supported by blurred fundamentals.'[50] It seems much more adequate to locate this problem in the almost futile effort to consolidate, to initiate the envisaged stage of change. In Pareto's terms, the behaviour of elites in crisis situations are subjectively distorted as they are believed to be motivated exclusively by scientific reasoning.[51] While the subjective assessment of political elites may recognize 1989 as the yardstick for change and normalization, quite a few central processes in politics and society indicate that Poland's transition lacks both a beginning and an end.

> One of the striking features of the Polish systemic transformation is, so to say, its intangibility, its complete invisibility – the result, I dare say, of the lack of any clear-cut landmark marking the end of one epoch and the beginning of the next one, the difficulty in indicating one, specific event which has impressed itself sufficiently strongly on the life and awareness of the public. . . . The political community's failure to complete the ritual of transition . . . has made it possible for opinions, which are not so much different as mutually inconsistent and delegitimizing . . . to coexist in public.[52]

Like pre-1989 Poland, post-1989 Poland is trapped in a liminal condition, when the institutional remainders of communism have been widely dismantled but new utopias simply cannot be re-aggregated.

Traditional values and symbols are abandoned and relayed by new values, represented by economic dynamism. Rapid changes have made the memory of Poles dwindle. A genuine state of transition exists, in which Poland is before the door of Europe. The high speed of change has deprived Poland of many historical roots and references to the past. There is, however, no clear idea where these changes will lead to. A circular spiral of changes dispenses with any beginning and any end. Authors such as Leslie Holmes argue that only a strong state can provide for more stability to the region (Holmes, L. 1997c). Yet distrust of the state and public institutions remains very high. The effects of the society of distrust include a high disposal to emigration as well as critical and hesitating attitudes towards the future. Sztompka's proposals for initiating the reconstruction of trust focus, above all, on two fronts: first, against tentativeness and for certainty; second, against arbitrariness and for accountability (Sztompka, 1996:57–8). As our analysis has shown, certainty and accountability are two values that are largely missing in post-1989 Poland. Although trust in institutions and individuals seems to be increasing (Sztompka, 1998:55), the decreasing approval for integration into European structures also shows that the appeal of one central image in Poland's permanent transition is weakening in turn.[53]

In this regard, one can speak of a vicious circle of normalization.[54]

> While the resolutely anti-partitocratic protest movements had paved the way for democratization in Central Eastern Europe, their persistent residues hinder the process of normalization. What was an asset at the time of mobilization becomes a liability at the time of normalization when uncompromising commitment has to give way to flexible pragmatism. . . . Thus, the change is ridden with tensions. Opposition to interest articulation and party formation finds strong resonance among both ex-movement leaders whose credentials are devalued, and among movement supporters who cultivate the moral idiom of politics and who see the movement ethos as the only healthy guide to political action. To many such supporters the processes of normalization that mark a shift to conventional party politics looks like a betrayal of principles and a restoration of the corrupt status quo.[55]

By the same token, Leslie Holmes pointed to various vicious circles. The cleansing of public office of corruption is in fact more than a mere metaphor. To clear away corruption is absolutely crucial to increase the legitimacy of the state. 'The fight against corruption is one of the most important undertakings in our new world. We must face this problem in order to eradicate it, as it causes not only economic damage but also poisons public trust.'[56] Another vicious circle, according to Holmes, is that 'many post-communist officials are loath to use too much state power in their fight against corruption, for fear that they will appear to be emulating the authoritarianism of their communist predecessors'.[57]

The desire to return to the start

Further indications of a missing cathartic reversal in the Polish transition can be gained from the existing widespread desire for such a
'reversal': the return to the start. The backward turn, with the aim of
reverting to a situation such as that of 1989, is intimated by a variety
of *communitas* situations that have played a significant role in post-
1989 politics. On the whole, I would claim that this desire for the
image of 1989 indicates the missing reaggregation of a *communitas*,
as assumed by Turner. 'There is a dialectic here, for the immediacy
of *communitas* gives way to the mediacy of structure, while, in rites
of passage, men are released from structure into *communitas* only to
return to structure revitalized by their experience of *communitas*.'[58]
As shown extensively in Chapter 2, the Polish case clearly contra-
dicts Turner's ideal-type. Polish politics even as long ago as the pre-war
era were in a condition of permanent liminality; the effects and the
duration of the round-table community were therefore limited and it
could not develop self-sustained new structures. Similarly, the underground state between 1939 and 1944, the reinstatement of Gomułka
in 1956, the rise to power of Edward Gierek in 1970, and the imposition of martial law in December 1981 could not engender stable
forms and structures, let alone predictability. They did not follow
conscious models, but were ad-hoc makeshift – or, in Sally Falk Moore's
terms, situational adjustments in order to avoid the worse. Thus,
experiences of *communitas* reinjected indeterminacy and reproduced
sequences of crises which prolong the state of permanent liminality.
'In new systems in the Third World (and potentially in the "new"
communist systems of Eastern Europe) the crises have not presented
themselves one by one but have come together, each one complicat-
ing the resolution of others. This inability to structure and handle
crises one by one has led in Poland and elsewhere to ongoing system
instability.'[59]

To a considerable extent, the round-table community reinforced
liminal conditions in politics and society. These could be sensed in
the widespread political apathy and non-participation which became
a profound conviction during the 1980s and have continued in
the 1990s (Kamiński, B. 1991:144; Mason *et al.* 1991, Kolarska-
Bobińska, 1994). The demobilization of elites has become one of
the outstanding features in post-1989 Poland.[60] Liminality also points
to the disappearance or the atomization of former opposition
movements (Michnik, 1995:367–8). The immaturity of political elites
is linked to 'relative deprivation in relation to the unrealistic

expectations and promises of the heroic-romantic period which preceded and accompanied the 1989 turning-point'.[61]

The structuring reference-points of post-1989 Polish politics and society have been those images that were shaped and stamped by liminal conditions in the pre-1989 period. In many domains of politics, such as the party system or civil society, the round-table pact could not leave a structuring impact behind. Rather, the round-table *communitas* became one further utopia of national salvation and unity. Hence it was hardly the beginning of transitory community experiences, but represented a further and most dramatic climax of a tendency that had been maturing during 44 years of communism.

In Turner's terms, there is 'normative *communitas*, where, under the influence of time, the need to mobilize and organize resources, and the necessity for social control among the members of the group in pursuance of these goals, the existential *communitas* is organized into a perduring social system'.[62] Such a spirit materialized in the creation of Solidarity's local and regional committees that were hastily set up in order to meet the organizational effort of the electoral campaign in June 1989. This enormous mobilization of human and financial resources was expected to last and to sustain enduring networks as the germs of civil society (Fehr, 1991:266ff.). Their official dissolution in mid-1990 showed how normative *communitas* had petered out.[63] And yet the emerging party system during the 1990s was stamped by recurrent aspects of *communitas*. The tradition of Solidarity governments between 1989 and 1993 and the reconstitution of the August community in Solidarity Electoral Action as of 1996 are indicators that have clearly impeded the emergence of a coherent party system. On the whole, political parties have not only rejected identification as parties or factions, but have also tried to convey an image of broad alliances (Subotic, 1996). In turn, 'the right–left division does not organize the political scene in the transitional period'.[64]

In moments of *communitas*, charismatic leadership is of particular importance. The initial success of the civic committees in the campaign of June 1989 heavily relied on the charismatic role of Lech Wałęsa. 'To become a candidate on the list of Solidarity it sufficed to be accepted by the Solidarity chairman. The electoral campaign was anchored in the idea: Lech Wałęsa and the candidate.'[65] By the same token, the spontaneous regrouping of the post-Solidarity camp in late 1995 was inspired by the short-term revival of Wałęsa's charisma. It restated the appeal of the August community of 1980, and thus became the basis for the reconstitution of Polish right-wing parties around the image of Solidarity. These intimated prolonged attempts at normative *communitas*, 'the attempt to capture and preserve spontaneous *communitas* in a system of ethical precepts and legal rules, something akin to Weber's "routinization of charisma"'.[66]

The greater the disillusionment became, whether with politics, economic reforms or deteriorating social conditions, the more often a settling of conflicts by social contract between state and society has been necessary since 1989. Accordingly, there has been a marked inclination to bypass norm-governed institutions such as parliament (Kamiński, A., 1995) and to settle conflicts by 'pacts', such as the pact on state enterprise, signed in February 1993.[67] Jacek Kuroń acknowledged the utopian character of social contracts: 'The myth of social justice can only stay alive in big social movements. Such movements need a utopia, a vision of social order in which this myth may be realized.'[68]

In resemblance to the pre-1989 period, social bonds or moral cohesion in post-1989 Poland are largely provided by the collective experiences of highly inclusive spontaneous communities. Among these communities one can find those of values or social movements as well as those of religious and national revivals, such as in the mass manifestations during the visit of Pope John Paul II in June 1997. By the same token, political and economic institutions seem to generate increasing solidarity and confidence (Sztompka, 1998:54–5). Yet while the communist regime did not manage to destroy moral cohesion, post-1989 Polish politics are still divided by pre-1989 cleavages as a consequence of the missed breaking-point in 1989.

The spirit of 1989 can be summarized as follows: 'Let us dismiss hatred. We do not want revenge. We are looking for the way to freedom, to replace distress by dialogue.'[69] In this way a new existential basis for a non-divided society should be set. In post-1989 Poland there has been extended and recurrent reference to the round table as a social contract or societal pact. The blur of differences at the round table (Herling-Grudziński, 1996b:13) was continued in the cordial contacts between Adam Michnik and representatives of the old regime, like General Jaruzelski or former prime minister Cimoszewicz (Michnik and Cimoszewicz, 1995). Their relationship became manifest in common TV shows and common articles. It is not therefore unreasonable to discover Kwaśniewski's electoral slogan 'Common Poland' (*Wspólna Polska*) of 1995 in the round-table community. Post-1989 was rather dominated by what Turner called ideological *communitas*, which 'one can apply to a variety of uto-pian models of societies based on existential *communitas*'.[70]

The recurrent appeal to communities may sustain anti-structure rather than support the development of new structures. This applies to the economy and to processes of constitution-making. In particular, the economic shock-therapy was launched in an atmos-phere of common popular support for a radical economic cure.[71] The extraordinary period in the aftermath of the round table makes a case for the continuation of *communitas*. 'At least during the first few months, Poland under the first non-communist government of prime minister Mazowiecki was almost unanimously envisaged as Citizens' Poland – a continuation of Solidarity, no longer in com-bat, but in united efforts of the whole nation to build democratic institutions and a market economy.'[72] Conversely, the economic hardship of Polish farmers at the end of the 1990s has led to a display of nationwide solidarity. The farmers' protests in early 1999 were considered by 96 per cent of the population to be entirely or partly justified.[73] Similarly, the emergence of a political commu-nity clustered around the Solidarity tradition as of 1996 entailed a protracted process of constitution-making. Solidarity managed to work out its own constitutional draft and to gather nearly 2 mil-lion signatures in support of it. As a result, the extra-parliamentary Polish right charged the governing post-communist coalition with illegitimacy and staged a highly contested political campaign over the final draft constitution.[74]

A further utopian model was embodied by a new version of a societal pact under conditions of nationwide community. The hope for consensus did not entirely disappear in the 1990s. 'What is happening in Poland? Fundamentally, there was a choice between a philosophy of "consensus", or the maintenance of the dynamics of disintegration' (Michnik, 1995:294). The general aim of a social contract was to fill the spiritual void with meaning. 'It seems that the strongest argument in favour of a social contract is the wide-spread feeling of hopelessness in Poland today.'[75] The programme of anti-communism was the deepening of the revolution consist-ing of the following aims: to convert society into the owner of capital (*powszechne uwłaszczenie*), to gain control of the state through society, and to replace the former elites entirely. One cannot but agree on the utopian character of this plan (Marciniak, 1996:122). Yet it was the same Marciniak who as an advocate of the 'pact on the state enterprise' made a case for a social contract that would restructure the whole social order. Thus, 'the object of a societal pact must be a fundamental correction of the whole of economic policy. And this cannot be divided into ten pieces ... a new concept of Poland's modernization must be negotiated with society.'[76] These demands point clearly to the utopia of a new social contract which would be based on the anti-structure of a societal community. At its roots is the suspension of differentiated norms, arguing for the bypassing of parliamentary institutions. As Wiktor Osiatyński expressed it, 'For many Poles, the very mechanism of solving conflicts by negotiations and the "spirit of the round table" continue to be dearly held values and guideposts for political behaviour.'[77]

A tiredness with repetitive changes that change little gradually replaced the zeal for reform with a zeal for reconstruction, with the desire to start from scratch. In his inaugural address as prime minister in late 1991, Jan Olszewski argued that his government represented the 'beginning of the end of communism'.[78] Five years later, he justified why his Movement for the Reconstruction of Poland (ROP) refused to take part in Solidarity's Electoral Action: 'Poland needs reconstruction and not reform. We have already had reforms.'[79] The zeal for starting anew is predominant. It sounds like an irony of history when a broad coalition in the manner of the civic committees was proposed as a solution for uniting the splintered opposition. Such a move was advocated under the slogan 'return to the start' (Roszkowski, 1996:18). It is this image of a 'return to the start' which expresses best the missing discontinuity.

The desire to return to the start has become manifest as the backwardness of Polish elites in politics has led to a search for identity patterns. The legacies of the past do not simply influence the present; they tend also to reinject indeterminacy and spawn new utopias. Expressions of national, political, or social unity are largely reserved for moments of *communitas*. In this vein, the continued spirit of 1989 as recurrence of communities evokes Tocqueville's remark on the spirit of 1789 as an emotional and memorable point. '*C'est 89, temps d'inexpérience sans doute, mais de générosité, d'enthousiasme, de virilité et de grandeur, temps d'immortelle mémoire, vers lequel se tourneront avec admiration et avec respect les regards des hommes, quand ceux qui l'ont vu et nous-mêmes auront disparu depuis longtemps*' ('This was in '89, a time of inexperience, certainly, but one also of rapturous enthusiasm, heroic courage and lofty ideals; a time to be remembered forever, to which the thoughts of men will still be turning with admiration and respect long after those who witnessed its achievement, and we ourselves, have passed away').[80] In the Polish case, the image of 1989 bears attributes of a new utopia, as the toothless politics of lustration and the constant politics of reform essentially address a second reality: the desire for a new start.

The continuity of the image of 1989

This chapter has conceptualized the image of 1989 as a non-contingent given in Poland's transition. The prolonged politics of reform and ritualized patterns of change strongly suggest that some expected discontinuities to the pre-1989 period were missed in 1989. It is crucial to recognize that 1989 as the factual end of the communist regime fulfilled in many respects the central expectation of discontinuity in institutional terms. Yet the lack of a starting-point of transition was a consequence of previous repetitive ruptures in Poland's permanent liminality.

As the dismantling of communism occurred on the grounds of an experience of the round-table community, the image of 1989 has reinjected indeterminacy and volatility into post-1989 political life. Short-term equality in a moment of undifferentiation and anti-structure has reinforced the confusion of identities and roles. The image of 1989 is thus to a large extent complementary with the image of the West and that of Solidarity. These too have had a broad and mythical appeal which prefigured what can be sensed as an expectation of discontinuity. Before 1989 this image of expecting discontinuities was nurtured by the very communist regime which regarded socialism as a transitional state to communism. In the 1980s political stalemate, economic crisis, and social conflicts mirrored the state of decay of communist Poland. To accomplish unity with the West, and to achieve a situation in which politics is in accordance with the will of society, were the primordial desires in pre-1989 Poland. Not by chance, the momentary success of an economic boom in the 'second Poland' in the early 1970s and the short-lived moment of *communitas* in autumn 1980 fullfilled this craving for a break.

As has been shown in this chapter, the continuity of the image of 1989 has a double-edged meaning. On the one hand, it perpetuates tendencies towards a way of conducting politics that relies upon identity-creating experiences of communities based on past images and unitary, utopian associations. On the other hand, it has aggravated conflicts in society, as can be sensed in the perpetuation of historical antagonisms and the undecidable issue of lustration. The recapturing of the past expresses a desire to finish a liminal state by identifying with images of utopias as exit routes from communism. The newly won autonomy in 1989 seemed to have liberated Poles from their own past. The continuity of expecting discontinuities which is rooted in a second reality, however, casts doubt on the widespread claim for autonomy. 'Recapturing the past is recapturing the original impression beneath the opinion of others which hides it; ... it is to understand that the process of mediation creates a very vivid impression of autonomy and spontaneity precisely when we are no longer autonomous and spontaneous.'[81]

8
The Continuity of Expecting Discontinuities

Commonly, post-1989 is associated with the expectation of a return to normality. The beginning of normality would be the consolidation of democracy, a further stabilization of economic growth, a gradual exit from the extraordinary: that is, a post-revolutionary phase. Inversely, the rise of anti-capitalist attitudes and the questioning of the new rules of the game would signify the search for a new utopia (Wnuk-Lipiński, 1996:274–5). The assumption of the break-up of 1989 implies a thinking that wishes to end the drama[1] of the disrupted East and West by a return to stability and normality. 'It would be nice to know how the drama of the revolutions of 1989 will end: then the history of these events could be written as a coherent play, with a beginning in the first half of the twentieth century, a development during the cold war, a climax in the late 1980s, an unfolding of the consequences of the climax in the 1990s, and a logically satisfying end at the start of the twenty-first century.'[2] With the advent of 1989 there was widespread hope that the transitory pre-1989 normality would discontinue and Poland would exit into the normality of Western-type structures. This prospect of an exit route opened up in a way comprehensible through a variety of conceptual approaches which relied mainly on expectations of stability. 'Normality is essentially coterminous with high levels of stability and predictability – with well-established and defined patterns of behaviour. After all, this is what norms are.'[3] In turn, normality was defined as the future status quo, to which Poles were supposedly returning after a long, forced separation caused by the Second World War and communism (Szacki, 1991:721).

In a similar vein, one can point to three major possible conceptions of normal politics (Holmes, 1997:337). First, there is normality from the perspective of the West; second, a return to the normal conditions of the pre-communist traditions of these countries; and third, the return to the past of the communist era. These three conceptions of normality are, to a large extent, mutually exclusive. This triad is almost equivalent to what Claus Offe defined as the guidelines for the East German situation.

> Social and political forces that emerge in the aftermath of state socialism are split among three centres of gravity, namely the ('golden') pre-Communist past, the ('better' aspects of the) Communist past. . . . and the 'better future' of prosperity to be achieved through an emulation of Western-style democratic capitalism. There is hardly anything that proponents of the three orientations making up this triangle of forces could easily agree upon.[4]

Normality of the new order is regarded as being impaired by the effects of institutional, mental, social, and political legacies of communism. 'The Leninist legacy, understood as the impact of Party organization, practice, and ethos, and the initial charismatic ethical opposition to it, favor an authoritarian, not a liberal democratic capitalist, way of life; the obstacles to which are (. . .) rather how to institutionalize public virtues.'[5] Such an inheritance would cause a new world disorder as a new way of life. While the first strand is about determination as regards expected results (dependent variables, democracy, and capitalism), the second strand rather derives a future non-consolidation from the determinating legacies of the past (Jowitt, 1992:268).

The standard approaches to normality are flawed by their bias towards dichotomies. Continuities in Eastern European transitions are generally conceived as sequential and evolutionary. In such a reading, communism as a system is followed by post-communism, which will be unique in human history, because communism itself was unique. In a similar vein, the presumed re-communization of Polish politics as of 1993 was followed by an attempt at de-communization in the second half of the 1990s. Any reference to the Western model is linked to the economic or political reality of capitalism or democracy. This sequential scheme focuses on continuities in terms of political outcomes that pertain to normal politics in the first reality.

This book has questioned the dichotomy of sequential continuities by analysing processes such as the jump to the market economy, the war at the top in Solidarity, or the politics of lustration from a triadic perspective. In its first part it has developed an analytical framework in order to grasp the second reality of continuities. The assumed cleavages, such as the antagonisms state *vs.* society, or communist power against Solidarity, played an important role but were subject to long-term continuities such as permanent liminality, mimetic conflict, and backwardness of elites. In these permanent conditions of crisis and the expected redress of crisis, processes of political and social change, such as the emergence of new political and economic order or party pluralism, were determined by the missing rupture-point of 1989 and the malleability of political identities. Part II of this book identified these steady and permanent reference-points as the images of Solidarity, the image of the West, and the image of 1989. Although distinguished in their historical genesis and their significance for institutional politics and ideologies throughout time, these images have been dominant in their impact on political and social identities. Continuities were considered as second realities that rule situations of shortages of legitimacy, welfare, and political stability. As the analysis in this book has suggested, continuities concern the invisible and unconscious realm of political passions. In situations of perpetuated crisis, endangered identities, and the lack of clear-cut belongings, identifications with communities and distant utopias appear to be guiding principles for collective actors. Thus, the continuity of second reality comes close to a circular movement by which Polish elites or collective groups seek discontinuities in a meta-reality but are largely precluded from achieving them.

On the grounds of the analysis that has been conducted throughout this book, normality is not a stable point of expectation in terms of a coherent systemic of political order, but a movement expressed in the recurrence of liminal threshold situations. If we follow Leslie Holmes' fourth approach to normality which would be equivalent to stability, 'the post-communist world is necessarily abnormal, since it has recently undergone revolution, is still transitional, and its end destination(s) remain(s) unclear'.[6] In such a process, elites and the populace are guided by political passions that constitute short-term communities or cherish utopian images as guiding principles of politics.

A great deal of the relevant literature examines post-1989 Poland on the outcome-level of normal politics. Contrary to systemic variables such as democracy, capitalism, or post-communism, my analysis has emphasized the cyclical character of Poland's transition. Continuities in Poland's transition are neither evolutionary nor linear, but repetitive and ritual-like. Several authors have likewise pointed to the tight relationship between the achievement of normality and the pursuit of new utopias as a persistent pattern in post-1989 Polish politics. To attempt an analysis of Poland's transition as a set of selected continuities means to deliberately abridge the view of the reality of complex political and social processes of change, and to locate them in an imaginary second reality. It has defined continuities as a persistent desire to leave the no-man's-land of an in-between state. While images provide for identities and the construction of new political and social structures, they may simultaneously flaw their success. Thus the second reality amounts to the expectation of discontinuities without achieving them.

As I have claimed throughout this book, this is what has happened, to a large extent, in post-1989 Poland. People have lost the framework of a socialist identity without acquiring the status of being a fully fledged peer of the democratic West. New norms and rules have remained widely contested, as is best illustrated in the long-term row over the Polish constitution, low turnouts in elections, a general distrust of institutions, as well as the problem of lustration and the politics of permanent reform. 'The longer the period after the collapse of communism, the more difficult it is to explain why catching up with Western economies is taking so long and encountering so many obstacles.'[7] The utopia-driven suspension in a transitory state of transition is tangible in the importance of feelings like nostalgia and the desire to return to the start. 'The insufficient control, if not the total absence of preparation for the rules of the democratic game, associated with the scope of problems to be resolved could entail a kind of nostalgia, a desire to return, more or less diffuse, to simpler politics.'[8] In this vein, 'to put it metaphorically, democratic reconstruction is currently suspended between nostalgia and hope'.[9]

I have suggested conceiving of pre- and post-1989 normality as a permanent transition. To elucidate the permanence of transition, a reference to Machiavelli is timely here. The collapse of norms and political order in late-fifteenth-century Italy prompted Machiavelli to make his famous plea for resistance against the arbitrariness of fortune:

Nevertheless, so as not to eliminate human freedom I am disposed to hold that fortune is the arbiter of half our actions, but that it lets us control roughly the other half. I compare fortune to one of those dangerous rivers that, when they become enraged, flood the plains, destroy trees and buildings, move earth from one place and deposit it in another. Everyone flees before it, everyone gives way to its thrust, without being able to halt it in any way. But this does not mean that, when the river is not in flood, men are unable to take precautions, by means of dykes and dams, so that when it rises next time, it will either not overflow its banks or, if it does, its force will not be so uncontrolled or damaging.[10]

Here Machiavelli claimed the possibility of controlling the outcomes of half our actions. His main intention seemed to have been to advocate a variable proportion with a fixed minimum (Pitkin, 1984:156). One can locate here the basis of the poignant metaphor supporting the philosophy of consolidating democracies. Prosaic overdetermination, as advocated by consolidologists, implies bringing the spiral of expecting discontinuities to a halt. Elite-centred approaches claim to control and predict fortune. 'And if one examines in detail the sorts of specific events that Machiavelli actually ascribes to fortune, they turn out to be perfectly ordinary (. . .) human choices or natural events of a sort that in principle are rationally comprehensible and often predictable.'[11] This book has made the reverse argument.

I would argue that the continuities developed in this book have been internalized as mentalities and have become an integral part of a Polish national and social habitus. As Norbert Elias showed, the various discontinuities and ruptures in the period after the end of the Thirty Years War shaped a specific national and social habitus of Germans (Elias, 1992). Similarly, non-contingent givens in Poland's transition can best be expressed by a social and political habitus of expecting discontinuities. Collective groups such as Solidarity, political alliances, and the populace have to a large extent internalized the habitus to identify with images of *communitas*. As I tried to show in my analysis, *communitas* in Polish politics and society were not only mental references or invented constructions, but relied on real experiences which came to develop a habitus that perpetuates the desire to pursue extra-institutional and community-based politics. The permanence of transition is not, therefore, primarily a rationally induced process. The habitus of expecting discontinuities aims at identification with images which have produced twofold results, one functional and the other moral and ethical.

First, intimations of market socialism and quasi-democratization in the independent society before 1989 referred to Western models embodying the economically prosperous and politically liberal. The image of Solidarity fulfilled a political function both in 1989, when Solidarity was re-legalized, and as of 1996, when AWS forged a political alliance to topple the post-communist government. Second, identity politics in Poland's transition were loaded with emotional appeals for moral and ethical renovation. Thus the image of the Solidarity *communitas* has maintained the myth of enchanted politics, while the ethos of Solidarity points to a moral crusade against post-communists. Conversely, identification with past images in moments of anti-structure may entail destabilizing effects, as can be seen in the wars at the top inside Solidarity or in the politics of lustration. Although the epoch of anti-politics as practised in the 1980s is over, there are intimations of large-scale *communitas* evoking a community of values, an ethics of non-violence, national unity, or religious revival (Sztompka, 1998).

As sources of identity are based on experiences, they have come to constitute an internalized habitus that is likely to rule Polish politics for a considerable time. This notion and image of *communitas* differs from 'imagined communities' that primarily draw on the invention or construction of communities.[12] Such an identification with images of *communitas* points to the passions of liberty and equality which have been treated in this book under the headings of permanent liminality and mimetic conflict in Chapters 2 and 3 respectively. The cycles of Poland's permanent revolution come close to what Tocqueville has expressed as the cyclical career of the passions for liberty and the constant desire for equality.[13] Given the pervasive impact of second realities in Poland's transition, the cyclical character of liberty and equality tends to prolong the transition. Political crafting, interest-driven politics, and the arrival of a confident political class are thus constantly weakened by images.

On the grounds of the permanence of transition as a habitus of expecting discontinuities, I would like to reconsider the significance of legacies that are understood as 'the past casting a long shadow on the present' (Crawford and Lijphart 1995:172). In contrast to such an evolutionary understanding of legacies, this book has argued that the permanence of transition is not evolutionary or linear.

The images conceptualized in this book were formed on the grounds of short-lived communities and mimetic utopias. They have had a double-edged effect, as they imply a backward orientation towards founding moments and a future orientation towards a utopian second reality. These disruptions have stamped collective mentalities, as can be seen in Solidarity's revival in 1989 and 1996, in the long-term allegiance to the image of the West, or in the pervasive desire to insert a rupture-point in the recent past. Distant 'nowhere-situations' of the second reality have retained their spell on Polish society, keeping it in emotional double-bind situations and thus at very low distance from these images. What actually influences the present is not so much the ensemble of past experiences, such as Solidarity's revolution in 1980/81, the Western model, or the round table. It is, rather, the constantly renewed desire for utopian projects, such as the reforging of the unity of Solidarity or the accession into the European Union at the risk of losing particular features of the national tradition. In many respects, the last words of Thomas More's *Utopia* express very well this mixed feeling of expectations, uncertainty, craving, and indecision. 'But I readily admit that there are very many features in the Utopian Commonwealth which it is easier for me to wish for in our countries than to have any hope of seeing realized.'[14]

An understanding of the habitus of expecting discontinuities has some bearing on the standard methodology in this field. It differs considerably from the concept of path dependence that is inspired by explanations of binding habits, routines, and legacies. 'The true strength of the concept of path dependence is precisely its analytic power in explaining outcomes where strategic actors are deliberately searching for departures from long-established routines.'[15] The concept of expecting discontinuities as a habitus is more modest than path-dependency, because it refrains from explaining outcomes. Yet it appears to be more appropriate, as it offers explanatory power where traditional path-dependence approaches fail. Most important of all, a triadic approach to continuities is not constrained by a historical timeframe, such as the legacies of the past or the path-dependent habits which essentially separate pre- from post-1989.

In order to elucidate this point, let me quickly review some of the flaws of path-dependence approaches before the non-contingent second realities as elaborated in this book. One central flaw of path-dependence approaches, it seems to me, concerns the claim that routines and habits are supposed to be exclusively located in the pre-1989 period. In a path-dependent scheme, the return of post-communist parties into power or the relapse into former practices would be seen as a corroboration of 'mental residues' (Elster *et al.*, 1998:296) of the pre-1989 East European past. Yet it would be too shortsighted to explain the return of the AWS in 1996–7 merely by the attraction of the image of the Solidarity community of 1980. An explanation of the reconstitution of the image of Solidarity needs to take account of liminal rupture-points in post-1989, such as the wars at the top in Solidarity or the end of the Solidarity governments in 1993. When, in the wake of the parliamentary elections in 1993, Solidarity and the bulk of right-wing parties were eliminated from parliament, this was seen as coterminous with the disintegration of the myth of Solidarity. Yet the liminal condition of Solidarity as a political organization ended with the reconstitution of the Solidarity camp in the AWS. To a considerable extent, the emergence of the AWS – although sustained by the image of Solidarity – was essentially stamped by a liminal condition in post-1989 Poland and not by a linear, path-dependent pre-1989 routine. Such a stamping effect through post-1989 rupture-points is perhaps more tangible with regard to the image of the West. While economic reforms and pro-European policies have been pursued almost unanimously by post-communist and post-Solidarity governments, the image of the West has remained a second reality, as catching up has not been completed and perceptions of backwardness among Polish elites and in the population have remained pervasive.

Double-binds are hypothetical by nature but can be extracted from evidence. Thus, I have argued that the institutional differentiation of post-1989 Solidarity in the war at the top, and the institutional regrouping under the heading of Solidarity in the AWS in 1996, strongly relied upon the unity of the image of Solidarity. There would be difficulties in using the duality between backward and forward linkages, as routines or habits are understood in path-dependent approaches (Elster *et al.*, 1998), to explain why and how Solidarity – after its disintegration and the momentary loss of effective influence on Polish politics since 1993 – rose from ashes. By the same token, there would also be difficulties in explaining why a feeling such as anti-communism assumed such a pervasive identity-creating dynamics and institutional impact from the mid-1990s onwards. Similarly, in path-dependent terms it would be paradoxical to argue that the round-table community as a consensual social contract could be causally connected with the missing rupture-point in the transition. Yet what the round-table community did, as argued in this book, was to reinforce continuities such as perpetual politics of reform or the desire to return to the start. Furthermore, path dependence has serious flaws when it comes to explain why the politics of memory in Poland, in the last resort, is not so much about the prosecution of former communists and retribution or disqualification, but rather, amounts to a belated and futile attempt to stage a cathartic purge. Due to several developments in post-round-table Poland, it has become almost impossible to decide the question of guilt. In turn, the politics of memory and lustration may perpetuate a political instability.

This set of considerations allows us to revise certain assumed stances on dependencies such as habits, routines, and legacies. The Polish case provides good evidence for the assumption that dependence cannot be reconstructed as emanating from a linear backward linkage in pre-1989. Rather, as the cases studied in this book suggest, it lies in the dependence on quickly changing double-binds. Hence the most important flaw of path-dependent habits concerns its evolutionary character. Path-dependent approaches are interested in the breaking with the past through the use of an appropriate strategy. Thus, a path-dependent approach must assume that 'starting from scratch' in 1989 is a myth, or is simply unreal (Stark, 1992:20). With cautious optimism, one might assume that the emerging spirit of new institutions is likely to eradicate the mental residues that were inculcated by the old regime (Elster *et al.*, 1998:296). Such a stance reckons that new (post-1989) institutional arrangements, habits, and beliefs are likely to suspend or reverse the binding power of habits and routines that point to legacies of the past. 'We believe that such material and cultural backward linkages – in which newly introduced arrangements serve to relativize the force of legacies and in a way even reverse the temporal structure of causality – are a possible, but by no means necessary outcome of institutional innovations that occur in the transition process.'[16]

As I have argued in this book, the analysis of second realities in Poland's transition provides for evidence that, throughout the 1990s, the habitus of expecting discontinuities has kept mythical images and utopias in high esteem. The particularity of social and political habitus in Poland and in other parts of Eastern Europe is that it has been shaped by many dis-continuities in terms of state sovereignty, national independence, and wars. Examining Poland's transition, one can perceive how the tradition of myth-based politics and the pursuit of second realities aim to discontinue the precariousness of political instability. Thus, the crucial pattern of reference for Solidarity's political leaders in 1989 was not the strategic choice to forge a consensus with the communists at the round table, but the re-legalization of the trade union. By the same token, the return to Europe was not so much induced by interest-driven or rationally induced options for an open society or democratic capitalism, as by a long-term habitus of cherishing the image of the West. Finally, the politics of continual reform, the politics of memory, and the malleability of norms, roles, and identities mirror the dependence on a second reality. Political elites that seek discontinuities find themselves in recurrent threshold situations between two points of reference, the images of the past on the one hand, and the images of utopias on the other. Being caught up in this circular movement, the elites in Poland and in Eastern Europe are not in a good condition to meet the Machiavellian prescription for keeping a check on *fortuna*. 'Only those defences that are under your control and based on your own ability are effective, certain, and lasting.'[17] As shown extensively throughout this book, the capacity of political elites to evade images indicates that the utopian appeal for images of *communitas* are likely to remain central points of reference.

Recent evidence about political and economic developments all over the region strongly suggests, therefore, that starting from scratch has become one of the most frequent formulae. Evidence from several countries in Eastern Europe supports the argument for the habitus of expecting discontinuities as they show a pattern of starting anew. In the Russian case, attempts for economic reform and two deep governmental crises between August 1998 and May 1999 have confirmed repetitive efforts to start from scratch.[18] Such a general desire to start from scratch has materialized under different conditions in many countries that had been regarded as being on the democratic track. The breakdown of the Bulgarian economy, with its disastrous inflation in early 1997, strongly differs from Russia's debt crisis and its insolvency. Anarchy in Albania was caused by pyramid investment schemes, while the Czech economic crisis is largely associated with the neo-liberal policies of former prime minister Vaclav Klaus, and was also caused by his premature resignation. After five years of Vladimir Meciar's rule, Slovakia started from scratch in order to catch up with the fast track for European integration.

In this vein, the de-Meciarizing of political life has become an equivalent of de-communization.

Although the modalities of starting from scratch are attuned to national particularities, one can safely claim that second realities of images, to a considerable extent, bind politicians and people all over Eastern Europe. Thus the framework of analysis developed in this book may be applied to a wider comparative setting in Eastern Europe. One might object to this extension by claiming that Poland's unique quality as a particularly crisis-ridden country which would exclude any extrapolation for more general purposes. However, it seems to be quite clear that the particularity of Poland with regard to other countries such as Czechoslovakia or Hungary is only one of degree, not of principle. 'Poland was, as is well known, more resistant to the Soviet model than any other country on which it was imposed, and the record of Polish communism in power comes closest to a permanent crisis. But it can also be argued that early adjustments enabled the regime to postpone an acute crisis for longer than in the two other [Hungary and Czechoslovakia] countries.'[19]

In the streets of Leipzig and Prague in 1989, but also in Belgrade and Sofia in the winter of 1996/7, scenes of a public happening, a spirit of reconciliation, and mutual forgiveness between opposition and state police, saw the unfolding of *communitas*. These communities were not imagined in terms of the collective representation of social facts: they were largely spontaneous manifestations of an anti-structure provoked by unbearable political and economic conditions. In scope and political ambition, the *communitas* of Solidarity in 1980 differed considerably from that of Solidarity in 1989–90 or in 1996. However, in all three cases, its image had a crucial influence on the reconstitution of its community and the ensuing political outcomes. The *communitas* with the West, as desired before the collapse of communism, was sustained by a deeply rooted identification with Western values, while the first reality of Westernization in post-1989 Poland has fragmented the image of the West.

A state of permanent transition suggests that communist society was driven by the prospective improvement of economic and social conditions. Most importantly, the struggle for legitimacy and societal consensus emerged as the prevailing pattern of political decisions. In this regard, pre-political passions focused on the hypothetical expectation of a second reality.

Concluding remarks

This assessment leads me to some remarks on prospective developments in Polish politics. Predictive efforts have rightly evoked high
scepticism among scholars. 'Any attempt to predict the course of
events in contemporary Eastern Europe is hazardous in the extreme
and highly likely to be somewhat off-course before the results are
published. Apart from the instabilities of the contemporary situation, the categories of analysis are themselves fluid and subject to
change.'[20] Given the highly contingent nature of political and social
change in Poland, such advice for caution is justified. Yet the conceptual design and the content of this book seem to vindicate an
attempt to establish some guidelines of a predictive nature on twofold grounds.

First, the claim for the permanence of transition itself requires
some guidelines of prediction. The methodological framework applied in this book has suggested that continuities consist of attempts
by collective groups in politics and society to base decisions on
hypothetical expectations which are linked to second realities.
However, the reference-points of second realities – the images of
identification – have a historical reality and institutional impact
on the outcome level of the first reality which makes the habitus
of expecting discontinuities relevant to politics and society. Second,
predictive efforts have been made by some authors. Leslie Holmes
has summarized the major future scenarios that are put forward in
the literature (Holmes, 1997a:343–5). The first scenario is that Poland
will become like the West. It assumes a gradual transformation into
a stable pluralist democracy typified by a general commitment to
the 'rules of the game'. The second scenario is that of an authoritarian system, be it under conditions of a democratic, strong leadership
or by military leaders. A third scenario apprehends an essentially
directionless, long-term transition, in which governments change
with abnormal frequency, and keep attempting to change direction. Despite predictive efforts, this book is more diagnostic than
predictive, and aims rather to illuminate the causes for current
problems and to suggest possible scenarios.[21]

This book has developed a theoretical framework for the study of
East European transitions by using empirical material from the Polish
case. An evaluation along critical lines might cause dissent and seem
bleak and pessimistic. Some aspects of post-1989 Polish politics appear
to be ruled by persistent instability. Rather than discouraging a

tentative forecast, I consider this quality of rapid change an advantage in gauging some future trends of development. A critical assessment is all the more justified because critique is something that must not be very fashionable.

> The false prophets are uncritical. They tell their listeners what they wish to hear, in that they express the aspirations of the group or individual in question regardless of the situation. The true prophets are critics, struggling against the violation of elementary principles of morality and justice. Micah therefore denounces those who cry 'Peace!' and foresee good even when the moral conditions of the society warrants no such proclamation.[22]

Politicians and scholars deplore low identification with systemic pillars of democracy and capitalism. The societies and states in Eastern Europe are distinguished by their weakness. What is needed is identity with democracy, a market economy and the state. It seems to me that the gist of this problem, however, is located in the social and political habitus of expecting discontinuities. There is good reason to subscribe to Ken Jowitt's prediction of turmoil over boundaries and identities as constitutive to post-1989 Eastern Europe. Yet Poland's lengthy transition before and after 1989 appears to be not simply the uncertainty of an unfinished system, but a repetitive reaching out for second realities and not accomplishing them. Thus continuities are not mere legacies of the pre-1989 past that influence the shaping of institutions and identities in a post-communist world. Mimesis is 'a process without end or beginning which cannot be but circular: a circle perfectly closed up around itself'.[23] What is impossible to know is the outcome of liminality and of mimetic conflict; however, what can be decided or at least suggested is that the continuities identified in this book will continue to exert a crucial influence on future Polish politics.

In the aftermath of the post-communist return to power in 1993, few observers would have predicted a reconstitution of the political right under the auspices of Solidarity, let alone a coalition between the AWS and the Freedom Union. Since the AWS has assembled some 40 parties into a successful Electoral Action, Solidarity has become a major structuring reference-point in Polish politics and society, both as a powerful myth and as political actor. There is good reason to assume that this influence is likely to remain considerable, although political coalitions and strategic options will be subject to constant change. The habitus of expecting discontinuities will perhaps even reinforce the identification with images, since political elites need to perform symbolic acts in order to forge social bonds with the masses. 'Also necessary is the need to perform spectacular symbolic acts of the type described by anthropologists as procedures of initiation, so that the nation can see that change is taking place at last.'[24] The malleability of political alliances and the constant reshaping of self-images in both camps (post-communist and anti-communist) may remain considerably high.

Given the weakness of the state, political parties, and civil society, and a widespread distrust in institutions, the West will continue to exert considerable influence as a structuring reference-point. This dependence may lead two ways. On the one hand, the West guarantees political and economic liberties and a certain degree of external control for reform processes. Similarly, the Western option is the most viable and promising way to leave the status of a country on the threshold between stable allegiances to Western security structures and dependence on Russia. On the other hand, it may exacerbate disillusionment with the unattainable, and entail a new double-bind between a missionary, universalizing Western Europe and a peripheral and dependent Central Europe. Polish foreign policy, both under Solidarity and post-communist governments, has been focused on access to NATO and the European Union. Accordingly, progress in adapting legal and economic frameworks to European standards has been considerable. Conversely, budget constraints, the pressure on accelerating reforms, and long-term transitory regulations before EU accession may risk the persistent status of Poles as second-class Europeans. At the same time, integration into the European Union may be threatened by what conservative forces consider a loss of national identity.

These concepts share the underlying principle of the liberation of a formerly repressive situation of which the subject(s) in question were victims. As Polish elites seek identification with second realities in order to accelerate discontinuities, these continuities have an arguably double-edged impact. Images in the permanent transition both endanger and stabilize the fledgling Polish democracy. If one were to express it in Machiavelli's terms, I would venture that the continuities in Poland's transition are simultaneously dangerous rivers, dikes, and dams. The obsessive desire for constant change points to the repetitiveness of a circular movement of liberating oneself. The dangers derive from pre-political passions that have guided the search for norms, identities, and structures. The continuity of an identity-seeking second reality suggests that the transitional situation of having left behind stable structures and not having arrived at new structures applies to both pre- and post-1989 Poland. At the same time, the images of the past keep politics in the circle of an imitative habitus of expecting discontinuities. Under these conditions, the future can hardly be predicted as lying in human choices and the rational action of elites.

Taking up Offe's suggestion about pulling oneself up by one's own bootstraps, this book has argued that non-contingent givens of second realities keep political elites and society caught up in the tensions between the recapturing of the past and utopian images for the future. Poland's permanent transition shows a highly emotional dependence on these images. In many respects, Poland and Eastern Europe as a whole suffer from the circularity of double-binds, where high exposure to dangers heightens the emotivity of human responses. The high emotivity in a situation of fear and insecurity lessens rational and realistic assessments, which provokes anew a high emotivity of response, and so on.[25] Lack of normativeness, ethical norms, interest-driven politics, and rational economic behaviour are sustained by backward-oriented and weak elites. Lustration addresses a non-event combined with a potentially boundless number of alleged scapegoats for it.

The images, however, have had a considerable ideological and institutional impact on post-1989 reality. The argument of the permanence of revolution or transition has already been made elsewhere (Curry and Fajfer, 1996; Poznański, 1996). In the most recent and elaborate study on institutional change and economic growth in Poland, an evolutionary approach suggested that the transition in Poland has stretched over more than two decades starting in the 1970s and is still far from being finished (Poznański, 1996). 'In any case it is practically impossible to identify the reasons why the transition process is such a long one, as there are no other cases with which the changes taking place in Eastern Europe could be compared.'[26] My understanding of transition should be separated both from the fashionable 'transition to democracy' and from transitional post-communism as an abnormal state of affairs.

Although the concept of transition has had a brillant career and has developed into the proto-science of transitology, the concept as such has been under attack since the early 1990s (Stark, 1992;

Stokes, 1997:201f.). I have argued that transition as a concept must not be dropped. However, in order to understand the vicious circle of transiting without end in Eastern Europe, political passions in a situation of dissolution of order need to be taken as the basis of analysis. As I have tried to show throughout this book, one must not confine the analysis of contingency to the regime transition in the post-1989 period. If the core problem of the political and economic modernization of former socialist societies lies in their lack of any non-contingent given (Offe, 1997:41), this book has proposed a shift in attention of analysis to the mythical second reality, in order to unveil how non-contingent images sustain repetitive changes and thus the permanence of transition. The habitus of expecting discontinuities underlines the significance of identity politics in a process of transition. In order to extricate the yardsticks and models of identity, a study of the modalities of the dissolution of order is needed.

Following the results of the analysis undertaken in this book, there seems to be good reason to debunk the prosaic routine of overdetermination that has become a key variable for the consolidation of democracies. Transition very much seems to be an unfinished project (Elster *et al.*, 1998:271ff.). The party system is fluid and shapeless, the state remains weak, elites are hardly playing their prescribed role, social trust in institutions is low, and allegiance to the West is becoming more and more volatile and contested. The images of Solidarity, of the West, and of the missing rupture-point in 1989 – although their shape and content might develop further – will continue to exert considerable influence on the shaping of political identities and behaviour. Even if their role must not be seen as exhaustive, they are likely to remain central reference-points for institutional change and will determine the choices of political power-holders.

On the grounds of the political and social habitus of expecting discontinuities, however, political outcomes do not necessarily have to be destabilizing. The continuities as examined throughout this book have exerted a double-edged influence on political stability and collective identities. The double-edged role of Solidarity is perhaps the most notable example. The tradition of nationwide community in Solidarity's peaceful self-limiting revolution of 1980–1 played a crucial role for the peacefully negotiated demise of communism. At the same time, the unresolved problem of accountabilities and the continuity of guiding the elites impeded any clear-cut rupture-point in terms of a zero hour. The utopian desire to meet these images has played an important role in preventing a cathartic moment of casting off the past. Thus, Polish politics are characterized by liminal conditions, mimetic conflict, and by a considerable distance from Western democracies in terms of political trust, social cohesion, and stable political identities. Political stability in terms of democratic legitimation and interest-driven economic and social policies are hampered by a recurrent recourse to images. On the other hand, these retain the stabilizing power of a democratic institutional framework, while the myth of Solidarity has created a viable political alternative in government.

Notes

Chapter 1. The Continuity of Second Reality

1 Schmitter and Karl 1994:176.
2 Staniszkis 1991a:127.
3 Pridham and Lewis 1996:2.
4 Marciniak 1996:108.
5 The expectations of GDP growth at 4.8 per cent remain the highest in East Central Europe, and for the estimated inflation rate of 8.9 per cent see *Central European Economic Review*, Vol. 6 No. 10, Dec. 1998–Jan. 1999, 10–11. Since 1992, there have been six consecutive years of economic growth. Growth rates of between 6 and 7 per cent up to 1998 have assured Poland, next to Ireland, the highest growth rates in Europe.
6 Szacki 1995:110.
7 Ash 1996:14.
8 Cited in Wandycz 1996: 9.
9 The Polish *rozrachunek z przeszłością* refers to the settling of accounts with the past and evokes the German *Vergangenheitsbewältigung* or *Geschichtsaufarbeitung*. There is no single English word for either the Polish or the German expression. Ash (1998) suggests it can best be translated as 'treating' the past, 'working over' the past, 'confronting it', 'coping, dealing or coming to terms with', even 'overcoming' the past.
10 Linz and Stepan 1996b:38.
11 O'Donnell and Schmitter 1986:6.
12 Linz and Stepan 1996b:71.
13 Huntington 1991:579.
14 Huntington 1991:579.
15 The German concept *Systemwechsel* (Beyme, 1994; Merkel, 1994) differs from change (*Systemwandel*), as it implies the dissolution of the old structure of political power followed by the construction of a new one. (Merkel, 1994:13) As such, it conveys a more rigid and less processual understanding than transition (Hartmann, 1995:287). Implying the shift to democratization, the dyadic structure of argument is evident here too.
16 Jowitt 1992:264.
17 Stark 1992:20.
18 Ibid. 18–19, n. 4.
19 Ibid. 22.
20 Ibid. 20–1.
21 Linz 1990:157.
22 See an extensive overview of definitions and the development of the literature on transitions and consolidations in Waldrauch (1996).

23 Schmitter and Karl 1994.
24 Offe 1997:41.
25 Machiavelli, The Prince, VI.
26 Ascherson 1981:26.
27 Curry and Fajfer 1996:3.
28 Elster *et al.* 1998:1.
29 Johan Huizinga's classical study of the waning of the Middle Ages provided the crucial insight that social habits of the epoch were inherent rather in that which links them to the past than in the germs which they contain of the future. In this vein, they were not the harbingers of a coming culture, but perfected and concluded the old one (Huizinga, 1955:7).
30 Szakolczai 1996:3.
31 Curry and Fajfer 1996:243.
32 White *et al.* 1994:1.
33 Kamiński, B. 1991:123.
34 Skilling 1989:234.
35 See Hankiss's elaborate classification for the Hungarian case which distinguishes dichotomized criteria for the first and the second society. According to this scheme, the first society is characterized by: homogeneity, vertical organization, the downward flow of power and influence, the predominance of state ownership, the total centralization of all spheres of social existence, priority given to political intentions, the predominance of official ideology, visibility to the ruling elite, legitimation and political acceptance. On the contrary, the second society is characterized by: differentiation, the horizontal organization of an upward flow of power and influence, the predominance of non-state ownership, growing autonomy of economic and social actors, priority of socio-economic factors, immunity to official ideology, partial invisibility to the ruling elite, and ambiguous legitimacy. Furthermore, the second society is sub-divided in areas such as the second economy, the second public sphere, the second culture, or the second social consciousness (Hankiss, 1990:87–104).
36 'The bulk of the Polish intelligentsia joined in an effort to rebuild the devastated country – for patriotic rather than ideological reasons – and many who had shared leftist or socialist traditions of old adopted the Communist faith. (. . .) to superimpose the situation of the 1960s and 1970s on the first postwar decade, and to maintain that communism in Poland lacked any support by intellectuals, would simply be wrong' (Kołakowski, 1983:58).
37 Kubik 1994a:73.
38 Ascherson 1981:276–7.
39 Kuroń and Żakowski 1995:216.
40 Not infrequently it is writers who are most capable of expressing difficult or paradoxical states of affairs. Under the communist regimes, many literary documents were intrigued by how to cope with the different realities which coexisted in communist systems. As Czesław Miłosz argued, the absurdity of communism's reality can only be lived by escape or by the artificial creation of another reality. This desirable different

reality provides harmony and happiness through the swallowing of pills (Murti-Bing) (Miłosz, 1953). In all these analyses, the logic of communist systems points to the existence of a different reality. The first reality of communism is thus based on the self-humiliating practices described by Ketman, which consist of systematic lies. Essentially, Ketman is a habit that mirrors a split sense of reality, praising the hated Russians (Miłosz, 1953:72). Miłosz's work was not only relevant to the heyday of Stalinism. Some decades later, Aleksander Zinoviev (Zinoviev, 1978) placed the penetrating and omnipresent power of communism in the individual. Communism's psychological, semantic, and spiritual control of the smallest communities leads to the constitution of *homo sovieticus* at the most fundamental level of communal life, where the normality of absurdity and the absurdity of the norm dominate.

41 See the appeals of Hungarian party leader Mátyás Rákosi for the strengthening of democracy. His never-ending repetition of a pathological state of being betrayed and of suffering is a good illustration of the reciprocity and interdependence of communism with imaginary democracy. This torment went together with 'a desire for a future happiness and a readiness to serve this purpose' (Horváth, 1998:338).

42 As Gross showed for the Polish underground during World War II, the black economy and corruption were fundamental, as they established a second reality. 'By means of corruption, normative and calculative modes of involvement were superimposed on the alientive mode and provided some social solidarity between the occupiers and the occupied' (Gross, 1979:303).

43 Engler 1992:82.

44 Krzeminski 1993:184.

45 Offe 1991:883.

46 Smolar 1996c:32.

47 Hankiss 1994a:535–6.

48 As Ernst Cassirer argued, scientific thought and mythical thought are very different but are fundamentally in quest of the same thing: reality. 'Myth has, as it were, a double face. On the one hand it shows us a conceptual, on the other hand a perceptual structure. It is not a mere mass of unorganized and confused ideas; it depends upon a definite mode of perception. If myth did not perceive the world in a different way it could not judge or interpret it in its specific manner. The mythical world is, as it were, at a much more fluid and fluctuating stage than our theoretical world of things and properties, of substances and accidents ... Mythical perception is always impregnated with these emotional qualities' (Cassirer, 1969:75).

49 As Tocqueville argued, the French revolution was basically a social and political one which did not destroy religious beliefs (Tocqueville, 1988:114).

50 Szacki 1996:73–4.

51 Nowak-Jeziorański 1995:120.

52 Schmitter and Karl 1995:978.

53 See Lipset and Bence 1994 and Osteuropa 4/1998:408–16.

54 Hankiss 1990:105.

55 Ibid. 107–8.

56 Szücs 1988:322. 'The region that lies between those two models . . . crossed the threshold of modern times amidst newly developing "Eastern European" conditions, but with defective "Western-like" structures. Precisely because of that duality, early modern times produced in this middle region a number of variant models instead of one unified one, as if all the permutations and possible combinations were being experimented with.'

57 'While the dyadic view treats Croatian and particularly Krajina Serbs as passive dupes, vehicles, or objects of manipulative designs originating in Serbia, the triadic view sees them as active participants in the intensifying conflict and as political subjects in their own right, construing (and misconstruing) the dangers of the present in the light of the atrocities of the past' (Brubaker, 1996:72).

58 'The first are of the kind in which people try to control their situations by struggling against indeterminacy, by trying to fix social reality, to harden it, to give it form and order and predictability. These are the kinds of processes that produce "conscious models", that produce rules and organizations, customs and symbols, rituals and categories and seek to make them durable. These attempts to crystallize and concretize social reality, to make it determinate and firm (are called) processes of regularization' (Falk Moore, 1976:50).

59 Ibid.

60 As Cassirer argued, while science restricts subjective qualities, it cannot destroy the reality of subjective qualities such as mythical perception. Arguing that every feature of our human experience has a claim to reality, Cassirer made a case for a three-tier scheme of reality. 'The world of our sense perceptions, of the so-called "secondary qualities", is in an intermediate position. It has abandoned and overcome the first rudimentary stage of our physiognomic experience, without having reached that form of generalization that is attained in our scientific concepts – our concepts of the physical world. But all these three stages have their definite functional value. None of them is a mere illusion; every one is, in its measure, a step on our way to reality' (Cassirer, 1969:77–8).

61 See Sztompka 1998:46.

62 For a recent treatment of this theme, see Glasman 1996.

63 Here one could point to the appeal of emigrants, who in the name of the liberation of the homeland fervently advocated a community of many different social layers and political currents (Wandycz, 1974). In the underground state between 1939 and 1994, the community was the fundamental aspect of maintaining identity as Poles (Gross, 1979).

64 Offe 1991:882.

65 To my knowledge, this is the only application of both theories to an empirical case.

Chapter 2. The Continuity of Transition

1 Poznański 1992:202.
2 According to the Social Science Citation Index, the predominant role of the concept 'transition' is proved through its widespread use in up to 350 titles each year between 1986 and 1989. In 1990 and 1991, there was an increase to about 400 titles per year, while from 1992 onward, the equilibrium point was reached at around 570 titles (Szakolczai, 1996:1).
3 The most notable exceptions are, to my knowledge, the thorough journalistic account by Skórzyński 1995 and the analytical account by Ekiert 1996.
4 This viewpoint was contested by Ekiert (1996:300, 1997) who underlined the crucial role of mass mobilization in 1989.
5 Geremek 1989:1.
6 Huntington 1991:608.
7 See Lijphart 1992:208–9. As Rokkan put it: 'The rising working class wanted to lower the thresholds of representation in order to gain access to the legislatures, and the most threatened of the old-established parties demanded proportional representation to protect their position against the new waves of mobilized voters created by universal suffrage.' Taking recourse to Rokkan, Lijphart stated: 'These logics are equally applicable to the East European democratic transitions around 1990. For Rokkan's "old-established parties" read ruling Communist parties, and for his "rising working class" read the new democratic forces.' See Lijphart 1992:208–9.
8 Michnik 1995:338.
9 Kowalski 1990b.
10 Kowalski 1990a:54.
11 Ibid. 49.
12 Ash 1991:23.
13 Michnik 1983:373.
14 Staniszkis 1991b:237.
15 See especially the conception of a self-governed republic that went 'far beyond the rules of the game in real existing socialism' (Holzer, 1984:343).
16 Kamiński, B. 1991:187.
17 See Chapter 6 of this book for an extensive discussion of the underground Solidarity.
18 Staniszkis (1984:327, n.13) pointed to an October 1981 research survey that revealed the inner differences and problems of identity in Solidarity. While 18 per cent of the delegates to the Solidarity Congress perceived their organization as a trade union and 69 per cent saw it as a social movement, the opposite tendency was visible among the rank-and-file members, of whom 47 per cent perceived Solidarity as a trade union and only 19 per cent as a social movement.
19 See for data: Smolar and Kende 1989:17–21.
20 Cited after Ost 1990:208.
21 Michnik *et al.* 1995:495.

22 Successive national polls showed fewer and fewer people identifying themselves as having belonged to Solidarity, from 37 per cent in 1981 to 22 per cent in late 1985. During the strike waves in late 1988, 47 per cent of those polled declared they had no intention of joining Solidarity (Mason *et al.*, 1991:208).

23 Michnik *et al.* 1995:530.

24 The number of party members declined from nearly 3.1 m in 1980 to nearly 2.7 m in 1981 and to some 2.1 m in 1984, remaining practically stable up to 1988; see the data in Ekiert 1996:318.

25 While the share of workers was at 46.1 per cent in 1980, it went down to 37.7 per cent in 1982. The share of young members (age 18 to 29) was in sharp decline. This cohort accounts for 24.8 per cent in 1980, 11.1 per cent in 1981, and 6.4 per cent in 1988; see Lewis (1988:32).

26 Withdrawal from 'rituals' refers to the withdrawal from party-controlled mass social organizations and the withdrawal from mass participation in elections, both of which are defined as 'highly ritualistic' (Kamiński, B., 1991:176–7).

27 This refers to the elections to People's Councils in 1984, to the Sejm in 1985, and to the Referendum on economic reform in 1987.

28 Staniszkis, 1991a:194.

29 Michnik 1995:134.

30 Ibid. 340.

31 Arnason 1993:154.

32 Gross 1994:181–2.

33 Heyns and Bialecki 1991:368.

34 Bauman 1994:15.

35 The Latin word *limen* can best be translated as threshold.

36 Turner 1969:94.

37 Ibid. 95.

38 Turner 1965:93.

39 Bauman 1994:17.

40 Ibid.

41 Hirsch 1985:10.

42 'Normative void was one of the most painful consequences of the dissolution of the Polish state. People did not know how to behave when they were forced to interact with the occupier; they could scarcely be expected to make decisions on their own. They sought advice frantically, looking for others who indirectly could share responsibility with them, or simply for someone who would tell them what to do' (Gross, 1979:137).

43 Kersten 1991:170.

44 See Kosiński 1977:26–27.

45 Kersten 1991:164. See also Mach 1996:5–11.

46 Cited in Gross 1989:204.

47 Polish Republican Party.

48 Polish Socialist Party.

49 Peoples' Alliance.

50 Cited in Kersten 1991:174–5. In this respect, a joke about communism as a daily life-experience is a good illustration of permanent liminality. According to one version, the participants of a party meeting in a remote district were repeatedly told by the comrade from the Central Committee that communism was already on the horizon. They did not understand the word, but were afraid to ask questions. Back home, they immediately picked up the dictionary, only to discover the following definition: 'horizon – something which the closer we get to it, the more it recedes'. See Szakolczai (1996:13, n.8).

51 Turner 1987:99–100.

52 In the definition of Václav Hável, 'living within the lie can constitute the system only if it is universal. The principle must embrace and permeate everything. There are no terms whatsoever on which it can coexist with living within the truth, and therefore everyone who steps out of the line denies it in principle and threatens it in its entirety' (Hável, 1985:40).

53 Michnik 1983b:105.

54 Curry and Fajfer 1996:3.

55 Turner 1985:121.

56 Kubik (1994a) used Turner's methodology to show the implementation of rituals and ceremonies in official discourse by the Gierek regime.

57 Kuroń and Żakowski 1995:147.

58 Staniszkis 1991a:202.

59 Brus and Laski 1989:33.

60 Poznański 1996:246–7.

61 Kolarska-Bobińska 1994:30.

62 Slay 1994:135.

63 Szakolczai 1996:5.

64 Wandycz 1974:330.

65 Cited in Davies 1981:78.

66 See Foreword by Jan T. Gross in Kersten 1991: p. xiv.

67 Walicki 1997:238.

68 Wandycz 1974:117–18.

69 Kubik 1994b:460.

70 Michnik 1989.

71 Kersten 1996:24.

72 Kubik 1994a:71. See in this regard also Horváth's study of the political psychology of the trickster clown as a paradigmatic feature of communism (Horváth, 1997).

73 Brus and Laski 1989:33.

74 Borkenau 1971:413.

75 Turner 1965:8.

76 Elster 1996:3.

77 Jedlicki 1990:57.

78 Skórzyński 1995:90–1.

79 Turner 1992:137.

80 Gross 1979:291.

81 'Gierek proclaimed that the present problems concern everyone in the

nation, both those inside and outside the party, both religious believers and non-believers, and there is a place for every citizen to resolve these problems.' Cited in Kubik, 1994a:31.
82 Ash 1991:32.
83 Kowalski (1990a:152) defined Solidarity as *społeczność* or *wspólnota*, while Kubik directly used Turner's concept of *communitas* to describe the suspension of the outside-world structures of power in the enclave of the striking shipyard (Kubik, 1994a:191).
84 Kuroń and Żakowski 1995:216.
85 Goodwyn 1991:379–80.
86 Havel 1991:212–13.
87 Cited in Osiatyński 1996:51.
88 Osiatyński 1996:59.
89 Michnik 1995:162–3.
90 Kamiński, B. 1991:160.
91 Turner 1987:95.
92 Cited in Skórzyński 1995:230.
93 Turner 1969:97.
94 See: Skórzyński 1995:227.
95 Turner 1992:137.
96 Turner 1969:127.
97 Turner 1969:132.
98 See Skórzyński 1995:225ff.
99 Ibid. 213.
100 Sewell 1996:871.
101 Wnuk-Lipiński 1996:271.
102 Skórzyński 1995:155.
103 O'Donnell *et al.* 1986:6.
104 Linz 1990:151.
105 Curry and Fajfer 1996:258.
106 Gross 1994:182–3.
107 Schmitter and Karl 1994:178.
108 O'Donnell *et al.* 1986:6.
109 The radicalism applied to modifications of the communist party's rules is reflected in the spirit of Solidarity's programme, whose thesis 1 claimed 'to smash into pieces the organizational structure of the economy, that serves the command system'. The proposals regarding self-management in enterprises of the Solidarity-congress were – despite changes – considered in the Law on State Enterprises of 25 September 1981; see Büscher *et al.* 1983:300. According to it, directors of state enterprises were to be elected by mixed commissions that would work on the principle of open competition.
110 In Graczyk's view, General Jaruzelski tried to accomplish the impossible in the wake of the proclamation of martial law: to reconcile liberal reforms with the communist party's monopoly of power. The introduction of 'liberal' institutions such as the state tribunal (*trybunał stanu*) in 1982, the Constitutional Court (1985), and the Ombudsman in 1987, are thus regarded as hybrid solutions (Graczyk 1997:80).

Chapter 3. The Continuity of Historical Antagonism

1 Ekiert 1996:312.
2 Ascherson 1981:251.
3 Kamiński, B. 1994:1.
4 Wnuk-Lipiński 1996:148.
5 First, per-capita GNP is considerably higher in the easy groups of cases (Czech Republic, Hungary) than in the unfavourable ones (Bulgaria, Slovakia). Second, the two favourable cases are without a significant minority population being present in the state's territory, while the other two countries have considerable minorities. Third, the easy cases have the experience of relatively stable democracies in the inter-war period plus significant industrialization prior to World War II. Fourth, reformist movements in the Czech Republic (1968) and Hungary (1956) and a growing opposition helped to debunk the ideological hegemony of state socialism, so dominant in Slovakia and Bulgaria, arguably the least dissident societies in the Eastern bloc. Finally, while in Hungary and in the Czech Republic political competition, coalition, and opposition unfolded quite well, Bulgaria and Slovakia were for a long time under the rule of uncompromising quasi-monopolistic parties.
6 Despite a great depression with huge drops in industrial production, Poland achieved growth of more than 49 per cent between 1925 and 1937. In comparison, Czechoslovakia achieved 22 per cent, Hungary 35 per cent (Chirot, 1989a:380).
7 Pasek 1997:21.
8 Gortat 1996:89.
9 Ziółkowski 1998:37.
10 The emblematic reform attempts linked to the Prague Spring proclaimed the slogan 'socialism with a human face', which was an attempt to reverse the dehumanizing aspect of Soviet communism.
11 See Rupnik 1988. As of 1968 and the failure of reform communism, Eastern European thinkers took up the term 'totalitarianism' in a different context than it had developed in the American social sciences of the 1950s. In the view of the Eastern European intellectuals, the 'essence' of the totalitarian system lay in the supremacy of ideology as the institutionalized lie. This totalitarian lie rests on two pillars: the destruction of memory and totalitarian language (Rupnik, 1988:269).
12 Mokrzycki 1995:76.
13 Linz and Stepan 1996b:49.
14 See Kuroń and Żakowski 1995:146–7. Between 1972 and 1974 national income increased by approximately 10 per cent annually, industrial production by 11 per cent and real wages by 7 per cent. Interestingly, the opening up towards Western economies led to a drop in turnover of imports from countries of the Council for Mutual Economic Aid from 69 per cent in 1970 to 54 per cent in 1978; see Landau and Roszkowski 1995:148.
15 Michnik 1995:336.
16 Kuroń and Żakowski 1995:97.
17 Meiklejohn Terry 1996:114.

18 Surdykowski 1985.
19 Ibid.
20 Kubik 1994a:147.
21 Kowalski 1990a:76.
22 Ibid.
23 Kuroń 1978:59.
24 Walicki 1988:19.
25 Ibid. 16.
26 Walicki 1997:242.
27 Ascherson 1981:183.
28 Cited in Michnik 1995:398.
29 The June riots in Poznań did not cause the changes in 1956 and neither did the stabilizing measures in the context of normalization. Gomułka would have probably returned to power without the workers' revolt (see Ascherson 1981:77).
30 This comes close to a 'ritualized drama', as exposed by Staniszkis 1984:279ff.
31 Malia 1996:52.
32 This account is based on Gombrowicz's *Gęba i twarz* (*Mug and Face*), printed in an anthology of Polish essays edited by Marek Klecel (1996).
33 Gombrowicz 1996:45–6.
34 See the establishment of PRON (Patriotic Movement for National Rebirth) in December 1982. This organization had little success, as did the citizens' committees of national salvation (OKON) that were set up in the wake of December 1981 (see Mink, 1989:141).
35 Kuroń and Żakowski 1995:147.
36 '*Perché in ogni città si trovono questi due umori diversi; e nasce da questo, che il populo desidera non essere commandato né oppresso da' grandi, e li grandi desiderano comandara e opprimere il populo*' ('For in every city these two diverse humours are found, which arises from this: that the people desire neither to be commanded nor oppressed by the *grandi*, and the *grandi* desire to command and oppress the people', The Prince, 9), and also in the Discourses, I, 4 '*E' sono in ogni republica due umori diversi, quello del populo, quello de' grandi*' ('In every republic there are two opposed humours, that of the people and that of the *grandi*'). Finally, the Florentine Histories III, 1: '*Le gravi e naturali nimicizie che sono intra gli uomini popolari e i nobili, causate da il volere questi comandare e quelli non ubbidire, sono cagione di tutti i mali che nascono nelle città*' ('The great and natural enmities that exist between the people and the nobles, caused by the wish of the latter to command and of the former not to obey, are the cause of all evils that arise in cities').
37 Tocqueville 1981:188. '*L'instabilité de l'état social vient favoriser l'instabilité naturelle des désirs. Au milieu de ces fluctuations perpétuelles du sort, le présent grandit; il cache l'avenir qui s'efface et les hommes ne veulent songer qu'au lendemain*' ('Social instability favours the natural instability of desires. Amid all these perpetual fluctuations of fate the present looms large and hides the future, so that men do not want to think beyond tomorrow').
38 A look at Lenin's positions shortly after the Bolshevik revolution clearly

testifies to the superiority of Western capitalist countries and the need to imitate them in order to stabilize the newly born Soviet Union (Lenin, 1918). The alleged sociological Bolshevik experiment was soon unmasked as a repetitive and destructive form of imitation in the wake of the collapse of the likewise tyrannical Tsarist order (Mauss, 1924–5:174).

39 Dembiński 1991:196.
40 Girard 1988:89.
41 Tocqueville, 1981:188. '*Mais, à mesure que les lumières de la foi, la vue des hommes se resserre, et l'on dirait que chaque jour l'objet des actions humaines leur paraît plus proche. Quand ils se sont une fois accoutumés à ne plus s'occuper de ce qui doit arriver après leur vie, on les voit retomber aisément dans cette indifférence complète et brutale de l'avenir qui n'est que trop conforme à certains instincts de l'espèce humaine. Aussitôt qu'ils ont perdu l'usage de placer leurs principales à long terme, ils sont naturellement portés à vouloir réaliser sans retard leurs moindres désirs, et il semble que du moment où ils désespèrent de vivre une éternité, ils sont disposés à agir comme ils ne devaient exister qu'un seul jour*' ('But as the light of faith grows dim, man's range of vision grows more circumscribed, and it would seem as if the object of human endeavours came daily closer. When once they have grown accustomed not to think about what will happen after their life, they easily fall back into a complete and brutish indifference about the future, an attitude all too well suited to certain propensities of human nature. As soon as they have lost the way of relying chiefly on distant hopes, they are naturally led to want to satisfy their least desires at once; and it would seem that as soon as they despair of living forever, they are inclined to act as if they could not live for more than a day').
42 Girard 1989:13. Most clearly, Girard argued in this direction by pointing out that, contrary to common belief, the war in former Yugoslavia is not borne out by differences, i.e. strong feelings of identity or belonging, be they ethnical, national or religious (Girard, 1996:26).
43 Morawski 1992:23.
44 Kowalik 1993:95.
45 See Kowalski 1990a:28ff.
46 Ibid. 29–30.
47 Girard 1987:299.
48 The historian Jerzy Jedlicki, cited in Kowalski 1990a:68.
49 Brus and Laski 1989:33.
50 Szacki 1995:44.
51 Linz and Stepan 1996b:272.
52 Miłosz 1953:21–2.
53 Hankiss 1994b:119.
54 Such was the case of the New Evolutionism in the 1970s which set out to self-organize social groups and movements and by these means wanted to arrive at the self-determination of Polish society.
55 Kearney 1979:39.
56 Hankiss 1994:118.
57 A mimetic image differs fundamentally from a utopian consciousness such as defined by Kołakowski (1974:24). 'I believe that an essential

part of utopian consciousness is to be found in the following idea: in the imagination of a situation that, whether desired or foreseen, is not only desired or foreseen but conforms to fundamental requirements of human beings; this situation not only realizes what single empirical human beings request but what the eidos, the essence of human kind, requires. Put differently, utopian consciousness reflects the more or less conscious heritage of Platonic structure of thought (in the case of Marx a Hegelian one); this heritage consists of the belief that a certain imagined form bears an essence, something that exists in terms of a higher, even though not empirical reality. This reality is not subject to simple observation but is nevertheless visible, if the earthly consciousnesss manages to be received in a finite consciousness.'

58 Bauman 1994:23–4.
59 As Lewis (1992:56) argued, politics were guided by resentment-driven policy options, the identification of scapegoats and the search for fall-guys: emotional and negative articulation led to the personalization of expression.
60 Gellner 1994:54.
61 Ibid. 12.
62 Weil 1948:32.
63 This credo was exposed by Adam Michnik in the programmatic and practical suggestions for the Polish opposition in his influential paper 'A New Evolutionism' of 1976, cited in Ost 1990:72.
64 See in this context Borneman 1997:23, who argued that scapegoating and the identification of culprits remain central mechanisms of judicial systems in the new East-Central European States.
65 Geremek 1990:103.
66 See Roszkowski 1994:290.
67 See Kuroń and Żakowski 1995:173.
68 Meiklejohn Terry 1996:114.
69 Michnik *et al.* 1995:572.
70 Holzer 1990b.
71 Michnik 1995:339.
72 Offe 1997:199.
73 Ibid. 200.

Chapter 4. The Continuity of Backwardness

1 Schöpflin 1993:5.
2 Feher 1995:61.
3 See: UNICEF Regional Monitoring Report: Public Policy and Social Conditions 1993: 7–8.
4 Kersten 1996:26.
5 Offe 1997:212.
6 Ibid. 185–6.
7 Hankiss 1990:91.
8 Kamiński 1991:6.
9 Such a desire was expressed by nearly 60 per cent of those polled; see Mason *et al.* 1991:216.

10 Bauman 1992a:84.
11 For extensive treatments of Polish economy see Kamiński (1991), Slay (1994), Landau and Roszkowski (1995), Poznański (1996).
12 Kamiński 1991:58.
13 Ibid., 4.
14 Interestingly, the idea of 'Finlandization' was popular among many Poles back into the Congress Kingdom in the 19th century. The Grand Duchy of Finland was a separate constitutional monarchy of which the Tsar was the hereditary Grand Duke. For a variety of reasons, such as Russian power politics and Poland's allegiance to Western religion and culture, to advocate a Finlandization in the middle of the 19th century meant to ignore fundamental political realities (Davies, 1981(II):367–8).
15 Sachs 1994:5.
16 Eberstadt 1990:368.
17 While Polish crude birth rates in 1980 and 1985 were 19.6 and 18.3 per 1000 of population, they declined to 15.0 in 1989 and 12.9 percent in 1993; see UNICEF Regional Monitoring Report (1993), pp.15ff. and p.70.
18 Rates of Polish in-migration into Germany increased considerably during the second half of the 1980s and decreased again as of 1990 (1986:10.981; 1987:15.194; 1988: 29.023; 1989: 26.092; 1990: 9.155; 1991: 3.348) (see Mihalka, 1994:40–42).
19 See Landau and Roszkowski 1995:287–9.
20 Bauman 1989:76.
21 'Intelligentsia' as a term appeared first in Russia in the 19th century. Not limited to Russia, it denotes a small educated class that has a special interest in modernizing society. 'The intelligentsia is a modern secular intellectual elite which, unlike those of the Western nations, has not grown up organically with its society – as happened in the West between the sixteenth and nineteenth centuries – but has been deliberately created by rulers who have set themselves the political task of bringing their countries at forced speed into the modern world' (Seton-Watson, 1964:13).
22 As Bauman (1989:72) put it: 'Karl Mannheim gave the old conception its modern rendition, better attuned to an age of advanced sociological awareness, in the idea of the *frei schwebende* intelligentsia: a loosely knit aggregate of people who collectively and *ex post facto* attain independence from particularizing social determinants, as they draw liberally from all particularized and socially determined categories and hence are not "at home" in any.'
23 Bauman 1992a:85.
24 See Szelényi and Szelényi (1994) and Wasilewski and Wnuk-Lipiński (1994).
25 Cited in Staniszkis 1991a:184.
26 Offe 1991:881.
27 The political engagement was clearly recognized: 'We want to change this system by means of progressive transformations, among which we use parliamentary methods.'
28 Kuroń 1991.

29 Michnik 1995:293.
30 Mosca 1950:147–8.
31 Bauman 1994:24.
32 Kamiński, A. and Kurczewska 1994:149–50.
33 Pańków 1998:200.
34 Staniszkis 1991a:184.
35 Szacki 1995:210.
36 Despite the cultural and historical fascination for the West, 'elsewhere' links up with the island of Utopia, as introduced by Thomas More into political theory. In the Eastern European context, this tendency of pulling 'elsewhere' closer was given a literary monument by Milan Kundera's 'Life is Elsewhere'.
37 Adam Michnik, cited in Szacki 1990:477.
38 Tiryakian 1995:259.
39 Rose 1991:7.
40 Turner 1992:52.
41 Jankowicz 1994:503.
42 Latour 1987:220ff.
43 Commonly, the idea of competition with the West is considered in the light of negative effects for Soviet-type societies. 'If only the Soviet Union were an island unto itself and the outside world did not exist or could be insulated, then, most certainly, far from feeling a need to reorganize and reconstruct, the system would have joyously celebrated its own triumph . . . But the Soviet Union was not an island unto itself. Far from it. On the contrary, it was locked in an ideological competition with the capitalist world, involved in a race for both economic and military preponderance, and for influence in the Third World' (Gellner, 1994:157).
44 Latour 1987:223.
45 Ibid. 10.
46 Turner 1992:52.
47 Post-1989 political elites resembled explorers who imitated models from islands in the West that were comparable to utopias. Thomas More's (1965) classical work on utopia is a treatise that relies on the account of a traveller who tries to convey to his listeners the utopian commonwealth through a distance. This utopia in terms of an ideal-type nowhere is aptly expressed in the words of the Croatian writer Slavenka Drakulić: 'Like other Eastern Europeans, I naively imagined that living in the West automatically guaranteed you a certain standard of living . . . The idea that I could be poor living in the West, perhaps unemployed; the fact that there is hardship and financial insecurity everywhere in the world, was beyond my imagination. If we are all poor here, they must all be rich . . . But the myth of the advantage of living in the West has not lost its power since the demise of communism' (Drakulic´, 1996:41–2).
48 Szacki 1995:44.
49 Norman Davies on the occasion of a lecture entitled 'Eastern Europe: myth or reality' held in July 1995 in Warsaw; see *Rzeczpospolita* 3 July 1995.
50 Miłosz 1953:59.
51 Ekiert 1996:286.

52 Bauman 1989:85.
53 Ekes 1994:55.
54 Staniszkis 1984:137.
55 In the first ballot, Solidarity obtained 252 of 261 available seats in the *Sejm* and the Senate. In the run-off-elections two weeks later, another eight seats were won, bringing the total to 260 of 261 seats.
56 Kuroń 1991:4.
57 Warszawski 1989:8.
58 Skórzyński 1995:223.
59 Warszawski 1989:9.
60 Balcerowicz 1995:204.
61 Sachs 1994:5.
62 Warszawski 1989:9.
63 Mannheim 1992:178.
64 Davies 1981:517.
65 Judt 1993:103.
66 Weber 1980:254.
67 Such a worship is also mirrored in the desire to be in a second reality. 'Post-communist societies from Vladivostok to Warsaw tune in every evening to a culture that is the culture of modern capitalist societies. Survey data clearly prove that the models to Polish TV-watchers are considerably more often the heroes of "Dynasty" than authentic Polish entrepreneurs or politicians' (Kurczewski, 1994:412). In this vein, Polish society shows striking parallels with Don Quixote, who 'trusting in the cultural reality of the chivalrous romance, tries to practise the ethos propounded therein, with the familiar outcome that in the end Don Quixote was ruined by it' (Kurczewski, 1994:411).
68 Joravsky 1994:848.
69 Tarde 1993:37.
70 Rogers and Joung – in 1985:87f.
71 Deutsch 1985:19f.

Chapter 5. The Continuity of the Image of the West

1 Kamiński, A. and Strzałkowski 1994:309.
2 Sachs 1994:5.
3 Offe 1997:38.
4 Feher 1995:57.
5 Staniszkis 1994a:10.
6 Ibid.
7 Interestingly, the social and national habitus of Germany and Poland were interdependent in crucial respects. Thus the needs for integration of the Prussian-German national state in the 19th century were incompatible not only with a solution of the Polish question but also with coexistence with a non-German, Polish population on the Polish territory occupied by Prussia. Therefore, in Bismarck's view, the Germanization of Poles in Prussia was an indispensable necessity of state formation (Müller, 1984:86).

8   Walicki 1988:10.
9   Szücs 1995:26.
10 'Broadly speaking, in eastern rural districts the aim was to nationalize the borderland East Slav population; in the cities and in the west, the aim was rather to nationalize the territory and economic life, by replacing Germans and Jews with Poles in key economic and political positions, and by encouraging their emigration' (Brubaker, 1996:86).
11 'While it was widely believed that Germans could not and Jews should not be assimilated, the assimilation of Belarussians and Ukrainians was seen as both possible and desirable, even as necessary. This stance was mainly caused by a fear for boundaries.' The crucial point about backwardness here is that 'in the eastern borderlands, the contours of national identity were more indeterminate. Between the Poles and Russians lay a vast zone extending from the Baltic to the Black Sea where national movements had developed only in the last few prewar decades, and where incipient national identities, articulated and propagated by a small urban intelligentsia, had yet to acquire a substantial social base among the still overwhelmingly peasant populations' (Brubaker, 1996:98).
12 See Jedlicki 1990:59.
13 Cited in Kersten 1991:51. This declaration, published by the Home Army *(Armia Krajowa)* in March 1944, was entitled 'What the Polish Nation is Fighting For'.
14 Chirot 1995:56.
15 Miłosz 1953:52.
16 Jedlicki 1990:60.
17 Ascherson 1981:78.
18 Offe 1997:196.
19 Feher 1995:64.
20 Miłosz 1953:46.
21 Ibid.
22 Ibid.
23 Despite its narrow margin for manoeuvre, Polish foreign policy started in the wake of de-Stalinization in the USSR and with the national road to socialism as of 1956. 'Abating global tensions fostered a gradual expansion of Poland's Western policies, but always within the parameters of Soviet priorities and limits, especially in all security-related matters. Thus, Poland championed denuclearization of Central Europe (the Rapacki Plan) in 1957 and a nuclear freeze in Central Europe (the Gomułka Plan) in 1964. Poland also took an active role in preparations for the Helsinki Accord in 1975 and in protracted negotiations for the reduction of conventional forces in Europe. Despite a sincere commitment to the alleviation of East–West hostilities, the Polish role was coordinated in Moscow as a component part of Soviet global and regional strategy. Still, the Polish effort to improve relations between the Soviet bloc and the West was in tune with a national search for security in a divided world. Although the politics of détente had a stabilizing effect on the communist order in Central Europe, it also relieved the danger of war and the likelihood of Soviet military intervention' (Rachwald, 1995:130).
24 Hankiss 1990:110.

25 Poznański 1996:96. The share of the CMEA in total turnover increased from 54.9 per cent to 65.2 per cent between 1978 and 1984 (1996:303, n.17).

26 While in 1986, the CMEA accounted for 46.6 per cent of Poland's trade turnover (with the Soviet Union's share at 27.6 per cent) in 1989, the share of the CMEA market was only 35.1 per cent, with the Soviet Union at 20.8 per cent.

27 Economist Intelligence Unit, 4th quarter 1995:25–6.

28 Kowalski 1990:87.

29 Ibid. 88.

30 Kuczyński and Nowotny 1994:249.

31 Offe 1991:880.

32 Among these were the introduction of private property, wage-differentiation, privatization of state enterprises, or the dismissal of workers.

33 See the studies by Borkowski (1994) and Morawski (1994).

34 Cited in Szacki 1994:171–2, n.74.

35 Jankowicz 1994:503.

36 Poznański (1996:106ff.) showed that the dismantlement of the traditional system of state planning and public ownership was carried out largely by the communist party itself. Important decisions regarded the decontrolling of prices for many of the subsidized industrial supplies for farming. 'With one stroke, the Rakowski government abandoned one of the pillars of the communist strategy, i.e., control over agriculture and protection of consumers against inflation for foodstuffs' (1996:107). 'Another pillar of communist economics – negotiable subsidization and job-guarantees for industrial enterprises – was abandoned by Rakowski's government as well' (107–8). Furthermore, paternalistic relations with state-owned industry were finished. Similarly, the state allocation of foreign currency, another fundamental element of the state-socialist economy, was abandoned.

37 Bauman 1993b:142.

38 Poznański 1996:273.

39 Kołakowski 1971:48.

40 Staniszkis 1991a:284.

41 Davies 1981 (II):636.

42 See extensive data on the desired economic order and the myth of the market in Kolarska-Bobińska 1990, Borkowski 1994 and Morawski 1994.

43 Gross 1994:179.

44 Cited in Ash 1990:220.

45 Davies 1981 (I):xvii. See the in-depth analysis of the Pope's first visit to Poland in Kubik 1994a.

46 Jedlicki 1973:231.

47 Joravsky 1994:844.

48 Hankiss 1994b:118.

49 Szacki 1995:120.

50 Szacki 1995:212.

51 Ash 1991:368.

52 Poland's hard-currency debts between 1975 and 1987 increased fivefold; see Poznański 1996:305, n.4.

53 Guerrieri 1995:120.

54 Szacki 1995:212.
55 Cited in Szacki 1995:177.
56 Gross 1994:184.
57 According to the chairman of the Freedom Union, Leszek Balcerowicz, the candidate for the Presidency, regardless of who it would become, had to divide the Freedom Union; see Gortat 1996:105.
58 See Karpiński 1997:64 and Juchler 1998:154–5. The Freedom Union attained 13.4 per cent of the votes and 60 seats in the Sejm in 1997, while the Democratic Union reached 10.3 per cent in 1993 (74 seats) and the KLD (4 per cent in 1993, no seat).
59 Ekiert 1993:18. In Ekiert's view, civil society managed to recover very quickly from four decades of communist rule. 'Polish civil society exploded as thousands of new organizations and movements were formed locally and nationally.' He gives the numbers of 1500 trade unions, 58 churches and religious denominations, hundreds of youth organizations, social and cultural movements, business associations, or ethnic minority organizations.
60 Nelson 1996:349.
61 Among the most important are Jerzy Hausner (1994), Witold Morawski (1995), and Melanie Tatur (1994).
62 Slay 1994:115.
63 Roberts and Jung 1995:187.
64 Slay 1994:187.
65 Solidarity Electoral Action (AWS) assembled as main parties the Solidarity trade union, the Confederation for an Independent Poland (KPN) and the Christian-National Alliance (ZChN).
66 Slay 1994:173.
67 Ibid. 149.
68 See Slay 1994:171. According to Slay, Poland's direct foreign investment rate in 1991 per capita was 50 per cent of the Czechoslovak level and only 10 per cent of the Hungarian level.
69 Cited in Berend 1995:143.
70 For 1997, labour costs per hour in Eastern Europe situated Poland (5.48 DM) second behind Slovenia (10.93 DM). While the Slovenian level approaches the value of labour costs per hour in Portugal, the gap with the level in Germany (nearly 48 DM) is yawning. In other Eastern European countries the levels are even lower than in Poland: Slovakia (4.85), Hungary (4.81), Czech Republic (4.80), Estonia (3.67), Latvia (3.37), Lithuania (3.24), Russia (3.03), Romania (1.81), and Bulgaria (1.42). See *Frankfurter Allgemeine Zeitung* of 28 January 1999 on the basis of data gathered by the Institute of the German Economy at Cologne.
71 Slay 1994:173.
72 Shafir 1994:33.
73 'The fact that there is now no Soviet Union fulfilling the two latent functions of securing peace and blocking migration is confronting the West European countries with problems and challenges which for the duration of its existence the imperial Soviet regime benevolently spared them' (Offe, 1997:198).
74 Jowitt 1992:260.

75 Offe 1997:161.
76 Ibid.
77 Girard 1987:26.
78 Offe 1997:160.
79 Weydenthal 1992:16.
80 Cited in Neumann 1993:364.
81 Cited in Potel 1999:9.
82 I owe this notion to Attila Agh, who characterized the Eastern perception of EU policies towards the Visegrád countries in these terms (Agh's talk at the European University Institute in Spring 1997).
83 Blaszczyk 1998:146–7. In surveys carried out between 1992 and 1997, between 70 and 80 per cent of those polled favoured integration into the European Union. By early 1999 the percentage had dropped to 60 per cent.
84 Smolar 1996b:169–70.
85 Hankiss 1994b:118.
86 Klimaszewski 1996:31.
87 Antall 1992:67.

Chapter 6. The Continuity of the Image of Solidarity

1 Some studies have examined the historical genesis and socio-structural composition of the trade union (Ash, 1991; Holzer, 1984; Goodwyn, 1991; Laba, 1991). Others have focused on aspects of Solidarity's mentality and the external public dimension (Staniszkis, 1984; Kowalski, 1990; Kubik, 1994a). For others, Solidarity was a modernizing and democratizing movement (Touraine, 1983; Tatur, 1989; Ost, 1990).
2 See Osteuropa 7/1986:540f. The very day of its foundation, 784 trade union groups and 108 inter-enterprise associations joined the OPZZ.
3 Kuczyński 1994:230.
4 Kamiński 1991:137.
5 Holzer and Leski 1990:173.
6 See Subotic 1996. The roster of the main post-Solidarity organizations and their emergence looks as follows: October 1989: ZChN; February 1990: KLD; May 1990: PC; June 1990: (FPD); July 1990: ROAD; December 1990: UD; February 1991: PSL 'Solidarity'. In May 1991 ROAD and FPD joined the UD; In October 1992 the FPD abandoned the UD; in autumn 1992 a split in the PC enabled the foundation of the RdR; in December 1993 a further split occurred in the PC; in April 1994 the UW was founded as an alliance of UD and KLD; in autumn 1995 the Patriotic Camp was founded which included amongst others: RdR; KPN; PSL-PL; in November 1995 ROP emerged.
7 Frybes and Michel 1996:18.
8 Ost 1990:25.
9 Jowitt 1992:295.
10 Pałubicki 1990.
11 Mason et al. 1991:208.
12 Ost 1990:208.

13   Cited in Skórzyński 1995:68.
14   Ibid. 91.
15   See the data in Mason *et al.* 1991:209–10.
16   Elias 1991:182–3.
17   As Michnik (1985:50) wrote: 'The crucial element in the strategy of new evolutionism is the conviction about the power of the workers. Firmly determined, they already forced the government some spectacular concessions. Without doubt they are the social group which the government really fears and before whose pressure it must cede.'
18   Kubik 1994b:446.
19   To avoid misunderstandings, especially frequent with the English term 'status', I keep using the German original.
20   The crucial passage in Weber says: *'Inhaltlich findet die ständische Ehre ihren Ausdruck normalerweise vor allem in der Zumutung einer spezifisch gearteten Lebensführung an jeden, der dem Kreise angehören will'.* . . . *'Sobald nicht eine bloß individuelle und sozial irrelevante Nachahmung fremder Lebensführung, sondern ein einverständliches Gemeinschaftshandeln dieses Charakters vorliegt, ist die "ständische" Entwicklung im Gang'* (Weber, 1980:535).
21   See Kuroń's pamphlet of 1982 (Kuroń, 1982), whose significance he reassessed in Kuroń and Zakowski 1995.
22   When martial law was proclaimed 425 persons were arrested. Of the 107 members of Solidarity's National Commission almost all were arrested, with the exception of Bujak, Kosmowski, Frasyniuk and Janas. During 1982 3616 persons were arrested, of which at the outset of 1983 still 1500 were in jail. These data draw on information provided by Holzer and Leski 1990:9 and 65; see also Staniszkis 1984:319, n.3.
23   Smolar 1989:31.
24   Michnik 1985:68.
25   Smolar and Kende 1989:19.
26   Whereas the average age of delegates was 36 years in 1981, it amounted to 42 in 1990. Only 36 of the 487 delegates to the Congress of April 1990 had participated in 1981. More important is the proportion concerning the members of the National Commission (*Komisja Krajowa)*, the highest directive board of the 'Solidarity' trade union, elected in September 1981. In 1981, this board had originally 107 members, made up of 69 elected by the National Congress, and the chairmen of 38 regional guiding boards. Out of these 107, only 20 came as delegates to the Congress in April 1990. Hence, 20 of the 36 delegates who participated in both Congresses were members of the guiding board (see *Tygodnik Solidarność* 22 April:24–7, and *Congress Post*, Gdańsk 6 September; cited after Strobel 1985).
27   By Solidarity II, I refer to the mainstream Solidarity organization as of 1989, while Solidarity I refers to the Solidarity trade union of 1980 and 1981.
28   Skórzyński 1995:133.
29   Kuroń and Żakowski 1995:269.
30   Skórzyński 1995:68.
31   Holzer and Leski 1990:154.

32 Michnik 1995:162–3.
33 Skórzyński 1995:141.
34 This civic committee was founded in May 1987.
35 Kuczyński and Nowotny 1994:249–50.
36 Michnik 1995:341.
37 Klimczak 1990:8.
38 There are different conceptualizations which, on the whole, boil down to the division into these two camps. Among the most known is Piotr Wierzbicki's division into three groups: the family, the suite and the court. The family (whose leading figures were Geremek, Kuroń, Michnik) was seen as ideologically united and leftist; the suite was regarded as a constellation of persons around the Mazowiecki government (Aleksander Hall, catholic left); while the court was rather made up of members of the trade union Solidarity around the pragmatic national leader Lech Wałęsa: see Wierzbicki, 1989. Later on, and most commonly, there is the distinction of a dualism between the government- (Mazowiecki) - camp and the Wałęsa-camp. Despite its slight bias perhaps the most concise treatment of this matter in the English language is provided by Kamiński, A. and Kurczewska 1991.
39 Michnik 1991a.
40 Cited in Maxwell 1991:47.
41 Michnik 1991:349.
42 Kozłowski 1995:88.
43 Girard 1988:147.
44 As a consequence, the Confederation for an Independent Poland (KPN) and other opposition parties or movements were excluded from both the civic committees and from the round table.
45 Gross 1994:176.
46 At the beginning of 1995 more than 250 political parties were officially registered in Poland; see Gebethner 1996:121.
47 Bujak 1990.
48 The etymological source of difference and, in its wake, of differentiation, is the double meaning of the French word *différer*. In an elaborate essay on *différence*, Jacques Derrida worked out two crucial meanings of *différer*. On the one hand, there is the action of putting off until later, of taking account of time, a detour, a delay. *Différer* in this sense is to temporize, to take recourse, consciously or unconsciously, to the temporal and temporizing mediation of a detour that suspends the accomplishment or fulfillment of 'desire' or 'will'. The second meaning refers to the more common usage: 'to be not identical, to be other, discernible'. Therefore 'whether it is a question of dissimilar otherness or of allergic and polemical otherness, an interval, a distance, spacing, must be produced between the elements other, and be produced with a certain perseverance in repetition' (Derrida, 1982:8).
49 Michnik 1995:241–2.
50 Michnik 1990.
51 *Gazeta Wyborcza* (Election Newspaper) was established as a result of the round-table talks offering to Solidarity the possibility of a daily press organ. It went into print in April 1989, shortly before the semi-free

elections of June 1989. Its editor became Adam Michnik, who grew into the role of one of Wałęsa's sharpest adversaries.

52 Michnik 1992:102.
53 Ibid. 88.
54 Michnik 1995:259.
55 Dehnel-Szyc and Stachura 1991:22.
56 Girard 1987:28.
57 Michnik 1995:260.
58 Zubek 1991:80.
59 A further reason for growing antipathy against Wałęsa was the 'envy inspired in Polish elites by the elevation to power in neighboring countries of rather sophisticated, even cosmopolitan, political leaders' (Zubek, 1991:75).
60 Michnik *et al.* 1995:384.
61 Girard 1977:158.
62 Girard 1965:102.
63 Skórzyński 1990.
64 Girard 1977:58.
65 Ibid. 62–3.
66 O'Donnell and Schmitter 1986:19.
67 Girard 1988:96.
68 See the programme passed by the II National Congress of 25 April 1990, point I.4.
69 Ibid.
70 See Milewicz 1997.
71 Gortat 1996:92.
72 Majcherek 1997.
73 This coalition embraces nearly 40 smaller and bigger political groups of a conservative-nationalist-catholic kind, amongst which there is the PC, the KPN and the ZchN. In the parliamentary elections of September 1997 the AWS obtained 33.8 per cent of the votes and 201 deputies in the *Sejm*. Prime minister Józef Buzek comes out of its ranks.
74 Majcherek 1997:3.

Chapter 7. The Continuity of the Image of 1989

1 Mazowiecki's exact formulation was 'Przeszłość odkreślamy grubą linią'; see *Gazeta Wyborcza* 25–7 August 1989.
2 Holmes, S. 1994:36.
3 Marciniak 1996:109.
4 Castle 1995:227.
5 I owe this notion of a third Solidarity to Bogdan Mach.
6 Michnik 1995:300.
7 Cited in Grabowski 1998:1017.
8 Frentzel-Zagórska 1993:186.
9 Grajewski 1996:8.
10 Offe 1997:93.
11 Adam Humer, a former UB officer, was sentenced to 9 years in prison

for the murder of members of the opposition at the end of the 1940s; see *Rzeczpospolita*, 9/10 March 1996. A Warsaw court sentenced two former policemen to 4 years and 18 months in prison respectively for their involvement in the events that led to the death of Grzegorz Przemyk in May 1983; see Open Media Research Institute, 10 April 1997:3.

12 See *Rzeczpospolita*, 23 and 26 April 1996.
13 Kuroń and Modzelewski 1996.
14 Sztompka 1996:50.
15 This includes hiding, stealing, and forging documents; their numbers increased from 6387 in 1990 to 40063 in 1995; see Holmes and Roszkowski 1997, chap. 12.
16 See Holmes 1997c:31, n.72. 'There might be a serious mismatch between perception of corruption and the actual situation in Poland (and probably in many other countries); but in terms of legitimacy, perceptions matter more than "reality". Moreover, this apparant discrepancy could well relate to the fact that many Poles do not personally experience corruption because they are not involved with high-ranking officials; if their perception is that corruption is worse higher up the state hierarchy than at lower levels, this too is bound to increase the legitimation problems of the state.'
17 See *Rzeczpospolita*, 25 April 1996.
18 Ibid. 23 May 1996.
19 Sztompka 1996:53.
20 See the opinion poll conducted by the CBOS in December 1997: 'Aktualne problemy i wydarzenia'.
21 Kowalski 1993:238.
22 *The Oxford English Dictionary*, 2nd edition, Vol. 9:121.
23 Offe 1997:95.
24 Marciniak 1996:109.
25 See Herling-Grudziński 1996a:15.
26 Ash 1998.
27 Michnik 1995:389.
28 Bracher 1970:72.
29 Orlos 1995:23.
30 This is also reflected in frequent incidents of anti-Semitism. As probably Europe's most mononational country, Poland has succumbed to anti-Semitic rhetoric not only against Jews, but also against intellectual, political, and economic elites (Gebert, 1991). 'Today, anti-semitism is the language of nostalgia, of resentment, of feeling victimized, and of economic wishful thinking' (Grudzińska-Gross, 1992:147).
31 Ash 1998.
32 The conflict patterns in Poland's lustration suggest that the pursuit of a cathartic effect is in vain, as antagonists are in a double-bind with past images which can hardly give concrete results in terms of judicial accountability. Both Girard (in his critique of Freud, 1989) and Bateson (1972:206) argued that double-binds do not invoke a single traumatic experience but refer to repeated experiences which make of the double-bind structure a habitual expectation. In Girard's account, the Oedipus drama is triggered by the oracle: 'A murderer is in your midst; get rid

of him and you will be rid of the plague. Only the discovery of the culprit cures the plague. The reciprocal witch hunt brings the crisis to a climax; the focusing of the guilt on Oedipus and his expulsion constitute a genuine resolution. The whole process is comparable to a cathartic purge' (Girard, 1988:145). Such a focus on clearly accountable scapegoats, as in the Nuremberg trials in post-1945 Germany, is not possible in Poland.

33 Kowalski 1993:238.
34 See Buzek 1998:19.
35 Kurczewski 1994:418–19.
36 Gortat 1996:105.
37 Kowalski 1993:237.
38 Hankiss 1994a:534–9.
39 See Szacki 1995:60.
40 Ibid. 45.
41 Slay 1994:135.
42 For a detailed account see Roszkowski 1997:12–17.
43 Polish United Workers' Party.
44 See the serious deliberations in both groups as to whether to form a coalition between the Freedom Union and the SLD.
45 Kuroń and Modzelewski 1996.
46 Cirtautas 1996:17.
47 Judt 1994:8.
48 In this regard, see the paradigmatic title of 'Changing Ru(o)les', in Holmes and Roszkowski 1997.
49 Herling-Grudziński 1996a:13–16.
50 Roszkowski 1996:17.
51 As Jon Elster has remarked about the motivations for transitional justice, people can deceive themselves about their true motivations. 'An emotional desire for vengeance, for instance, is often presented as an impartial desire for retribution' (Elster, 1998:34).
52 Kowalski 1997:294–95.
53 See Sołtyk 1999:8. Approval rates of the Polish public regarding integration in the European Union have been dropping for the last three years from around 80 per cent to nearly 60 per cent in December 1998. As Bronisław Geremek, the Polish minister of Foreign Affairs, declared in June 1998 in view of rising frustrations, 'The party is over.'
54 Jan Pakulski has examined normalization under four aspects: 1. from moral principles to group interests; 2. from civic forums to parties and interest groups; 3. from charismatic leaders to statesmen and party politicians; 4. from plebiscitary to parliamentary democracy (Pakulski, 1995:417–18).
55 Pakulski 1995:421.
56 The President of the Hungarian State Audit Office, as cited in Holmes 1997b:46.
57 Ibid. The vicious circle of transition is based on pervasive images of the past that cannot simply be removed. As Girard (1977:81) argued, 'The mechanism of reciprocal violence can be described as a *vicious circle*. Once a community enters the circle, it is unable to extricate

itself. We can define this circle in terms of vengeance and reprisals, and we can offer diverse psychological descriptions of these reactions. As long as a working capital of accumulated hatred and suspicion exists at the centre of the community, it will continue to increase no matter what men do. Each person prepares himself for the probable aggression of his neighbours and interprets his neighbour's preparations as confirmation of the latter's aggressiveness. In more general terms, the mimetic character of violence is so intense that once violence is installed in a community, it cannot burn itself out. To escape from the circle it is first necessary to remove from the scene all those forms of violence that tend to become self-propagating and to spawn new, imitative forms.'

58 Turner 1969:129.
59 Curry and Fajfer 1996:6.
60 See also Schmitter and Karl 1994.
61 Sztompka 1998:53.
62 Turner 1969:132.
63 For a recent extensive account of the civic committees' dissolution, see Grabowski, Tomek (1996).
64 Frentzel-Zagórska 1993:184.
65 See Kurowski 1991: 'The electoral campaign was not won by the camp that backed Wałęsa, it was won by Wałęsa himself. Therefore, it is a complete misunderstanding to speak about a Wałęsa-camp. There is no such a camp. There is Wałęsa, there are groups and circles that support him and there are opposed groups.'
66 Turner 1992:59.
67 This pact of February 1993 convened the government, trade unions, and employer organizations at one table and aimed to establish fundamental rules as to the process of privatization, collective bargaining, and the financing of state enterprises.
68 Kuroń 1993:23.
69 Michnik 1995:156.
70 Turner 1969:132.
71 Stabilization measures were backed by the majority of Poles, who were persuaded that this way was the only one to save Poland; see Gomułka 1993:188.
72 Frentzel-Zagórska 1993:203.
73 CBOS report 2/1999.
74 Finally, the constitution was passed by a tight margin in the referendum in May 1997, with 53 in favour and 46 per cent against, although with a low turnout of only 43 per cent (Batt and Wolczuk, 1998:90–3).
75 Kowalik 1993:95.
76 Marciniak 1992:4.
77 Osiatyński 1996:21–2.
78 Vinton 1992:4.
79 Cited in Smolar 1996a:450.
80 Tocqueville 1988:296.
81 Girard 1965:38.

Chapter 8. The Continuity of Expecting Discontinuities

1 The references to Polish history and politics as drama or tragedy are
   bountiful. Thus, the quasi-permanent Polish post-war crisis was regarded
   as the Polish drama (Staniszkis, 1984:35; Kersten, 1991: p. xxv). The
   conditions of the principal actors in 1988 and 1989 were characterized
   as a classical revolutionary drama with three basic *dramatis personae*
   (the moderates, the radicals, the counter-revolutionaries) (Smolar,
   1996a:440). Solidarity was seen as 'dramatized history' (Kowalski, 1990a:9).
   The destruction of Solidarity by martial law in 1981 was equated to
   Greek tragedy (Holzer, 1990:105–6; Wnuk-Lipiński, 1996:147).
2 Chirot 1991:x.
3 Holmes, L. 1997:337.
4 Offe 1996b:186.
5 Jowitt 1992:293.
6 Holmes, L. 1997:337.
7 Kolarska-Bobińska 1994:60–1.
8 Frybes and Michel 1996b:81.
9 Wnuk-Lipiński 1996:275.
10 Machiavelli, *The Prince*, XXV.
11 Pitkin 1984:163.
12 I think here of Benedict Anderson's (1983) account of nations as imag-
    ined communities. As he wrote, a nation 'is imagined because the members
    of even the smallest nation will never know most of their fellow-mem-
    bers, meet them, or even hear of them, yet in the minds of each lives
    the image of their communion' (Anderson, 1983:15). In turn, Offe criti-
    cized the inauthenticity of ethnic politics in Eastern Europe by arguing
    that supposedly self-evidently valid foundations of the community are
    'in fact "invented", imagined, construed and designed by invoking lin-
    guistic, religious, cultural, historical or dynastic group characteristics
    which are thus a matter of strategic choice rather than collective es-
    sence' (Offe, 1997:206, n.9).
13 'A plusieurs reprises, depuis la Révolution a commencé jusqu'à nos jours, on
    voit la passion de la liberté s'éteindre, puis renaître, puis s'éteindre encore,
    et puis encore renaître; ainsi fera-t-elle longtemps, toujours inexpérimentée et
    mal réglée, facile à décourager, à effrayer et à vaincre, superficielle et passagère.
    Pendant ce même temps la passion pour l'égalité occupe toujours le fonds des
    cœurs dont elle s'est emparée la première. . . . Tandis que l'une change sans
    cesse d'aspect, diminue, grandit, se fortifie, se débilite suivant les événements,
    l'autre est toujours la même, toujours attachée au même but avec la même
    ardeur obstinée et souvent aveugle'* (On several occasions during the pe-
    riod extending from the outbreak of the Revolution up to our time we
    find the desire for freedom reviving, succumbing, then returning, only
    to die out once more and presently blaze up again. This presumably
    will be the lot for many years to come of a passion so undisciplined
    and untutored by experience; so easily discouraged, cowed and van-
    quished, so superficial and short-lived. Yet during this same period the
    passion for equality, first to entrench itself in the hearts of Frenchmen,
    has never given ground; for it links up with feelings basic to our very

nature. For while the urge to freedom is forever assuming new forms, losing or gaining strength according to the march of events, our love of equality is constant and pursues the object of its desire with a zeal that is obstinate and often blind, ready to make every concession to those who give it satisfaction'). (Tocqueville, 1988:298).

14 More 1965:245–7.
15 Stark 1992:20.
16 Elster *et al.* 1998:296.
17 Machiavelli, The Prince XXIV.
18 See Yeltsin's ambitions to start from scratch a long-delayed second term of economic reform, in 'Start from Scratch', *International Herald Tribune*, 18 March 1997.
19 Arnason 1993:154.
20 Lewis 1993:291.
21 See Comisso (1994:187–8) for a critique of predictive efforts in the field of East European transitions. In her view, a good theory is characterized not so much by its ability to predict, but rather, should clarify and suggest possible scenarios for the future.
22 Zeitlin 1984:234.
23 Dupuy 1982:135.
24 Kowalski 1993:238.
25 This mixed record of the simultaneity of images bears striking resemblance with Elias's sociological interpretation of Edgar Allan Poe's *Fishermen in the Maelstrom*. In this tale, a fishing boat sailed by two brothers is sucked into the abyss of an enormous whirlpool. The older brother, immobilized by fear, cannot escape his fate and is drawn into the maelstrom. The younger brother, exercising more self-control over his emotions, observes the objects being drawn into the abyss and manages to notice certain regularities in their process. By using this information he behaves in such a way that he avoids his brother's fate. Uncritical and fearful involvement is contrasted with critical and detached reflection on one's own situation (see Elias, 1987:48).
26 Kolarska-Bobińska 1994:60–1.

Bibliography

Adam, J. 1993. *Planning and Market in Soviet and East European Thought, 1960s–1992*. New York: St. Martin's Press.

Anderson, Benedict. 1983. *Imagined Communities*. London and New York: Verso.

Antall, Józef. 1992. *East European Reporter* V (II), March–April 1992, 67.

Arato, A. 1981. 'Civil Society against the State', *Telos*, 47, 23–47.

Arendt, H. 1951. *The Origins of Totalitarianism*. London: George Allen.

Arnason, J. P. 1993. *The Future that Failed*. London and New York: Routledge.

Ascherson, N. 1981. *The Polish August: The Self-Limiting Revolution*. London: Penguin.

Ash, T. G. 1990. *Ein Jahrhundert wird abgewählt: aus den Zentren Mitteleuropas 1980–1990*. Translated from the English by Yvonne Badal. München: Hanser.

Ash, T. G. 1991. *The Polish Revolution: Solidarity*. London: Granta Books.

Ash T. G. 1996. 'Neo-Pagan Poland?', *The New York Review of Books*, 11 January 1996, 10–14.

Ash, T. G. 1998. 'The Truth about Dictatorship', *The New York Review of Books*, 19 February 1998.

Ash, T. G. 1999. 'The Puzzle of Central Europe', *The New York Review of Books*, 18 March, 18–23.

Balcerowicz, L. 1995. 'Lessons from the Shock-Therapy', *Journal of Economic Policy*, 1, 1–25.

Balcerowicz, L. 1995. Interview in: *Zmiana warty czyli jak to się stało*. Warszawa: Rzeczpospolita.

Bateson, G. 1972. *Steps to an Ecology of the Mind*. San Francisco/Scranton/London/Toronto: Chandler.

Batt, J. and Wolczuk, K. 1998. 'Redefining the State: The Constitutional Process', in White *et al.* (eds). *Developments in Central and East European Politics*, 83–102.

Bauman, Z. 1989. 'Intellectuals in East-Central Europe. Continuity and Change', in Schoepflin, G. and Wood, N. (eds) *In Search of Central Europe*. Cambridge: Polity Press, 70–90.

Bauman, Z. 1992a. 'Love in Adversity: On the State and the Intellectuals, and the State of Intellectuals', *Thesis Eleven*, 31, 81–104.

Bauman, Z. 1993a. 'A Post-Modern Revolution?', in Frentzel-Zagórska, Janina (ed) *From a One-Party State to Democracy*. Amsterdam Atlanta: Rodopi, 3–19.

Bauman, Z. 1993b. 'Dismantling the Patronage State', in Frentzel-Zagórska, Janina (ed) *From a One-Party State to Democracy*. Amsterdam Atlanta: Rodopi, 139–54.

Bauman, Z. 1994. 'After the Patronage State. A Model in Search of Class Interests', in Bryant, C. and Mokrzycki, E. (eds) *The New Great Transformation? Change and Continuity in East-Central Europe*. London and New York: Routledge, 14–35.

Berend, I. T. 1995. 'Alternatives of Transformation: Choices and Determinants – East-Central Europe in the 1990s', in Crawford, Beverley (ed), 130–49.

Bertschi, C. C. 1995. 'Lustration and the Transition to Democracy: The Cases of Poland and Bulgaria', *East European Quarterly*, 28, No. 4, 435–51.

Beyme, Klaus. 1994. *Systemwechsel in Osteuropa*. 2. Aufl. Frankfurt/Main: Suhrkamp.

Bibò, I. 1992. *Die Misere der osteuropäischen Kleinstaaterei*. Frankfurt/Main: Neue Kritik.

Blaszczyk, C. 1998. 'European Policy-Making in Poland – Institutional and Political Framework', in Lippert, B. and Becker, P. (eds) *Towards EU-Membership. Transformation and Integration in Poland and the Czech Republic*. Bonn: Europa Union Verlag, 129–52.

Borkenau, F. 1971. *World Communism: A History of the Communist International*. Ann Arbor: University of Michigan Press.

Borkowski, A. 1994. 'Zmiany przekonań na temat pożądangeo ładu gospodarczego', in Morawski, W. (ed.). *Zmierzch Socjalizmu Państwowego*, 256–63.

Borneman, J. 1997. *Settling Accounts: Violence, Justice and Accountability in Postsocialist Europe*. Princeton: Princeton University Press.

Bos, E. 1994. 'Die Rolle von Elite und kollektiven Akteueren in Transitionsprozessen', in Merkel, W. (ed.). *Systemwechsel 1*, 81–109.

Bracher, K.-D. 1970. *The German Dictatorship: the Origins, Structure and Effects of National Socialism*. London: Weidenfeld & Nicolson.

Brubaker, R. 1996. *Nationalism Reframed*. Cambridge: Cambridge University Press.

Brus, W. and Laski, K. 1989. *From Marx to the Market*. Oxford: Oxford University Press.

Bujak, Z. 1990. 'Na Zachód od Centrum', interview with Zbigniew Bujak, in *Polityka*, 28 July 1990.

Bunce, V. and Csanádi, M. 1993. 'Uncertainty in the Transition: Post-Communism in Hungary', *Eastern European Politics and Societies*, 7(2), 240–75.

Büscher, B. *et al.* (ed.). 1983 *Solidarność. Die polnische Gewerkschaft Solidarität in Dokumenten, Diskussionen und Beiträgen*. Köln.

Buzek, J. 1998. 'Wyobraźnia władzy', interview in *Wprost*, 11 October 1998, 19–21.

Cassirer, E. 1969. *An Essay on Man*. New Haven and London: Yale University Press.

Castle, M. 1995. *A Successfully-Failed Pact. The Polish Political Transition of 1989*. Stanford: Stanford Univ. Ph.D.

Chirot, D. (ed.). 1991. *The Crisis of Leninism and the Decline of the Left. The Revolutions of 1989*. Seattle and London: University of Washington Press.

Chirot, D. 1989a. 'Ideology, Reality, and Competing Models of Development in Eastern Europe Between the Two World Wars', *Eastern European Politics and Societies*, 3(3), 378–411.

Chirot, D. 1989b (ed.). *The Origins of Backwardness in Eastern Europe: Economics and Politics from the Middle Ages until the Early Twentieth Century*. Berkeley and Los Angeles: University of California Press.

Chirot, D. 1995. 'National Liberation and Nationalist Nightmares: The Consequences of the End of Empires in the Twentieth Century', in Crawford, Beverley (ed.), 43–68.

Cirtautas, A. M. 1996. 'Constitutional Development in Post-Communist Poland', *Polish Sociological Review*, 113(1), 17–24.

Comisso, E. 1994. 'Prediction versus Diagnosis: Comments on a Ken Jowitt Retrospective', *Slavic Review*, 53(1), 186–92.

Crawford, B. (ed.). 1995. *Markets, States and Democracy: the Political Economy of Post-Communist Transformations*. Boulder, Co.: Westview Press.

Curry, J. and Fajfer, L. (eds). 1996. *Poland's Permanent Revolution. People vs. Elites, 1956 to the Present*. Washington: The American University Press.

Curry, J. 1997. 'Which Way is Right?', *Transitions*, October 1997, 74–9.

Dahrendorf, R. 1959. *Class and Class Conflict in Industrial Society*. London: Routledge & Kegan Paul.

Dahrendorf, R. 1990. *Reflections on the Revolution in Europe*. London: Chatto & Windus.

Davies, N. 1981. *God's Playground. A History of Poland*. Vols. I and II. Oxford: Clarendon Press.

Davies, N. 1996. *Europe. A History*. Oxford: Oxford University Press.

Dehnel-Szyc, M. and Stachura, J. 1991. *Gry Polityczne*. Warszawa: Oficyna Wydawnicza.

Dembiński, P. 1991. *The Logic of the Planned Economy*. Oxford: Oxford University Press.

Derrida, J. 1982. 'Différence', in *Margins of Philosophy*. Brighton: Harvester Press.

Deutsch, K. 1985. 'On Theory and Research in Innnovation', in Merritt, R. and Merritt, A. (eds). *Innovation in the Public Sector*. Beverly Hills/London/New Delhi: Sage, 17–35.

Die Gewerkschaften in Polen nach dem 13. Dezember 1981, in *Osteuropa* 7/1986:534–548.

Drakulić, S. 1996. *Café Europa*. London: Abacus.

Drweski, B. 1995. 'Que sont les communistes devenues?', *La Nouvelle Alternative*, 38, Juin 1995, 7–11.

Dupuy, J.-P. 1982. *Ordres et Désordres*. Paris: Seuil.

Dwernicki, C. and Zalewski, F. 1995. 'La transition polonaise à la lumière de la présidentielle', *La Nouvelle Alternative*, 40, December 1995, 40–3.

Eberstadt, N. 1990. 'Health and Mortality in Eastern Europe 1965–1985', *Communist Economies*, 2(3), 347–71.

Ekes, J. 1994. Polska. *Przyczyny słabości i podstawy nadziei*. Warszawa: Instytut Wydawniczy Pax.

Ekiert, G. 1993. 'Public Participation and Politics of Discontent in Post-Communist Poland 1989–1992.' Program on Central and Eastern Europe Working Paper Series #30 Minde de Gunzburg Center for European Studies. Harvard University.

Ekiert, G. 1995. 'Democratization Processes in East Central Europe: A Theoretical Reconsideration, *British Journal of Political Sciences*, 21 (1991), 285–313, reprinted in Pridham, G. (ed.). *Transitions to Democracy*. Aldershot: Dartmout, 329–57.

Ekiert, G. 1996. *The State Against Society. Political Crises and Their Aftermath in East Central Europe*. Princeton: Princeton University Press.

Ekiert, G. 1997. 'Rebellious Poles: Political Crises and Popular Protest under State Socialism', 1945–89, *East European Politics and Societies*, 11(2), 299–338.

Elias, N. 1978. *Was ist Soziologie?* Third edition. München: Juventa.

Elias, N. 1987. *Involvement and Detachment*. Oxford: Basil Blackwell.

Elias, N. 1991. *The Society of Individuals*. Oxford: Blackwell.

Elias, N. 1992. *Studien über die Deutschen*. Frankfurt: Suhrkamp.

Elster, J. 1993. *Political Psychology*. Cambridge: Cambridge University Press.

Elster, J. (ed.). 1996. *The Roundtable Talks and the Breakdown of Communism*. Chicago and London: The University of Chicago Press.

Elster, J. 1998. 'Coming to terms with the past. A framework for the study of justice in the transition to democracy', *Archives Européennes de Sociologie*, 39(1), 7–48.

Elster, J./Offe, C./Preuss, U. 1998. *Institutional Design in Post-Communist Societies*. Cambridge: Cambridge University Press.

Engler, W. 1992. *Die zivilisatorische Lücke. Versuche über den Staatssozialismus*. Frankfurt/Main: Suhrkamp.

Feher, F. 1995. 'Imagining the West', *Thesis Eleven*, 42, 52–68.

Fehr, H. 1991. 'Solidarność und die Bürgerkomitees im neuen politischen Kräftefeld Polens', in Deppe, R. *et al.* (eds). *Demokratischer Umbruch in Osteuropa*. Frankfurt/Main:Suhrkamp, 256–80.

Frentzel-Zagórska, J. 1993. 'The Road to a Democratic Political System in Post-Communist Eastern Europe', in Frentzel-Zagórska, J. (ed.). *From a One-Party State to Democracy*. Amsterdam/Atlanta, 165–93.

Friedrich, C. J. and Brzeziński, Z. 1956. *Totalitarian Dictatorship and Autocracy*. Cambridge: Harvard University Press.

Frybes, M. and Michel, P. 1996a. *Après le communisme. Mythes et légendes de la Pologne contemporaine*. Paris: Bayard Éditions.

Frybes, M. and Michel, P. 1996b. 'La "transition" polonaise', *Revue Internationale de Politique Comparée*, 3(1), 69–83.

Fukuyama, F. 1992. *The End of History and the Last Man*. New York: Free Press.

Furet, F. 1978. *Penser la révolution française*. Paris: Gallimard.

Furet, F. 1995. *Le passé d'une illusion*. Paris: Robert Laffont.

Gąciarz, B. 1994. 'Samorząd pracowniczy wobec zmian systemowych', in Hausner, J. and Marciniak, P. (eds). *Od socjalistycznego korporacjonizmu do . . .?* Warszawa: Fundacja Polska Praca, 257–75.

Gebethner, S. 1996. 'Parliamentary and Electoral Parties in Poland', in Lewis, P. (ed.). *Party Structure and Organization in East-Central Europe*. Cheltenham and Brookfield: Edward Elgar, 120–33.

Gellner, E. 1994. *Conditions of Liberty. Civil Society and its Rivals*. London.

Geremek, B. 1989. 'Warszawska wiosna?', *Tygodnik Powszechny*, 23 April 1989, 1.

Geremek, B. 1990. 'Between Hope and Despair', *Daedalus*, 119(1), 91–109.

Geremek, B. 1991. *La rupture: La Pologne du communisme à la démocratie*. Paris: Seuil.

Gerschenkron, A. 1962. *Economic Backwardness in Historical Perspective*. Cambridge: Harvard University Press.

Girard, R. 1965. *Deceit, Desire, and the Novel*. Baltimore: The Johns Hopkins University Press.

Girard, René. 1977 *Violence and the Sacred*. Baltimore: The Johns Hopkins University Press.

Girard, R. 1987. *Things Hidden Since the Foundation of the World*. London: The Athlone Press.

Girard, R. 1988. *To Double Business Bound*. Baltimore: The Johns Hopkins University Press.

Girard, R. 1989. *The Scapegoat*. Baltimore: The Johns Hopkins University Press.

Girard, R. 1990. *Les feux de l'envie*. Paris: Grasset.

Girard, R. 1994. *Quand ces choses commenceront. . . .* Entretiens avec Michel Treguer. Arléa.

Girard, R. 1996. 'In principio c'era il capro', *Il Sole-24 ore*, 5 May 1996, 26.

Glasman, M. 1996. *Unnecessary Suffering*. London:Verso.

Gombrowicz, W. 1996. 'Fratze und Gesicht', in Klecel, M. (ed.) *Polen zwischen Ost und West*. Frankfurt/Main: Suhrkamp, 38–49.

Gomułka, S. 1993. 'Poland: Glass Half Full', in Portes, R. (ed.). *Economic Transformation in Central Europe: A Progress Report*. London: CEPR, 187–210.

Goodwyn, L. 1991. *Breaking the Barrier. The Rise of Solidarity in Poland*. New York, Oxford: Oxford University Press.

Gortat, R. 1996. 'Trudny egzamin: partie polityczne w wyborach prezydenckich', *Przegląd Społeczny*, 1–2/1996, 6–107.

Gowin, J. 1996. *Kirche-Staat-Gesellschaft. Polen in den neunziger Jahren*. Warszawa.

Grabowska, M. 1997. 'Czy polskie społeczeństwo jest podzielone', *Rzeczpospolita* 25 March 1997.

Grabowski, S. 1998. 'Vom "dicken Strich" zur "Durchleuchtung"', *Osteuropa*, 10/98, 1015–23.

Grabowski, T. 1996. 'The Party that Never Was: The Rise and Fall of the Solidarity Citizens' Committees in Poland', *Eastern European Politics and Societies*, 10(2), 214–54.

Graczyk, R. 1997. *Konstytucja dla Polski. Tradycje, doświadczenia, spory*. Kraków: Znak.

Grajewski, A. 1996. 'Lustracja po polsku', *Przegląd Polityczny*, 31, Summer 1996, 8–14.

Gross, J. T. 1979. *Polish Society under German Occupation. The Generalgouvernement, 1939–1944*. Princeton: Princeton University Press.

Gross, J. T. 1989. 'Social Consequences of War: Preliminaries to the Study of Imposition of Communist Regimes in East Central Europe', *Eastern European Politics and Societies*, 3(2), 198–214.

Gross, J. T. 1991. 'Polen nach der Revolution', *Transit*, 3, 69–78.

Gross, J. T. 1994. 'Poland after the Revolution-the Obfuscated Autonomy of Politics', in Kovacs, J. M. (ed.). *Transition to Capitalism? The Communist Legacy in Eastern Europe*. New Brunswick and London: Transaction Publishers.

Grudzińska-Gross, I. 1992. 'Post-Communist Resentment, or the Rewriting of Polish History', *Eastern European Politics and Societies*, 6(2), 141–51.

Guerrieri, P. 1995. 'Trade Integration of Eastern Europe and the Former Soviet Union in the World Economy: A Structuralist Approach', in Crawford, Beverley (ed.), 103–29.

Guruita, B. 1998. 'The Shadow of Securitate', *Transitions*, 9, September 1998.

Hankiss, E. 1990. *East European Alternatives*. Oxford: Clarendon Press.

Hankiss, E. 1994a. 'Our Recent Past: Recent Developments in East Central Europe in the Light of Various Social Philosophies', *Eastern European Politics and Societies*, 8(3), 535–41.

Hankiss, E. 1994b. 'European Paradigms: East and West, 1945–1994', *Daedalus*, 123(3), 115–26.

Hartmann, J. 1995. 'Alte Luft in neuen Reifen? Demokratie, Osteuropa und der Rest der Welt – Literatur zum Systemwechsel', *Neue Politische Literatur*, 40(2), 287–94.

Hassner, P. 1995. *La Violence et la Paix*. Paris: Esprit.

Hausner, J. 1994. *Tendencje i perspektywy rozwoju systemu reprezentacji interesów w krajach Europy Wschodniej*. Biuletyn 3. Kraków: Akademia Ekonomiczna.

Havel, V. 1985. *The Power of the Powerless*. Edited by John Keane. London: Hutchinson.

Havel, V. 1991. *Open Letters. Selected Prose 1965–1990*. Selected and edited by Paul Wilson. London/Boston: Faber and Faber.

Herling-Grudziński, G. 1996a. 'Dziennik pisany nocą', *Rzeczpospolita*, 9/10 March 1996, 13–16.

Herling-Grudziński, G. 1996b. 'Prawo ponad polityką', interview in *Przegląd Pol-ityczny*, Summer 1996, 15–17.

Heyns, Barbara and Bialecki, I. 1991. 'Solidarność: Reluctant Vanguard or Makeshift Coalition?' *American Political Science Review*, 85(2), 351–70.

Higley, J./Pakulski, J./Wesołowski, W. (eds) 1998. *Postcommunist Elites and Democracy in Eastern Europe*. London: Macmillan.

Hirsch, H. 1985. *Bewegungen für Demokratie und Unabhängigkeit in Polen 1976–1980*. München and Mainz.

Hirschman, A. 1977. *The Passions and the Interests*. Princeton: Princeton University Press.

Holmes, L. 1997a. *Post-Communism*. Durham: Duke University Press.

Holmes, L. 1997a. 'The Democratic State or State Democracy? Problems of Post-Communist Transition'. Jean Monnet Chair Paper RSC No. 97/48. Florence: European University Institute.

Holmes, L. and Roszkowski, W. (eds) 1997b. *Changing Ru(o)les?* Warsaw: ISPPAN (mimeo).

Holmes, L. 1997c. 'Corruption in Post-Communist Countries, with Particular Reference to Poland', in Holmes, L. and Roszkowski, W. (eds) *Changing Ru(o)les?* Warsaw: ISPPAN (mimeo).

Holmes, S. 1994. 'The End of Decommunization', *East European Constitutional Review*, 3(3–4), 33–6.

Holzer, J. 1984. *'Solidarność' 1980–1981. Geneza i historia*. German version: 1985. *'Solidarität'. Die Geschichte einer freien Gewerkschaft in Polen*. München: Beck.

Holzer, J. 1990a. 'Solidarity's Adventures in Wonderland', in Gomułka, S. and Pol-onsky, A. (eds). *Polish Paradoxes*. London and New York: Routledge, 97–115.

Holzer, J. 1990b. 'Dekada Solidarności', *Tygodnik Powszechny*, 2 September 1990.

Holzer, J. and Leski, K. 1990. *Solidarność w podziemiu*. Łódź: Wydawnictwo Łódzkie.

Horváth, A. 1997. *The Political Psychology of Trickster-Clown. An Analytical Experiment Around Communism as a Myth*. EUI Working Paper SPS No. 97/5. San Domenico: European University Institute.

Horváth, A. 1998. 'Tricking into the Position of the Outcast: A Case Study in the Emergence and Effects of Communist Power', *Political Psychology*, 19(2), 331–47.

Horváth, A. and Szakolczai, A. 1992. *The Dissolution of Communist Power*. London: Routledge.

Huizinga, J. 1955. *The Waning of the Middle Ages*. London and Tonbridge. Penguin Books.

Huntington, S. P. 1991. 'How Countries Democratize', *Political Science Quarterly*, 106(4), 579–616.

Jankowicz, A. D. 1994. 'The New Journey to Jerusalem: Mission and Meaning in the Managerial Crusade to Eastern Europe', *Organization Studies*, 15/4, 479–507.

Janos, A. 1982. *The Politics of Backwardness in Hungary 1825–1945*. Princeton: Princeton University Press.

Jedlicki, J. 1973. 'Polskie nurty ideowe lat 1790–1863 wobec cywilizacji Zachodu', in *Swojskość i cudzoziemszczyzna w dziejach kultury polskiej*. Warszawa.

Jedlicki, J. 1990. 'Holy Ideals, and Prosaic Life, or the Devil's Alternatives', in Gomułka, S. and Polonsky, A. (eds). *Polish Paradoxes*. London and New York: Routledge, 40–62.

Joravsky, D. 1994. 'Communism in Historical Perspective', *American Historical Review*, June 1994, 837–57.

Jowitt, K. 1992. *New World Disorder. The Leninist Extinction*. Berkeley, Los Angeles, Oxford: University of California Press.

Juchler, J. 1998. 'Machtwechsel in Polen. Die Parlamentswahlen und ihre Folgen', *Osteuropa* 2/98, 148–59.

Judt, T. 1993. 'Die Vergangenheit ist ein anderes Land', *Transit*, 6, Sommer 1993, 87–120.

Judt, T. 1994. 'Nineteen Eighty-Nine. The End of Which European Era?', *Daedalus*, 123(3), 1–17.

Jurczyk, M. 1990. 'Jurczyk o Solidarności 80', *Trybuna*, 28 June 1990.

Kamiński, A. 1995. 'Jak buduje się 'Trzecia Rzeczpospolita', *Rzeczpospolita*, 156, 7 July 1995.

Kamiński, A. and Kurczewska, J. 1991. 'Letter from Poland', *Government and Opposition*, 26(2), 215–28.

Kamiński, A. and Kurczewska, J. 1994. 'Institutional Transformations in Poland: The Rise of Nomadic Political Elites', in *The Transformation of Europe*. Warszawa: IFiS Publishers.

Kamiński, A. and Strazałkowski, P. 1994. 'Strategie zmian instytucionalnych w gospodarkach krajów Europy Wschodniej', in Morawski, W. (ed.). *Zmierzch Socjalizmu Państwowego*. Warszawa: Wydawnictwo Naukowe PWN, 301–12.

Kamiński, B. 1991. *The Collapse of State Socialism*. Princeton: Princeton University Press.

Kamiński, B. 1994. *The Institutional Dimension of the Transition from Communism*. PPRG Discussion Papers, 26. Warsaw University.

Karpiński, J. 1982. *Count-Down. The Polish Upheavals of 1956, 1968, 1970, 1976, 1980. . . .* New York: Karz-Cohl.

Karpiński, J. 1996. 'Polish Security Services and the Oleksy Case', *Transition*, 2(22), 1 November 1996, 9–13.

Karpiński, J. 1997. 'In Poland, a Long-Standing Tradition of Resistance', *Transition* 3(3), 21 February 1997, 14–19.

Karpiński, J. 1997. 'Poland's Phoenix Rises', *Transitions*, 4(6), 62–5.

Keane, J. 1988. *Civil Society and the State*. London: Verso.

Keane, J. 1996. *Reflections on Violence*. London: Verso.

Kearney, R. 1979. 'Terrorisme et Sacrifice. Le cas de L'Irlande du Nord', *Esprit* 28, April 1979, 29–44.

Kennedy, M. 1991. *Professionals, Power, and Solidarity in Poland. A Critical Sociology of Soviet-Type Society*. Cambridge: Cambridge University Press.

Kennedy, M. (ed.) 1995. *Envisioning Eastern Europe*. Ann Arbor: University of Michigan Press.

Kersten, K. 1991. *The Establishment of Communist Rule in Poland 1943–1948*. Berkeley/Los Angeles/Oxford: University of California Press.

Kersten K. 1996. 'Bilans zamknięcia', in *Spór o PRL*. Kraków: Znak, 17–27.

Kiss, C. 1989. 'Central European Writers about Central Europe: Introduction to a Non-Existent Book of Readings', in Schöpflin, G. and Wood, N. (eds). *In Search of Central Europe*. Cambridge: Polity Press.

Klimaszewski, B. 1996. 'McDonaldization of Polish Culture', *Periphery*, 2(1/2), 29–31.

Kojder, A. 1998. 'Systemic Transformation in Poland', *Polish Sociological Review* 3/98, 247–66.

Kolankiewicz, G. 1994. 'Elites in Search of a Political Formula', *Daedalus*, 123(3), 143–57.

Kolarska-Bobińska, L. 1990. 'The Myth of the Market and the Reality of Reform', in Gomułka, S. and Polonsky, A. (eds). *Polish Paradoxes*. London/New York: Routledge, 160–79.

Kolarska-Bobińska, L. 1994. *Aspirations, Values and Interests. Poland 1989–94*. Warsaw: IFiS Publishers.

Kołakowski, L. 1967. *Der Mensch ohne Alternative*. München: Piper & Co.

Kołakowski, L. 1971. 'Hope and Hopelessness', *Survey*, 17(3), 35–52.

Kołakowski, L. 1974. *Marxismus – Utopie und Anti-Utopie*. Stuttgart: Kohlhammer.

Kołakowski, L. 1983. 'The Intelligentsia', in Brumberg, A. (ed.), *Genesis of a Revolution*. New York, 54–67.

Kołakowski, L. 1996. 'PRL-Wesoły nieboszczyk?', in *Spór o PRL*. Kraków: Znak, 146–58.

Korboński, A. 1996. 'Crisis of Legitimacy or Palace Revolution', in Curry, Jane Leftwich/Fajfer, Luba (eds), 17–54.

Kornai, J. 1992. *The State Socialist System*. Oxford: Oxford University Press.

Koselleck, R. 1988. *Critique and Crisis: Enlightenment and the Pathogenesis of Modern Society*. Oxford/New York/Hamburg: Berg Publishers. Originally 1959. *Kritik und Krise. Eine Studie zur Pathogenese der bürgerlichen Welt*. Freiburg/ München: Verlage Karl Alber.

Kosiński, L. A. 1977. 'Demographic Characteristics and Trends in North-eastern Europe: German Democratic Republic, Poland, Czechoslovakia, and Hungary', in Kostanick, H. L. *Population and Migration Trends in Eastern Europe*. Boulder: Westview Press, 23–48.

Kowalik, T. 1993. 'Can Poland Afford the Swedish Model?', *Dissent*, Winter 1993, 88–96.

Kowalik, T. 1995. 'Czy umowa społeczna jest utopia?', in *Negocjacje droga do paktu społecznego*. Warszawa: Instytut Pracy i Spraw Spolecznych.
Kowalski, S. 1990a. *Krytyka solidarnościowego rozumu*. Warszawa: Wydawnictwo PEN.
Kowalski, S. 1990b. 'Wziąść wszystko', *Rzeczpospolita*, 8 August 1990.
Kowalski, S. 1993. 'Poland's New Political Culture: the Relevance of the Irrelevant', *Economy and Society*, 22(2), 233–42.
Kowalski, S. 1997. 'Prawo moralne i rządy prawa. Czy wolność można wynegocjować?' in Czyżewski, M./Kowalski, S./Piotrowski, A. (eds). *Rytualny chaos. Studium dyskursu politycznego 1997*. Kraków: Wydawnictwo Aureus.
Kozłowski, K. 1991. 'Le gouvernement Mazowiecki n'a pas suivi un programme d'épuration', *La Nouvelle Alternative*, 21, 18–20.
Kozłowski, K. 1995. 'Rewolucja dwóch tysięcy', interview in *Zmiana warty czyli jak to się stało*, Warszawa: Presspublica, 86–92.
Kozłowski, P. 1995. *Szukanie sensu, czyli o naszej wielkiej zmianie*. Warszawa: Wydawnictwo Naukowe PWN.
Krockow, C. 1990. *Die Deutschen in ihrem Jahrhundert 1890–1990*. Reinbek: Rowohlt.
Krzeminski, A. 1993. *Polen im 20. Jahrhundert. Ein historischer Essay*. München: Beck.
Kubik, J. 1994a. *The Power of Symbols Against the Symbols of Power: The Rise of Solidarity and the Fall of State Socialism in Poland*. University Park: Penn State University Press.
Kubik, J. 1994b. 'Who done it: Workers, Intellectuals, or Someone Else? Controversy over Solidarity's Origins and Social Composition', *Theory and Society*, 23, 441–66.
Kuczyński, W. 1992. *Zwierzenia zausznika*. Warszawa: Polska Oficyna Wydawnicza 'BGW'.
Kuczyński, P. and Nowotny, S. 1994a. 'Elita Solidarności', in Morawski, W. (ed.), *Zmierzch socjalizmu państwowego*, 247–55.
Kuczyński, P. 1994b. 'Propaganda pomaga mówieniu' in Morawski, W. (ed.). *Zmierzch socjalizmu państwowego*, 214–31.
Kundera, M. 1984. 'The Tragedy of Central Europe', *New York Review of Books*, 26 April 1984.
Kurczewski, J. 1994. 'Poland's Seven Middle Classes', *Social Research*, 61(2), 395–421.
Kuroń, J. 1978. *Zasady Ideowe*. Paris.
Kuroń, J. 1982. Tezy o wyjściu z sytuacji bez wyjścia, in *Kontakt*, April 1982.
Kuroń, J. 1991. 'Dlaczego?', *Życie Gospodarcze*, 23/1991.
Kuroń, J. 1993. 'Man muß träumen. Soziale Gerechtigkeit als soziale Bewegung', *Transit*, 6, 6–24.
Kuroń, J. and Modzelewski, K. 'List otwarty', *Gazeta Wyborcza*, 22 January 1996.
Kuroń, J. and Żakowski, J. 1995. *PRL dla początkujących*. Wrocław: Wydawnictwo dolnośląskie.
Kwiecień, A. 1996. 'Pyrrusowe zwycięstwo Aleksandra Kwaśniewskiego?' *Periphery*, 2(1/2), 11–13.
Laba, R. 1991. *The Roots of Solidarity*. Princeton, New Jersey: Princeton University Press.

Lagowski, B. 1994. 'Realizm Tradycja Europe', Interview in *Przegląd Polityczny*, 25, Autumn 1994, 23–7.

Landau, Z. and Roszkowski, W. 1995. *Polityka Gospodarzca II RP i PRL*. Warszawa: Wydawnictwo Naukowe PWN.

Latour, B. 1987. *Science in Action*. Milton Keynes: Open University Press.

Lavenex, S. 1997. 'Transgressing Borders. The Emergent European Refugee Regime and "Safe Third Countries"', Paper presented at the Annual Convention of the International Studies Association (ISA), Toronto 18–22 March 1997.

Lenin, W. I. 1918. 'The Immediate Tasks of the Soviet Government' (April 1918), in Connor, James E. (ed.). *Lenin on Politics and Revolution. Selected Writings*, 248–74.

Lewis, P. 1988. *Political Authority and Party Secretaries in Poland 1975–86*. Cambridge: Cambridge University Press.

Lewis, P. 1990. 'Non-Competitive Elections', *Parliamentary Affairs*, 43(1), 90–107.

Lewis, P. 1992. 'Beyond Stalinism: Communist Political Evolution', *Communist Studies*, 41–62.

Lewis, P. 1993. 'Democracy and its Future in Eastern Europe', in Held, David (ed.). *Prospects for Democracy*. Cambridge: Polity Press.

Lijphart, A. 1992. 'Democratization and Constitutional Choices in Czecho-Slovakia, Hungary and Poland 1989–91', *Journal of Theoretical Politics*, 4(2), 207–24.

Lindblom, C. 1977. *Politics and Markets*. New York: Basic Books.

Linz, J. 1990. 'Transitions to Democracy', *The Washington Quarterly*, Summer 1990, 143–64.

Linz, J. and Stepan, A. 1996a. 'Towards Consolidated Democracies', *Journal of Democracy*, 7(2), 14–33.

Linz, J. and Stepan, A. 1996b. *Problems of Democratic Transition and Consolidation. Southern Europe, South America, and Post-Communist Europe*. Baltimore and London: The Johns Hopkins University Press.

Lipset, S. M. and Bence, G. 1994. 'Anticipations of the Failure of Communism', *Theory and Society*, 23, 169–210.

Livingston, P. 1992. *Models of Desire*. Baltimore: Johns Hopkins University Press.

Mach, Z. 1996. 'Reconstruction of Collective Identity after Migration'. Paper presented at the ICCR-Conference on Collective Identity in Paris 3–6 July 1996.

Machiavelli, N. 1988. *The Prince*. (ed.) Quentin Skinner/Russell Price. Cambridge: Cambridge University Press.

Machiavelli, N. 1984. *Discorsi sopra la prima deca di Tito Livio*. Milano: Biblioteca Universale Rizzoli.

Maier, C. S. 1997. *Dissolution. The Crisis of Communism and the End of East Germany*. Princeton: Princeton University Press.

Malia, M. 1994. *Vollstreckter Wahn: Rußland 1917–1991*. Stuttgart: Klett-Cotta. Translated from the English original: *The Soviet Tragedy. A History of Socialism in Russia 1917–1991*. New York: Free Press.

Malia, M. 1995. 'Totalitarismus und Sowjetideologie', *Transit*, 9, 115–27.

Malia, M. 1996. Interview in *Esprit*, 218, Jan.–Fév. 1996, 40–53.

Mannheim, K. 1992. *Essays on the Sociology of Culture*. London and New York: Routledge.

Marciniak, P. 1992. 'Umowa społeczna', *Życie Gospodarcze*, 6 September 1992.

Marciniak, P. 1996. 'Wybory prezydenckie '95 – prawdziwy koniec Okrągłego Stołu?', *Przegląd Społeczny*, 1–2/1996, 108–24.

Marody, M. 1988. 'Sens zbiorowy a stabilność i zmiana ładu społecznego', in Rychard, A. and Sułek, A. (eds). *Legitymacja: Klasyczne teorie i polskie doświadczenia*. Warsaw: PTS, 280–5.

Mason, D./Nelson, D./Szklarski, B. 1991. 'Apathy and the Birth of Democracy: The Polish Struggle', *East European Politics and Societies*, 5(2), 205–33.

Mauss, M. 1924–5. 'A Sociological Assessment of Bolshevism', in Gane, Mike (ed.). 1992. *The Radical Sociology of Durkheim and Mauss*. London and New York: Routledge, 165–211.

Maxwell, K. 1991. 'Spain's Transition to Democracy: a Model for Eastern Europe?', *Proceedings of the Academy of Political Science*, 38(1), 35–49.

Mazowiecki, T. 1989. 'Un tournant dans l'histoire polonaise', Interview in *La Nouvelle Alternative*, June 1989, 15–17.

Mazowiecki, T. 1993. 'L'Expérience du gouvernement en Pologne', Interview in *L'Esprit*, 196, Novembre 1993, 149–62.

Meiklejohn T. S. 1996. 'June 1976: Anatomy of an Avoidable Crisis', in Curry, J. and Fajfer, L. (eds), 109–65.

Mennell, S. 1992. 'The Formation of We-Images: A Process Theory', in Calhoun (ed.) *Social Theory and the Politics of Identity*. Oxford and Cambridge: Blackwell, 175–97.

Merkel, W. (ed.). 1994. *Systemwechsel 1. Theorien, Ansätze und Konzeptionen*. Opladen: Leske & Budrich.

Merritt, R. and Merritt, A. 1985 (eds). *Innovation in the Public Sector*. Beverly Hills: Sage.

Michnik, A. 1983. 'Polnischer Krieg', in Büscher, Barbara *et al.* (eds). *Solidarność: Die polnische Gewerkschaft Solidarität in Dokumenten, Diskussionen und Beitraegen 1980–1982*. Köln.

Michnik, A. 1985. *'Polnischer Frieden' – Aufsätze zur Konzeption des Widerstandes*. Berlin.

Michnik, A. 1989. 'Związek zawodowy już nie wystarczy', *Gazeta Wyborcza*, 6–8 October 1989.

Michnik, A. 1990. 'Akcja Demokratyczna, czym nie będzie', (Democratic Action: what it is not going to be), in *Po Prostu*, 16 August 1990.

Michnik, A. 1991a. 'Egzamin z odpowiedzialności', *Gazeta Wyborcza*, 29 October 1991.

Michnik, A. 1991b. 'Zwei Visionen eines posttotalitären Europas', in Deppe, R. *et al.* (eds). *Demokratischer Umbruch in Osteuropa*. Frankfurt/Main: Suhrkamp.

Michnik, A. 1995. *Diabeł Naszego Czasu*. Warszawa: Niezależna Oficyna Wydawnictwa.

Michnik, A. 1998. 'Hero or Traitor?', *Transitions*, 9, September 1998.

Michnik, A. and Cimoszewicz, W. 1995. 'O prawdę i pojednanie', *Gazeta Wyborcza*, 9–10 September.

Michnik, A./Tischner, J./ Zakowski, J. 1995. *Między Panem i Plebanem*. Kraków: Znak.

Michta, A. 1995. 'Safeguarding the Third Republic: Security Policy and Military Reform', in Prizel and Michta (eds). *Polish Foreign Policy Reconsidered*, 73–94.

Mihalka, M. 1994. 'German and Western Response to Immigration from the East, *RFE/RL Research Report*, 3(23), 10 June 1994, 36–48.

Mildenberger, M. 1998. 'Zwischen Konsens und Polarität. Zur Entwicklung der demokratischen politischen Kultur in Polen', *Aus Politik und Zeitgeschichte* B 6–7, 39–45.

Milewicz, E. 1997. 'Dobrze, bo skutecznie', *Gazeta Wyborcza*, 16 October 1997.

Miller, P. and Rose, N. 1990. 'Governing Economic Life', *Economy and Society*, 19(1), 1–31.

Miłosz, C. 1953. *The Captive Mind*. New York: Alfred A. Knopf.

Mink, G. 1989. *La force ou la raison. Histoire sociale et politique de la Pologne 1980–1989*.

Modzelewski, K. 1995. *Quelle voie après le communisme?* La Tour d'Aiges: Editions de l'Aube.

Mokrzycki, E. 1995. 'Revenge of the Utopia', in Kennedy, Michael D. (ed.). *Envision-ing Eastern Europe*. Ann Arbor: University of Michigan Press, 73–86.

Morawski, W. 1992. 'Poland on the Road to Capitalism: Between Imitation and the Unknown', in Lengyel, G. and Offe, C. (eds). *Economic Institutions, Actors and Attitudes: East Central Europe in Transition*.

Morawski, W. 1994. 'Modele reformy a zmiana systemowa w Polsce', in Morawski, W. (ed.). *Zmierzch socjalizmu państwowego*. Warszawa: Wydawnictwo Naukowe PWN, 286–300.

Morawski, W. 1995. 'Korporatyzm: Wyłananie sie nowych stosunków przemysłowych w Polsce', in *Negocjacje drogą do paktu społecznego*. Warszawa: Instytut Pracy i Spraw Społecznych.

More, T. 1965. *The Complete Works of St. Thomas More*, iv, eds Surtz, E. and Hexter, J. H. New Haven and London: Yale University Press.

Mosca, G. 1950. *Elementi di scienza politica*. German translation: *Die herrschende Klasse. Grundlagen der politischen Wissenschaft*. München: Leo Lehnen Verlag.

Müller, M. 1984. *Die Teilungen Polens: 1772, 1793, 1795*. München: Beck.

Narojek, W. 1991. *The Socialist 'Welfare State'*. Warsaw: PWN.

Nelson, D. 1996. 'Civil Society Endangered', *Social Research*, 63(2), 345–68.

Neumann, I. B. 1993. 'Russia as Central Europe's Constituting Other', *East European Politics and Societies*, 7(2), 349–69.

Nowak-Jeziorański, J. 1995. *Rozmowy o Polsce*. Warszawa.

Nowak-Jeziorański, J. 1996. 'Od Trzeciej Rzeczypospolitej do Drugiej Polski Ludowej', in *Spór o PRL*. Kraków: Znak.

O'Donnell, G. 1996. 'Illusions about Consolidation', *Journal of Democracy*, 7(2), 37–51.

O'Donnell, G. and Schmitter, P. 1986. 'Tentative Conclusions about Uncertain Democracies'. Vol. iv in O'Donnell *et al.* (eds). *Transitions from Authoritarian Rule: Prospects for Democracy*. Baltimore and London: Johns Hopkins University Press.

Oberman, J. 1992. 'Czechoslovakia Overcomes its Initial Reluctance', *RFE/RL Research Report*, 1(23), 5 June 1992, 19–24.

Offe, C. 1991. 'Capitalism by Democratic Design? Democratic Theory Facing the Triple Transition in East Central Europe', *Social Research*, 58(4) (Winter 1991), 865–92.

Offe, C. 1994. *Der Tunnel am Ende des Lichts. Erkundungen der politischen Transformation im neuen Osten.* Frankfurt/Main und New York: Campus.

Offe, C. 1996. 'Designing Institutions in East European Transitions', in Goodin, R. E. (ed.). *The Theory of Institutional Design.* Cambridge: Cambridge University Press, 199–226.

Offe, C. 1997. *Varieties of Transition. The East European and East German Experience.* Cambridge: MIT Press.

Okey, R. 1992. 'Central Europe/Eastern Europe: Behind the Definitions', in *Past & Present*, 137, Nov. 1992, 102–33.

Orlos, K. 1995. 'Co zostało z naszej solidarności?' in *Zmiana warty czyli jak to się stało.* Warszawa: Presspublica, 21–7.

Osiatyński, W. 1996. 'The Roundtable Talks in Poland', in Elster, Jon (ed.). 1996, 21–68.

Ost, D. 1990. *Solidarity and the Politics of Anti-Politics.* Philadelphia: Temple University Press.

Ost, D. 1995. 'Labor, Class and Democracy: Shaping Political Antagonism in Post-Communist Societies', in Crawford, B. (ed.). *Markets, States and Democracy.* Boulder: Westview Press.

Oughourlian, J.-M. 1982. *Un mime nommé désir.* Paris: Bernard Grasset.

Paczkowski, A. 1996. 'Przeszłość w naszej pamięci' *Przegląd Polityczny*, 31, Summer 1996, 18–20.

Paczkowski, A. 1997. 'Pologne, la nation-ennemi', in Courtois, S. *et al. Le livre noir du communisme.* Paris: Robert Laffont, 397–428.

Paczkowski, A. 1998. *Pół wieku dziejów Polski 1939–1989.* Warszawa: Wydawnictwo Naukowe PWN.

Pakulski, J. 1993. 'Mass Social Movements and Social Class', *International Sociology*, 8(2), 131–58.

Pakulski, J. 1995. 'Mass Movements and Plebiscitary Democracy: Political Change in Central Eastern Europe', *International Sociology*, 10(4), 409–26.

Pałubicki, J. 1990. 'Długi Marsz', *Gazeta Wyborcza*, 23 April 1990.

Pańków, I. 1998. 'A Self-Portrait of the Polish Political Elite', in Higley, J./ Pakulski, J./Wesołowski, W. (eds), 188–202.

Parel, A. J. 1992. *The Machiavellian Cosmos.* New Haven and London: Yale University Press.

Pareto, V. 1968. *The Rise and Fall of the Elites.* Totowa, New Jersey: The Bedminster Press.

Pasek, B. 1997. 'Poland's Contentious Communist Legacy', *Transition*, 10 January, 3(1), 20–1.

Patora, T. 1997. 'Wciąż brakuje sędziego do Sądu Lustracyjnego. Ostateczne rozwiązanie w Olsztynie', *Gazeta Wyborcza*, 292, 16 December 1997.

Pietkiewicz, B. 1998. 'Sąd nad sędziami', *Polityka*, 3, 17 January 1998.

Pitkin, H. F. 1984. *Fortune is a Woman. Gender and Politics in the Thought of Niccolò Machiavelli.* Berkeley/Los Angeles/London: University of California Press.

Potel, J.-Y. 1992. 'Enjeux et risques d'une Union européene élargie', *Le Monde diplomatique*, 539, February 1999, 8–9.

Poznan´ski, K. 1992. *Constructing Capitalism: The Re-Emergence of Civil Society and Liberal Economy in the Post-Communist World.* Boulder, Colo.: Westview Press.

Poznański, K. 1996. *Poland's Protracted Transition. Institutional Change and Economic Growth 1970–1994.* Cambridge: Cambridge University Press.

Pridham, G. and Lewis, P. (eds). 1996. *Stabilising Fragile Democracies.* London/New York: Routledge.

Prizel, I. and Michta, A. 1995. *Polish Foreign Policy Reconsidered.* New York: St. Martin's Press.

Przeworski, A. 1993. 'Economic Reforms, Public Opinion, and Political Institutions: Poland in the Eastern European Perspective', in Bresser Pereira, *et al.* (eds). *Economic Reforms in New Democracies.* Cambridge: Cambridge University Press.

Rachwald, A. 1995. 'Looking West', in Prizel and Michta (eds). *Polish Foreign Policy Reconsidered*, 129–55.

Raina, P. 1978. *Political Opposition in Poland 1954–1977.* London: Poets and Painters Press.

Reisch, A. 1992. 'Hungary Sees Common Goals and Bilateral Issues', *RFE/RL Research Report*, 1(23), 5 June 1992, 19–24.

Roberts, K. and Jung (eds). 1995. *Poland's First Post-Communist Generation.* Aldershot/Brookfield: Avebury.

Rogers, E. and Joung-Im, K. 1985. 'Diffusion of Innovation in Public Organizations', in Merritt, R. and Merritt, A. (eds). *Innovation in the Public Sector.* Beverly Hills/London/New York, 85–108.

Rosati, D. 1993. 'Poland: Glass Half-Empty', in Portes, R. (ed.) *Economic Transformation in Central Europe: A Progress Report.* London: CEPR, 211–73.

Rose, R. 1991. 'What is Lesson-Drawing?', *Journal of Public Policy*, II, 1, 3–30.

Roszkowski, W. 1994. *Historia Polski 1914–1993.* 3rd edition. Warszawa: Wydawnictwo Naukowe PWN.

Roszkowski, W. 1996. 'Powrót do początku', *Periphery*, 2(1/2), 17–18.

Roszkowski, W. 1997. 'The Afterlife of Communism in Poland', in Holmes, L. and Roszkowski, W. (eds.) *Changing Ru(o)les.* Warsaw: ISPPAN (mimeo).

Rothschild, J. 1974. *East Central Europe between the Two World Wars.* Seattle and London: University of Washington Press.

Rupnik, J. 1988. 'Totalitarianism Revisited', in Keane, J. (ed.). *Civil Society and the State*, 263–89.

Sachs, J. 1994. *Poland's Jump to the Market Economy.* Cambridge: MIT Press.

Sakwa, R. 1995. 'Subjectivity, Politics and Order in Russian Political Evolution', *Slavic Review*, 54(4), 943–64.

Samsonowicz, H. 1995. *Miejsce Polski w Europie.* Warszawa: Wydawnictwo Bellona.

Schmitter, P. and Karl, T. 1994. 'The Conceptual Travel of Transitologists and Consolidologists: How Far to the East Should They Go?' *Slavic Review*, 53(1), 173–85.

Schmitter, P. and Karl, T. 1995. 'From an Iron Curtain to a Paper Curtain: Grounding Transitologists or Students of Postcommunism?', *Slavic Review*, 54(4), Winter 1995, 965–78.

Schöpflin, G. 1993. *Politics in Eastern Europe 1945–1992.* Oxford and Cambridge: Blackwell.

Sewell, W. H. 1996. 'Historical Events as Transformations of Structures: Inventing Revolution at the Bastille', *Theory and Society*, 25, 841–81.

Shafir, M. 1994. 'Immigrants, Refugees, and Post-Communism', *RFE/RL Research Report*, 3(23), 10 June 1994, 33–5.

Shlapentokh, D. 1995. 'The French Revolution in the Intellectual and Political Context of the Last Years of the Soviet Regime', *International Journal of Politics, Culture and Society*, 9(1), 87–112.

Sienkiewicz, W. 1991. *Mały słownik historii Polski*. Warszawa: Wiedza Powszechna.

Simecka, M. 1984. *The Restoration of Order. The Normalisation of Czechoslovakia 1969–1976*. London: Verso.

Skilling, H. G. 1989. *Samizdat and an Independent Society in Central and Eastern Europe*. Houndmills: Macmillan Press.

Skórzyński, J. 1990. 'Solidarność, kryzys tożsamości', *Tygodnik Solidarność*, 20 April 1990.

Skórzyński, J. 1995. *Ugoda i Rewolucja*. Warszawa: Rzeczposplita.

Slay, B. 1994. *The Polish Economy*. Princeton: Princeton University Press.

Smolar, A. 1996a. 'Revolutionary Spectacle and Peaceful Transition', *Social Research*, 63(2), 439–64.

Smolar, A. 1996b. 'Kwaśniewskis Polen', *Transit*, 11, 162–75.

Smolar, A. 1996c. 'From Opposition to Atomization', *Journal of Democracy*, 7(1), 24–38.

Smolar, A. and Kende, P. 1989. *Die Rolle der oppositionellen Gruppen am Vorabend der Demokratisierung in Polen und Ungarn (1987–89)*, Köln.

Soltyk, R. 1999. 'L'opinion polonaise hésite', *Le Monde diplomatique*, 539, 8.

Sorel, G. 1914. *Reflections on Violence*. Repr. 1975. New York: B.W. Huebsch.

Sperber, M. 1987. *Die Tyrannis und andere Essays aus der Zeit der Verachtung*. München: dtv.

Stachowski, Z. 1993. 'Kosciół katolicki a proces transformacji społecznej', in Stachowski, Z. and Wojtowicz, A. (eds). *Antynomie transformacji w Polsce*. Warszawa.

Staniszkis, J. 1984. *Poland's Self-limiting Revolution*. Princeton: Princeton University Press.

Staniszkis, J. 1991a. *The Dynamics of the Breakthrough in Eastern Europe: The Polish Experience*. Berekeley: University of California Press.

Staniszkis, J. 1991b. '"Political Capitalism" in Poland', *Eastern European Politics and Societies*, 5(1), 127–41.

Staniszkis, J. 1991c. 'Dilemmata der Demokratie in Osteuropa', in Deppe, Rainer/Dubiel, Helmut/ Roedel, Ulrich (eds). *Demokratischer Umbruch in Osteuropa*. Frankfurt/Main: Suhrkamp, 326–47.

Staniszkis, J. 1994a. 'Ontology, Context and Chance: Three Exit Routes from Communism', in Program on Central and Eastern Europe. Working Paper Series, 31, Minda de Gunzburg Center for European Studies, Harvard University.

Staniszkis, J. 1994b. 'Solidarność jako związek zawodowy', in Morawski, Witold (red.). *Zmierzch socjalizmu państwowego*. Warszawa: Wydawnictwo Naukowe PWN, 112–35.

Stark, D. 1992. 'Path Dependence and Privatization Strategies in East Central Europe', *East European Politics and Societies*, 6(1), Winter 1992, 17–54.

Stokes, G. 1997. *Three Eras of Political Change in Eastern Europe*. Oxford: Oxford University Press.

Subotic, M. 1996. 'Nic nie zostało uporządkowane', *Rzeczpospolita*, 9 January 1996.

Surdykowski, J. 1985. *Tygodnik Powszechny*, 15 December 1985.

Szacki, J. 1990. 'A Revival of Liberalism in Poland', *Social Research*, 57(4), 463–91.

Szacki, J. 1991. 'Polish Democracy: Dreams and Reality', *Social Research*, 58(2), Winter 199, 711–22.

Szacki, J. 1995. *Liberalism after Communism*. Budapest: Central European University Press.

Szacki, J. 1996. 'Dwie historie', in *Spór o PRL*, Kraków: Znak, 68–74.

Szakolczai, A. 1996. 'In a Permanent State of Transition: Theorising the East European Condition', *EUI Working Paper SPS, No. 96/9*. San Domenico: European University Institute.

Szakolczai, A. 1998. 'In a Permanent State of Transition. Theorizing the East European Condition'. Paper presented at the conference Die Osterweiterung der Europäischen Union, 6–7 May 1998. Bonn.

Szelényi, I. and Szelényi, B. 1994. 'Why Socialism Failed: Towards a Theory of System Breakdown – Causes of Disintegration of East European State Socialism', *Theory and Society*, 23, 291–332.

Sztompka, P. 1996. 'Trust and Emerging Democracy: Lessons from Poland', *International Sociology*, 11(1), 37–62.

Sztompka, P. 1998. 'The Cultural Imponderables of Rapid Social Change: Trust, Loyalty, Solidarity', *Polish Sociological Review*, 1/98, 45–56.

Szücs, J. 1988. 'Three Historical Regions of Europe', in Keane, John (ed.). *Civil Society and the State*. London: Verso, 291–332.

Szücs, J. 1995. *Trzy Europy*. Lublin: Instytut Europy Srodkowo-Wschodniej.

Tajne Dokumenty Biura Politycznego i Sekretariatu KC. Ostatni rok wladzy 1988–1989. London: Aneks.

Tarde, G. 1993 (1895). *Les Lois de l'Imitation*. Paris: Seuil.

Tatur, M. 1989. *Solidarność als Modernisierungsbewegung*. Frankfurt/Main: Campus.

Tatur, M. 1994. '"Corporatism" as a Paradigm of Transformation', in Staniszkis, J. (ed.). *W poszukiwaniu paradygmatu transformacji*. Warszawa: Instytut Studiów Politycznych, 93–130.

The Oxford English Dictionary. Second Edition, xix. Oxford: Clarendon Press.

Thibaud, P. 1992. 'Westernism and the Eastern Left', *Thesis Eleven*, 32, 108–13.

Tiryakian, E. A. 1991. 'Modernization: Exhumetur in Pace (Rethinking Macrosociology in the 1990s)', *International Sociology*, 6(2), 165–80.

Tiryakian, E. 1995. 'Modernization in a Millenarian Decade', in Grancelli, Bruno (ed.). *Social Change and Modernization*.

Tocqueville, A. 1988. *L'ancien régime et la révolution*. Paris: Flammarion.

Tocqueville, A. 1981. *De la démocratie en Amerique*. Vol. II. Paris: Flammarion.

Touraine, A. *et al.* 1983. *Solidarity: The Analysis of a Social Movement: Poland 1980–1981*. Cambridge: Cambridge University Press.

Toynbee, A. 1979 (1939). *A Study of History*, v. Oxford: Oxford University Press.

Turner, V. 1965. 'Betwixt and Between: The Liminal Period in Rites de Passage', in *New Approaches to the Study of Religion (proceedings of the Annual Meeting of the American Ethnological Society, 1964)*. Seattle: University of Washington Press.

Turner, V. 1969. *The Ritual Process. Structure and Anti-Structure.* New York: de Gruyter.

Turner, V. 1974. 'Liminal to Liminoid, in Play, Flow, and Ritual: An Essay in Comparative Symbology', *Rice University Studies*, 53–92.

Turner, V. 1985. *On the Edge of the Bush.* Tucson: University of Arizona Press.

Turner, V. 1987 (1967). 'Betwixt and Between: The Liminal Period in *Rites de Passage*', in *The Forest of Symbols.* New York: Cornell University Press.

Turner, V. 1992. *Blazing the Trail*, ed. Turner, Edith. University of Arizona Press.

UNICEF Regional Monitoring Report. 1993. *Central and Eastern Europe in Transition. Public Policy and Social Conditions*, 1, November 1993.

Van Gennep, A. 1960 (1909). *Les Rites de Passage.* Paris: Picard.

Vinton, L. 1992. 'Olszewski's Ouster Leaves Poland Polarized', *RFE/RL Research Report*, 1(25), 19 June 1992, 1–10.

Vinton, L. 1995. 'Domestic Politics and Foreign Policy 1989–1993', in Prize, I. and Michta, A. (eds). *Polish Foreign Policy Reconsidered.* New York: St. Martin's Press, 23–71.

Wągrowska, M. 1997. 'Polityka zagraniczna' in: Raport: Bilans koalicji SLD-PSL, *Rzeczpospolita*, 11 September 1997.

Waldrauch, H. 1996. 'Was heißt demokratische Konsolidierung? Über einige theoretische Konsequenzen der osteuropäischen Regimewechsel'. Working paper. Wien: Institut für höhere Studien.

Walicki, A. 1988. 'The Three Traditions in Polish Patriotism and Their Contemporary Relevance'. Bloomington: The Polish Studies Center.

Walicki, A. 1997. 'Intellectual Elites and the Vicissitudes of Imagined Nation in Poland', *East European Politics and Societies*, 11(2), 227–53.

Wandycz, P. 1974. *The Lands of Partitioned Poland, 1795–1918.* Seattle and London: University of Washington Press.

Wandycz, P. (ed.) 1996. *Spór o PRL.* Kraków: Znak.

Warszawski, D. 1989. 'Une période difficile de transition', *La Nouvelle Alternative*, 14, 7–9.

Wasilewski, J. 1998. 'Elite Circulation and Consolidation of Democracy', in Higley, J. *et al.* 1998. *Postcommunist Elites and Democracy in Eastern Europe*, London: Macmillan, 163–87.

Wasilewski, J. and Wnuk-Lipiński, E. 1994. 'Poland: Winding Road from the Communist to the post-Solidarity elite', *Theory and Society*, 24/5, 669–96.

Weber, M. 1980. *Wirtschaft und Gesellschaft*, ed. Johannes Winckelmann, 5th edition. Tübingen: Mohr.

Wedel, J. 1988. *The Private Poland.* New York: Facts on File Publications.

Weil, S. 1948. *La pesanteur et la grâce.* Paris: Union Générale Edition.

Weydenthal, J. B., 'Poland Supports the Triangle as a Means to Reach other Goals', *RFE/RL Research Report*, 1(23), 5 June 1992, 15–18.

White, S./Batt, J./Lewis, P. G. 1998. *Developments in Central and East European Politics.* London: Macmillan.

White, S./Gill, G./Slider, D. 1994. *The Politics of Transition. Shaping a Post-Soviet Future*. Cambridge: Cambridge University Press.

Wierzbicki, P. 1989. 'Familia, swita, dwór', *Tygodnik Solidarność*, 10 November 1989.

Winiecki, J. 1992. 'The Polish Transition Programme: Underpinnings, Results, Interpretations', *Soviet Studies*, 44(5), 809–35.

Wnuk-Lipiński, E. 1995. *After Communism*. Warsaw: ISP PAN.

Wnuk-Lipiński, E. 1996. *Demokratyczna Rekonstrukcja*, Warszawa: Wydawnictwo Naukowe PWN.

Wydra, H. 1997. *Imitating Capitalism and Democracy at a Distance*. EUI Working Paper SPS 97/2. San Domenico: European University Institute.

Wydra, H. 1999. 'Democracy in Eastern Europe as a Civilizing Process', in Smith, D. and Wright, S. *Whose Europe? The Turn towards Democracy*. Oxford: Blackwell/Sociological Review, 288–310.

Wydra, H. 2000 (forthcoming). 'Human Nature and Politics: A Girardian Reading of Crisis and Conflict in the work of Niccolò Machiavelli', *Contagion*, 7.

Zeitlin, I. M. 1984. *Ancient Judaism. Biblical Criticism from Max Weber to the Present*. Cambridge: Polity Press.

Zieliński, M. 1994. 'Czy istnieje w Polsce kapitalizm', *Przegląd Polityczny*, 25, Autumn 1994, 34–7.

Ziemer, K. 1998. 'Konsolidierung der polnischen Demokratie in den neunziger Jahren', *Aus Politik und Zeitgeschichte*, 6–7, 29–38.

Ziemkiewicz. 1997. 'W poszukiwaniu straconego centrum', *Rzeczpospolita*, 27 May 1997.

Zinoviev, A. 1978. *The Yawning Heights*. New York: Random House.

Ziółkowski, M. 1998. 'On the Diversity of the Present: Suspended between Tradition, the Legacy of Socialism, Modernity and Postmodernity', *Polish Sociological Review*, 1/98, 21–43.

Zubek, V. 1991. 'Walesa's Leadership and Poland's Transition', *Problems of Communism*, January–April.

Zubek, V. 1992. 'The Rise and Fall of Rule by Poland's Best and Brightest', *Soviet Studies*, 44(4), 579–608.

Index

Subject Index

antagonism(s)
  between East and West, 67
  between state and society, 50
  historical, 5, 51–2, 168
  replica of, 53, 71
antagonists
  weakness of, 43, 70
anti-politics, 3, 40, 51, 116
anti-structure, 25–6, 42–3, 54, 69,
    145, 148, 166, 168
  of *communitas*, 148
  of the round-table community,
    25, 148
  of a societal community, 167
  of permanent liminality, 69

backwardness, 22, 74, 77–8, 105,
    127
  leap out of, 81
  continuity of, 74–95
  state of, 22
Balcerowicz-plan, 111
Bielecki government, 118

capitalism
  logic of, 101–2, 110, 114
Catholic Church, 28–9, 70, 72,
    116, 130–2, 134, 137, 145, 157
  heritage of the, 113
Catholic Electoral Action, 138
Centre Alliance (PC), 140
Christian National Alliance
    (ZChN), 138, 200
civil society, 69–70, 116
Civic Parliamentary Club (OKP), 135,
    142
Committee for the Defence of
    Workers (KOR), 36
communitas, 22–3, 48, 133, 173
  continuation of, 166
  moments of, 148, 167

existential, 44
experience(s) of, 42–4, 139, 149,
    163
  liminal experience of, 48
  normative, 164
  round-table, 44–8
  Solidarity, 43–4, 138, 140, 143, 145,
    173
  spirit of, 148
  in 1980, 44, 163
  of 1989, 148
community
  anti-structural, 49
  August, 164–5
  Gdańsk, 125
  imaginary, 69
  national, 43, 58
  of a third Solidarity, 148
  recurrent appeal to, 166
  underground polity as a, 43
  with Western Europe, 98, 106, 113,
    115
Confederation for an Independent
    Poland (KPN), 46, 200
conflict
  see also mimetic conflict
  Girard's theory of, 62
  identity-based, 51–2, 76
  ideological, 51–2, 76
  interest-based, 52
  political, 50–3
consciousness
  double, 15
  utopian, 55, 193
consolidology, 1, 10, 172–3
contingency
  in politics, 9–10, 20, 28
  in Poland's transition, 21
continuity
  of a gap between the first and
    second reality, 161
  of backwardness, 74–95
  of distance, 95

Index of Persons